American Sports History Series

edited by
David B. Biesel

1. *Effa Manley and the Newark Eagles* by James Overmyer, 1993
2. *The United States and World Cup Competition: An Encyclopedic History of the United States in International Competition* by Colin Jose, 1994
3. *Slide, Kelly, Slide: The Wild Life and Times of Mike "King" Kelly, Baseball's First Superstar* by Marty Appel, 1996
4. *Baseball by the Numbers* by Mark Stang and Linda Harkness, 1997
5. *Roller Skating for Gold* by David H. Lewis, 1997
6. *Baseball's Biggest Blunder: The Bonus Rule of 1953–1957* by Brent Kelley, 1997
7. *Lights On! The Wild Century-Long Saga of Night Baseball* by David Pietrusza, 1997
8. *Windy City Wars: Labor, Leisure, and Sport in the Making of Chicago* by Gerald R. Gems, 1997
9. *The American Soccer League: The Golden Years of American Soccer, 1921–1931* by Colin Jose, 1998

A related title by the series editor:

Can You Name That Team? A Guide to Professional Baseball, Football, Soccer, Hockey, and Basketball Teams and Leagues by David B. Biesel, 1991

The Windy City Wars

Labor, Leisure, and Sport in the Making of Chicago

Gerald R. Gems

American Sports History Series, No. 8

The Scarecrow Press, Inc.
Lanham, Md., & London
1997

SCARECROW PRESS, INC.

Published in the United States of America
by Scarecrow Press, Inc.
4720 Boston Way
Lanham, Maryland 20706

British Library Cataloguing in Publication Information Available

Library of Congress Cataloging-in-Publication Data

Gems, Gerald R.
  Windy city wars : labor, leisure, and sport in the making of
Chicago / Gerald R. Gems.
     p.   cm. -- (American sports history series , no. 8)
  Includes bibliographical references and index.
  ISBN 0-8108-3305-0 (alk. paper)
  1. Sports--Illinois--Chicago--History. 2. Leisure--Illinois-
-Chicago--History.   3. Popular culture--Illinois--Chicago--History.
  4. Chicago (Ill.)--History. I. Title. II. Series.
  GV534.5.C4G46   1997
  796'.09773' 11--dc21   97-12133
                                                                     CIP
ISBN 0-8108-3305-0 (cloth : alk. paper)

⊖™ The paper used in this publication meets the minimum requirements of
American National Standard for Information Sciences—Permanence of
Paper for Printed Library Materials, ANSI Z39.48–1984.
Manufactured in the United States of America.

Dedication

To my extended family, who have contributed more to this work than they can ever imagine.

Contents

Acknowledgments

I wish to extend my sincere gratitude to my parents, for their research assistance and whose lives present the basis for this work; Marian Owen, for her generous support of the project; and Frank Di Benedetto, for sharing his life and his invaluable resources.

Dr. Joan Hult planted the initial seeds for this work as the topic for a doctoral dissertation. She provided valuable input and support throughout the project.

I especially want to thank Dr. Nancy Struna, whose guidance and editorial skills brought years of research to fruition. Any scholarly merits inherent in this work are due, largely, to her. She has presented an exemplary model as a teacher, historian, and friend.

In the course of research one entails numerous debts that deserve public thanks: to Lillian Chorvat, curator of the Czech Museum in Berwyn, Illinois, for translation of Czech materials; and the helpful staff at the Chicago Historical Society.

North Central College, in particular Dr. Jerry Berberet, former Dean of the Faculty and Vice-President for Academic Affairs, facilitated financial assistance in the form of two grants, made possible by the Lilly Foundation and the Leadership, Ethics, and Values Program. Sandy Lassiter, Barbara Anderson, Cheryl Bryan, and Becky Botos provided invaluable word processing skills over the years.

Lastly, I owe my wife and children my gratitude and much more, for they settled for less of my time than they deserved.

Introduction

In a city often torn by ethnic, racial, and political strife, the Chicago Bears' 1986 Super Bowl season arguably presented the greatest display of cultural unity in over a century. Although I did not get to participate in the festivities that followed the football season, I certainly joined in the spirit of the occasion as a native Chicagoan. Many others evidently shared my passion for sport.

My own interests and involvement in sporting endeavors started at an early age, consumed my youth, and continue throughout my adult life. That interest was fanned by my parents, whose own leisure lives revolved largely around sporting practices and associations. I had clearly learned from my parents. But as the children of ethnic and immigrant parents with little or no sporting traditions, my parents had developed their interests under the guidance of others in different historical circumstances. The same could be said for each of the estimated 300,000 who welcomed the Bears home after their victory and countless others, like me, who shared their feelings.

The messages conveyed by signs, T-shirts, and cheers gave ample evidence that sport did not operate in a vacuum. Many in the crowd cheered for particular heroes based on their ethnic, racial, or class affiliations. Some inherited these convictions from parents. Others were nurtured and reinforced by their own historical experiences. Despite their various beliefs and values derived from the particular perspectives of ethnicity, class, religion, and gender, they shared in a communal celebration.

These same factors had long promoted discord within the city. An estimated million or more arrived for the celebration when the Chicago Bulls won the first of their four national championships, but the festivities were marred by looting, rampages, and deaths. Such actions symbolized the tensions still inherent in the city. Whereas harmony reigned in the Bears' triumphal moment, the Bulls' revelers produced mixed results. How did sports generate such extreme behavior? How did such diverse groups come to agree on anything? How did athletic events foster a cohesive spirit and common interest? How did they engender violence? The answers to such questions lie enclosed in our collective pasts—in the pattern of historical developments and the human efforts that created a popular culture.

This work attempts to arrive at some understanding of the process by examining its chronological development. The role of sport in the process of transition from the earliest communal village life to a commercialized, industrial city remains the central theme. The definition of sport, along with its practice and uses, also changes in the process, from that of a voluntary leisure activity to more utilitarian functions, eventually culminating in highly structured, regulated, competitive contests subject to a particular ideology. That continual process of inculcating an ideological hegemony evolved through various stages—repression, coercion, accommodation, adoption, and adaptation—to fit particular needs based on cultural differences. Racial, class, ethnic, religious, and gender values intruded and continue to intrude upon the process.

Several American sport historians have examined aspects of such development with varying conclusions. Early studies, such as Frederic Paxson's "The Rise of Sport" and Dale Somers' *The Rise of Sport in New Orleans,* perceived sport as an urban safety valve that provided for the release of pent-up energies. John R. Betts provided a comprehensive survey in *America's Sporting Heritage,* emphasizing the effect of urbanization and industrialization on the growth of sport, as did Benjamin G. Rader in *American Sports: From the Age of Folk Games to the Age of Spectators.* Allen Guttmann, in *From Ritual to Record,* identified the characteristics of modern sport and the process of development as a reflection of society. Melvin Adelman used modernization theory in his study of

New York to posit that modern sports evolved in commercial rather than industrial cities. Adelman contends that sport is more than a simple reflection of society and has its own dynamic processes related to urbanization, class, religion, nationalism, sectionalism, ethnicity, and masculinity. Ron Smith, *Sports and Freedom,* differs with Adelman on the relationship of commercialization and professionalization. Like Adelman, Stephen Hardy, *How Boston Played,* and Roy Rosenzweig, *Eight Hours for What We Will,* have further analyzed the complex relationships of class, ethnicity, and religion on leisure activities with particular insights relative to power and the ability to effect change. George Kirsch, *The Creation of American Team Sports,* reinforces Adelman's perceptions on the nature of urban sport, while demonstrating the effects of nationalism and class on the development of a sporting culture. Steven Reiss, *City Games,* invokes the modernization framework in his investigation of demographic changes and the relationships between sport and urban structures, organizations, and ideology.[1]

Revisionist historians have taken a more critical view of organizers and their motives. Dominick Cavallo, *Muscles and Morals: Organized Playgrounds and Urban Reform,* and Cary Goodman, *Choosing Sides: Playground and Street Life on the Lower East Side,* analyze the supervised play movement during the Progressive era. The former assesses ideological foundations, while the latter assumes a Marxist paradigm and elements of social control to impose a particular value system and subordinate status on immigrants. Gary Ross Mormino, however, found that sport could reinforce ethnic communal values while it assimilated individuals. Like historians, other sport scholars disagree on the assimilative capabilities of sport in their studies of particular subcultures.[2]

Elliott Gorn, *The Manly Art,* Warren Goldstein, *Playing for Keeps,* and Ned Polsky, *Hustlers, Beats, and Others,* have supplied invaluable insights into the characteristics, values, and meanings of sporting subcultures. Gorn and Polsky, in particular, explore alternative groups in opposition to the mainstream. Both Randy Roberts, in *Papa Jack: Jack Johnson and the Era of White Hopes,* and Rob Ruck, *Sandlot Seasons: Sport in Black Pittsburgh,* detail the capabilities of human agency in building community pride and racial consciousness.[3]

Sport historians have focused largely on male activities. Feminist scholarship has produced a surge of new gender studies; but these, too, are mostly concerned with middle class women and neglect the majority. A notable exception is Kathy Piess, *Cheap Amusements: Working Women and Leisure in Turn-of-the-Century New York.* Studies of particular ethnic groups, their sporting practices, and meanings are similarly lacking. While most sport historians agree on the city as the setting for the development of sports in America, we still know too little about the myriad residents who comprised the urban sporting culture.[4]

Despite an abundance of native histories and numerous accounts of their sporting practices, there is a dearth of material on the origin of popular culture. Sport is a primary ingredient in the cultural stew that comprises the popular culture of shared values and practices; yet we still know too little about promoters, participants, and patrons. Examinations of ethnic experiences have proposed various theories of assimilation, but the nature and function of sport as a component of such change has attracted little scholarly attention. Past histories, like Betts's *American Sporting Heritage,* have assumed a functionalist role for sporting interests and enterprises, emanating from the belief in a cultural consensus. Others, like Guttmann, who subscribe to the view of sport as a reflection of society, negate the ability of humans to change conditions. Such studies as Adelman's assume a linear process of acculturation based on ethnics' passive acceptance of native American dictates. They invariably draw upon native sources and accounts, usually gleaned from newspapers that exhibit a distinct middle class bias, and fail to examine ethnic perceptions. Given the nature of sequestered ethnic residential patterns, the maintenance of traditional cultural practices, and the political strife that has characterized the history of Chicago, such a modernization theory of culture seems untenable. While this study exhibits similarities to modernization proponents in the characteristics and in the way that sport developed, it was not a linear process, but one of starts and stops and hardly one of consensus. Immigrant groups and their values continually intruded upon the process of culture formation.[5]

Immigrant histories, such as Oscar Handlin's *The Uprooted,* posited that the migratory experience was one of alienation, resulting in ethnic seclusion and isolation in America. While Handlin stressed the deleterious effects of cultural loss, Rudolph Vecoli effectively refuted such claims by demonstrating that such conditions did not apply in Chicago.[6] Moreover, some immigrant groups, such as the German Turners, Czech Sokols, and Polish Falcons, had long-established sporting traditions that revolved around religious or social customs and nationalistic objectives that were not always compatible with the aims of the native Americans. Despite differences, particular groups and communities vied for athletic supremacy, though they shunned contact in other spheres of life. Sporting interests came to serve as the most visible social bond among a host of factions. No study has yet examined the developmental process that led to the formation of a common sporting culture in Chicago. This study seeks to answer the questions how and why sporting practices and relationships contributed to that phenomenon.[7]

Chicago provided more than just a setting for sport. Within one lifetime it virtually erupted from a frontier outpost to a city of more than a million inhabitants of various racial and ethnic groups, each with its own interests and values. The process of cultural transformation occurred at a more rapid rate than in the older urban centers of the East and South, offering a basis for comparison. In Chicago, change often occurred in a volatile fashion; yet sporting practices eventually served an integrative function among such dissimilar groups. As a largely ethnic, Catholic, working class city, distinguishable by particular neighborhoods and lifestyles, a study of Chicago allows the opportunity to assess not only the patterns of development, but the pluralistic meaning of sport, seemingly unrecognized by modernization theorists.[8]

A multitude of factors is involved in such a study, as different racial, ethnic, and religious groups arrived in Chicago at different times. Such chronological and cultural differences colored their perspectives and the meanings of life in America. Actions, reactions, and the lifestyles of each group modified with time as ethnic Americans lost their hyphenated status to become simply "Americans." Beginning in the late seventeenth century, each of these groups imposed themselves upon a preexisting culture. The French expeditions of that period interrupted and changed the lives of the first true native Americans, to be followed by the British after the conclusion of the French and Indian War in 1763 and later by the independent American settlers. By the mid-nineteenth century, large numbers of Europeans began to seek new lives in the United States. By that time, however, the descendants of the English colonists, largely white, Anglo-Saxon Protestants, had established a society that promised equality and opportunity, yet promulgated such particular values along racial, religious, and gender lines. Cultural leadership came to rest with these white, Anglo-Saxon Protestant males, and all others assumed a subordinate relationship within the early American society. Subordinate groups eventually questioned the rhetoric of democracy and opportunity against the realities of their social condition, which required rationalization.

Such an hierarchical social structure enables the more powerful faction greater access and control over resources and the ability to influence others. This concept of hegemony serves as the framework for analysis. Hegemony assumes that a dominant group has the power to define and shape a society by establishing particular values and practices that become accepted as social norms. Subordinate groups can then accept, reject, adapt, and accommodate to the dominant ideology and the structures that reinforce or reproduce it. Acceptance suggests a unidirectional, passive process, while rejection results in struggle, as was often the case in nineteenth century Chicago. The adaptation and accommodation that occurred thereafter produced a popular culture more agreeable to divergent groups.[9]

Any power relationship is always a tenuous one that requires constant reinforcement and safeguarding in order to maintain the status quo. This proved especially true in Chicago, where ethnics soon outnumbered the native born and threatened their dominant position. The ethnics often resisted native impositions, resulting in relationships characterized by force, coercion, negotiation, alliance, and persuasion to achieve the consent and conformity of subordinate groups. A limited and incomplete acceptance produced, in its final form, a hegemonic culture as the product of both dominant and subordinate groups.[10]

The evolution of such a popular culture, as opposed to the high culture of the elites, is readily discernible in the sporting practices of Chicagoans. Sport provided a common interest that transcended ethnic, racial, religious, political, and class lines and spurred relationships between divergent groups. The lines of social division were, and to a large degree still are, clearly drawn in the city that served as a major labor center and depository for European refugees. Their leisure interactions eventually proved more successful than confrontation in the inculcation of the dominant group values and a more homogeneous culture.

In analyzing the social relations of people and the meanings and role of sport in the process of culture formation, sport must necessarily be considered in a broader context. Cultures cannot be dictated or imposed; they are created and recreated by humans within and over time. As the old and new residents of Chicago made decisions that required them to adopt, reject, accommodate, or adapt elements of the established culture, they created an ever-evolving culture. For immigrants and wage laborers, both work and leisure issues initiated concerns over personal freedom, democracy, equality, and the nature of the society. Industrialization, with its regulated work schedules, allotted what time would be available for leisure. Commercialization changed the nature and form of leisure activities, including sport. Sporting practices became integral to the struggle over the work and leisure processes as debates ensued over the nature of leisure, its wholesome uses, and its relationship to productive capabilities for work. Within this larger context, the historical records attest to a particular pattern of development imposed by a like-minded group of commercial interests. The reaction of subordinate groups to such impositions was anything but passive, dictating that the product was a collaborative and, not infrequently, antagonistic process.

xviii   Introduction

John Hargreaves has asserted that such a pattern inculcated the dominant group ideology in four phases. The first was repressive in nature and involved the transition to capitalism. The successive stage brought some accommodation of folk sports with those of the dominant group. The following diffusion of such reconstructed sports throughout the society also served to "remake" the working class. The final massification of sport in the twentieth century secured such practices within the domain of capitalism as commercialized entertainment. Hargreaves' model is applicable to Chicago in the repressive transition from a frontier settlement to a commercial city and the clash of conflicting cultures. Americanized ethnic youth adopted the new sports and games during the Progressive era, and alternative sport organizations incorporated their practices within the established mainstream structures thereafter.[11]

By adopting such a model to the study of sport and culture formation in Chicago, it might help to explain the enigma that has long plagued historians, i.e., the lack of class consciousness among the American working class. Chicago provides a particularly useful location for such a study. Whereas most other studies of sport or leisure have focused primarily on the East, Chicago served as the national headquarters for the anarchist movement. As the site of the Haymarket Massacre, the Pullman Strike, and the birthplace of the radical "Wobblies" (Industrial Workers of the World), Chicago provided ample evidence of an astute class consciousness. Not coincidentally, Chicago provided a significant measure of the leadership and innovation in the Progressive reform movement, particularly in the field of recreation, where it served as the model for programs on a national level. Given the cosmopolitan nature of the city, the intensity of its political and labor issues, and its racial turmoil, how did Chicagoans come to agree upon anything, particularly sport? What role did such sporting relations play in the waning of class consciousness? Why does the working class continue to perceive sport as a meritocracy, and its youth favor athletics as a more acceptable means of social mobility than education? The answers lie in our collective historical experience.

This is the story of that experience—the impositions of a dominant group, the reactions of groups who possessed alternative values and beliefs, and the making of a mass culture through leisure practices and associations that transcended political, ethnic, racial, religious, and gender divisions. It focuses on a pluralistic popular culture capable of absorbing factional differences and yet allowing for multiple goals and values within a dominant ideology. Such breadth, however, requires the imposition of some limits. It is, primarily, the story of white ethnic males. As white males, whether American or ethnic, most often established the terms under which sport was practiced, race and gender have been relegated to peripheral issues. Race does not become an issue in Chicago until the large-scale migration of southern blacks to the North during World War I. Also, while middle class women took a more active role in the sporting culture by the late nineteenth century, working class women did so largely through the playground movement, industrial recreation programs, and religious agencies somewhat later. By that time both blacks and women reacted to a system established by white males. The variables of race and gender warrant their own more complete studies beyond the scope of this one, for which there is abundant data in Chicago that yet awaits collection and analysis. Any criticism based on such omission is both warranted and justified, for I admittedly present only a portion of the whole story.[12]

The story follows the transition from a frontier town to a commercialized city, with the advent of sporting practices that reinforced the capitalist system. The immigration of ethnic groups with alternative values, and industrialization which heightened class consciousness, produced conflict. Sport, as a common interest, provided a less overt means to infuse a particular ideology, allayed tensions, and brought some accommodation between divergent interests. Sport proved to be an integral part of the popular culture that merged shared interests as it allowed for pluralistic values. It transcended the lines of race, class, ethnicity, religion, and gender to promote American patriotism by World War II.

Notes

1. Frederic Paxson, "The Rise of Sport," *Mississippi Valley Historical Review*, 4 (1917), 143-68; Dale Somers, *The Rise of Sports in New Orleans, 1850-1900* (Baton Rouge: Louisiana StateUniversity Press, 1972); John R. Betts, *America's Sporting Heritage, 1850-1950* (Reading, MA: Addison-Wesley, 1974); Benjamin G. Rader, *American Sports: From the Age of Folk Games to the Age of Spectators* (Englewood Cliffs, NJ: Prentice-Hall, 1983); Allen Guttmann, *From Ritual to Record: The Nature of Modern Sports* (New York: Columbia University Press, 1978); Melvin L. Adelman, *A Sporting Time: New York City and the Rise of Modern Athletics, 1820-1870* (Urbana: University of Illinois Press, 1986); Stephen Hardy, *How Boston Played: Sport, Recreation and Community, 1865-1915* (Boston: Northeastern University Press, 1982); Roy Rosenzweig, *Eight Hours for What We Will: Workers and Leisure in an Industrial City, 1870-1920* (New York: Cambridge University Press, 1983); George B. Kirsch, *The Creation of American Team Sports, 1838-72* (Urbana: University of Illinois Press, 1989); Rob Ruck, *Sandlot Seasons: Sport in Black Pittsburgh* (Urbana: University of Illinois Press, 1987). Steven Riess, *Touching Base: Professional Baseball and American Culture in the Progressive Era* (Westport, CT: Greenwood Press, 1980); and, Riess, *City Games: The Evolution of American Urban Society and the Rise of Sports* (Urbana: University of Illinois Press, 1989).

2. Dominick Cavallo, *Muscles and Morals, Organized Playgrounds and Urban Reform, 1880-1920* (Philadelphia: University of Pennsylvania Press, 1981); Cary Goodman, *Choosing Sides: Playground and Street Life on the Lower East Side* (New York: Schocken Books, 1979); Gary Ross Mormino, "The Playing Fields of St. Louis: Italian Immigrants and Sport, 1925-1941," *Journal of Sport History*, 9 (Summer 1982): 5-16. On assimilation studies, see J. A. Fox, "Pueblo Baseball: A New Use for Old Witchcraft," *Journal of American Folklore*, 74 (1961): 9-16; Maria T. Allison, "Sport, Ethnicity, and Assimilation," *Quest*, 34:2 (Nov. 1982): 165-75; idem, "On the Ethnicity of Ethnic Minorities in Sport," *Quest*, 31 (1979): 50-6; John C. Pooley, "Ethnic Soccer Clubs in Milwaukee: A Study in Assimilation," in John W. Loy, Gerald S. Kenyon, and Barry McPherson, eds., *Sport, Culture, and Society* (Philadelphia: Lea & Febiger, 1981), 168-78.

3. Elliott Gorn, *The Manly Art: Bare-Knuckle Prize Fighting in America* (New York: Cornell University Press, 1986); Warren Goldstein, *Playing for Keeps: A History of Early Baseball* (Ithaca, NY: Cornell University Press, 1989); Ned Polsky, *Hustlers, Beats, and*

Others (Chicago: Aldine, 1967). Randy Roberts, *Papa Jack: Jack Johnson and the Era of White Hopes* (New York: The Free Press, 1983); Rob Ruck, *Sandlot Seasons: Sport in Black Pittsburgh.*

4. See, for example, most of the articles in the special issue on Sport and Gender, *Journal of Sport History,* 18:1 (Spring 1991); Kathy Piess, *Cheap Amusements: Working Women and Leisure in Turn-of-the-Century New York* (Philadelphia: Temple University Press, 1986).

5. For discussion of modernization theory, see Joyce Appleby, "Modernization Theory and the Formation of Modern Social Theories in England and America," *Comparative Studies in Society and History,* 20:2 (1978), 259-85; Peter Stearns, "Modernization and Social History: Some Suggestions and a Muted Cheer," *Journal of Social History,* 14 (1980): 189-209; and Richard S. Gruneau, "Modernization or Hegemony: Two Views on Sport and Social Development," in Jean Harvey and Hart Cantelon, eds., *Not Just a Game* (Ottawa: University of Ottawa Press, 1988), 9-32. Stephen Hardy, "Entrepreneurs, Structures, and the Sportgeist: Old Tensions in a Modern Society," in Donald G. Kyle and Gary D. Stark, eds., *Essays on Sport History and Sport Mythology* (College Station: Texas A & M Press, 1990), 45-82, offers a model for sport studies that challenges the modernization theory.

6. Oscar Handlin, *The Uprooted: The Epic Story of the Great Migrations that Made the American People* (New York: Grosset & Dunlap, 1951); Rudolph J. Vecoli, "Contadini in Chicago: A Critique of the Uprooted," *Journal of American History,* 51 (December 1964): 404-17. On immigrant histories, see Stow Persons, *Ethnic Studies at Chicago, 1905 45* (Urbana: University of Illinois Press, 1987); Ronald H. Bayor, *Neighbors in Conflict: The Irish, Germans, Jews, and Italians of New York City, 1929-1941* (Baltimore: Johns Hopkins University Press, 1978); Peter Kivisto and Dag Blanck, eds., *American Immigrants and Their Generations* (Urbana: University of Illinois Press, 1990); Peter Kivisto, *Immigrant Socialists in the United States* (Cranbury, NJ: Associated University Presses, 1984); Lawrence J. McCaffery, et al., *The Irish in Chicago* (Urbana: University of Illinois Press, 1987).

7. In addition to studies already cited, see Steven Riess, "Race and Ethnicity in American Baseball, 1900-1919," *Journal of Ethnic Studies,* 4 (Winter 1977): 39-55; Riess, "A Fighting Chance: The Jewish-American Boxing Experience," *American Jewish History,* 74 (March 1985): 223-54; Gerald Redmond, *The Caledonian Games in Nineteenth Century America* (Rutherford, NJ: Fairleigh Dickinson Uni-

versity Press, 1971); Richard Sorrell, "Sports and Franco-Americans in Woonsocket, 1870-1930, *Rhode Island History,* 31 (Fall 1972): 117-26; Benjamin Horowitz, "Hakoah in New York (1926-1932): A New Dimension for American Jewry," *Judaism,* 25 (Summer 1977): 375-82; Peter Levine, *Ellis Island to Ebbets Field: Sport and the American Jewish Experience* (New York: Oxford University Press, 1992); George Eisen and David Wiggins, eds., *Ethnicity and Sport in North American History and Culture* (Westport, CT: Greenwood Press, 1994).

8. Stephen Hardy, "The City and the Rise of American Sport," *Exercise and Sport Sciences Review,* 9 (1982): 183-219; John Marshall Carter and Arnd Kruger, eds., *Ritual and Record: Sports Records and Quantification in Pre-Modern Societies* (Westport, CT: Greenwood Press, 1990); Donald Mrozek, "Thoughts on Indigenous Western Sport: Moving Beyond the Model of Modernity," *Journal of the West,* 22 (Jan. 1983): 3-9; Maria T. Allison, "On the Ethnicity of Ethnic Minorities in Sport," *Quest,* 31:1 (1979): 50-6; Maria T. Allison and Gunther Luschen, "A Comparative Analysis of Navaho Indian and Anglo Basketball Sport Systems," *International Review of Sport Sociology,* 14:3-4 (1973): 75-86; Alice Taylor Cheska, "Revival, Survival, and Revisal: Ethnic Identity through 'Traditional Games'," in Gary Fine, ed., *Meaningful Play, Playful Meaning* (Champaign, IL: Human Kinetics Press, 1987), 145-53; Leonard M. Wankel and Bonnie G. Berger, "The Psychological and Social Benefits of Sport and Physical Activity," *Journal of Leisure Research,* 22:2 (1990): 167-82, all offer refutation to Guttmann's influential work. For case studies of Chicago groups, see Gerald R. Gems, "Sport, Religion, and Americanization: Bishop Sheil and the Catholic Youth Organization," *International Journal of the History of Sport* (August 1993): 233-41; Gems, "Sport and the Forging of a Jewish-American Culture: The Chicago Hebrew Institute," *Journal of American Jewish History,* 83:1 (March 1995): 15-26; Gems, "The Neighborhood Athletic Club: An Ethnographic Study of a Working-Class Athletic Fraternity in Chicago, 1917-1984," *Colby Quarterly,* 32:1 (March 1996): 36-44.

9. The concept of hegemony is attributed to Antonio Gramsci, a communist member of the Italian parliament, imprisoned by the fascists in 1928. See Quintin Hoare and Geoffrey N. Smith, eds., *Selections from the Prison Notebooks of Antonio Gramsci* (New York: International Publishers, 1971); Dante Germino, *Antonio Gramsci: Architect of a New Politics* (Baton Rouge: Louisiana State University Press, 1990); T. J. Jackson Lears, "The Concept of Cultural Hegemony: Problems and Possibilities," *American Historical Review,* 90 (June 1985): 567-83. Stephen Steinberg, *The Ethnic Myth: Race,*

Ethnicity, and Class in America (Boston: Beacon Press, 1989), 7-8, states that 80 percent of colonists at the time of independence emanated from the British Isles, while 99 percent were Protestants. On popular culture, see Eileen and Stephen Yeo, eds., *Popular Culture and Class Conflict, 1590-1914* (Atlantic Highlands, NJ: Humanities Press, 1981). For developments in Chicago, see Lawrence W. Levine, *Highbrow/Lowbrow: The Emergence of Cultural Hierarchy in America* (Cambridge: Harvard University Press, 1989), 116-18, 140-2, 208.

10. George H. Sage, *Power and Ideology in American Sport* (Champaign, IL: Human Kinetics, 1990), 15-26; David Whitson, "Sport and Hegemony: On the Construction of the Dominant Culture," *Sociology of Sport Journal,* 1 (1984): 64-78; Jean Harvey and Hart Cantelon, eds., *Not Just a Game*; John Hargreaves, *Sport, Power, and Culture: A Social and Historical Analysis of Popular Sports in Britain* (New York: St. Martin's Press, 1986); Stephen G. Jones, *Sport, Politics, and the Working Class* (Manchester: Manchester University Press, 1988); T. J. Jackson Lears, "The Concept of Cultural Hegemony: Problems and Possibilities."

11. John Hargreaves, "Sport, Culture and Ideology," in Jennifer Hargreaves, ed., *Sport, Culture and Ideology* (London: Routledge & Kegan Paul, 1982), 30-61.

12. James R. Grossman, *Land of Hope: Chicago, Black Southerners, and the Great Migration* (Chicago: University of Chicago Press, 1989). For insights and preliminary investigations of race and gender, see Grant Jarvie, ed., *Sport, Racism, and Ethnicity* (London: The Falmer Press, 1991); George Eisen, "Sport, Recreation and Gender: Jewish Immigrant Women in Turn-of-the-Century America (1880-1920)," *Journal of Sport History,* 18:1 (Spring 1991): 103-120; Gerald R. Gems, "Sport and the Americanization of Ethnic Women in Chicago," in George Eisen and David Wiggins, eds., *Ethnicity and Sport in North American History and Culture,* 177-200; J. A. Mangan and Roberta Park, eds., *From Fair Sex to Feminism* (Totowa, NJ: Frank Cass, 1987); Gems, "Working Class Women and Sport: An Untold Story," *Women In Sport and Physical Activity Journal* (Spring 1993): 17-30; and Gems, "Blocked Shot: The Development of Basketball in the African-American Community of Chicago," *Journal of Sport History* (Summer 1995): 135-48.

CHAPTER 1

Early Chicago — The Making of a Commercial City and Its Leisure Culture

Though situated on marshy lowlands and swamp of limited promise, Chicago was, from the beginning, a great meeting place. Indian trails of the nine major tribes that ringed the Great Lakes region had long converged at the site. The nomadic tribes frequented the region known as the place of the wild onion. Early French explorers introduced Christianity to the Indians in the seventeenth century, and the fur trade brought French and English trappers to the region. The first permanent settler, Jean Baptiste Point du Sable, a black man engaged in the fur trade, arrived with his Indian wife in the 1770s. Du Sable's trading post was considered elegant by wilderness standards, with a well-furnished cabin, bakery, dairy, smokehouse, stables, and barns. His residence signaled an inauspicious start to the cultural interplay that would transpire over the next century and a half and transform the region into a major urban metropolis.[1]

Only a few hardy souls ventured into the Illinois territory in the late eighteenth century. The lifestyles of these early settlers, trappers, and frontiersmen meshed with those of the native Indians, with whom they lived in relative harmony. The Indian tribes lived a rustic, nomadic, and warlike existence, interspersed with periods of leisure in which they danced and engaged in ball games, such as lacrosse. Early French-Canadian settlers also experienced an autonomous and idyllic lifestyle. For these hardy types, hunting provided both enjoyment and sustenance, while other recreations occupied the rest of one's waking hours. Both French-Canadians and the Indians admired and practiced a generous hospitality in their relationships. They shared in festivities, particularly the dancing and drinking which came to be centered at Mark Beaubien's Sauganash Hotel, home to as many as thirty boarders by 1831. For both groups, life's rhythms remained unregulated by the clock.[2]

Languid summer days provided occasions for sailing parties among the white settlers, while sleighing and skating vied with more dancing and drinking during the winter months. Young French-Indian women cavorted with the newly arrived white men from the eastern states throughout the seasons. Foot races, shooting matches, dancing, and storytelling provided popular amusement and brought status to some.

Mark Beaubien, described by his biographer as "jolly, generous, and athletic," ran the Sauganash Hotel, named after an Indian friend, more for fun than for profit.[3] Beaubien enjoyed company and he allowed all townspeople the free use of his ferry. Acquaintances stated that "two minutes with him cured the blues."[4]

Drunken brawlers and Indians often shared sleeping space on the floor of his hotel when they were not dancing to the owner's fiddle or laughing at his tales. Mark's older brother, Jean, served the official needs of the community, acting in a variety of roles as militia leader, school trustee, justice of the peace, and election judge.[5]

For many others, gambling often reinforced or diminished one's economic standing. Land and houses were bartered for other goods or changed hands on the fortunes of cards or horse races. As in other frontier societies, socioeconomic status, influence, and power were often transitory in Chicago. Luck was ephemeral, and fortunes changed rapidly in the carefree society unencumbered by too many material wants.[6]

The Anglo-American Invasion

The westward expansion of Anglo-Americans in the early nineteenth century encroached upon such peaceful settlements. John Kinzie, of English-Scotch parentage, arrived

from Detroit and bought the DuSable cabin in 1804. He began
selling liquor to the Indians and that same year five Sac and
Fox chieftains, under the influence of alcohol, sold fifty million
acres of their land to the United States government. Moreover,
they assumed that their annual gifts over the next two decades were friendly gestures rather than the consummation of
business contracts. The War of 1812 brought additional white
faces from the East to occupy a garrison of the United States
government. The local inhabitants resisted the intrusion with
the infamous Fort Dearborn massacre. Further white incursions and the duplicitous treaties that they entailed led to the
Winnebago and Black Hawk Wars by the early 1830s. By that
time, however, speculators had already sold the first town lots
on the southwestern shore of Lake Michigan. The dozen
buildings that marked the landscape near the Chicago River
in 1832 numbered 180 the next year, and the population
approached 4,000 by mid-decade.[7]

The federal government appropriated $25,000 for the con-
struction of a harbor, built by a then little-known engineer
named Jefferson Davis. Land sales, conducted by speculators
operating with eastern capital, were to finance a proposed
canal, which was begun on the Fourth of July. Whites chased
many of the Indians from the region in the Black Hawk War.
The treaty that ended the hostilities in 1831 eventually removed the tribes to land west of the Mississippi River and
opened the area to rapid white settlement.[8]

For a time, some of the early settlers and their offspring
managed to bridge the divergent cultures. Medore Beaubien,
a half-breed son of Jean, had been educated at Princeton and
was elected a trustee. Billy Caldwell, a Sauganash Indian
chief of mixed parentage, became justice of the peace.
Caldwell even offered to buy schoolbooks for Indian children
if they would adopt the white style of dress. They declined,
and the Indians attended a Beaubien family wedding dressed
in traditional garb, including tomahawks and scalps. Boys of
both races continued to hunt together, but the half-breeds
were forced to choose between the divergent worlds as additional settlers arrived from the East in search of new opportunities. The growing number of Yankees gradually

supplanted the bucolic lifestyle with a more urban and commercial one.[9]

In August 1833 the state legislature incorporated Chicago as a chartered town, an event that marked the beginning of a rapid change in the frontier society. Henry Whitehead, a Methodist minister, arrived the following month to proselytize the Indians, 5,000 of whom had gathered at Chicago to cede more of their land to the U.S. government. Agents paid Indians in fifty-cent pieces, and white traders quickly relieved them of their money by selling pints of whiskey for one dollar and all other goods at fifty cents. Subsequent land speculation by the easterners began to transform the once communal society into a profit-oriented marketplace. The early settlers, such as Jean Beaubien, lost much of their land to scheming lawyers.[10]

Beaubien's rival, John Kinzie, and Gurdon S. Hubbard, already operated within such a system. Serving as an Indian agent and fur traders, both proved adept in the commercial world and became two of the town's leading citizens. As the sole credit line to the East, Hubbard functioned as the town financier. The privatization of property resulted in the subjugation of communal values. Animals that previously roamed the streets were required to be penned, and neighbors sued Chief Alexander Robinson for allowing his horses to graze upon their land.[11]

The white settlers brought a different set of cultural values to the community, and they disrupted the existing social practices and relationships. Easterners conscripted territory by force and treaty, and the American Fur Company and other creditors received much of the payment for Indian holdings. In the rush for land, both the French-Canadian and Indian cultures were quickly subsumed. In a final show of defiance, Indians donned war paint and paraded through the streets of Chicago as they departed for their reservation. Medore Beaubien, Caldwell, and Antoine Ouilmette, who had resided in the area nearly fifty years, joined the Indians in their exodus of 1835.[12]

As the Anglo-American community emerged, easterners introduced urban amenities, such as three dancing schools, even as residual hunting and gambling practices persisted.

Bears and wolves were still shot with some regularity, and a billiard hall was also established at Couche's Hotel in 1836. Weekly wolf hunts continued, and shooting within the city limits caused great concern for the public safety as late as 1847. The staying power of these events was, however, short. Concerned citizens formed a committee to abolish gambling. As early as 1837, legislation forbade billiards, along with shuffleboard and cards. Such regulations imposed restrictions on the boisterous and undisciplined lifestyles of the early settlers. As informal practices became subject to government and laws, a more clearly defined pattern of acceptable leisure practices emerged.[13]

Anglo-American newcomers did more than regulate existing leisure practices, however. They also regularized particular sports in highly organized structures. Impromptu horse races, such as an 1834 winter match run on the frozen river, gave way to a three-day schedule of races arranged by the Chicago Sporting Club in 1840. The event consisted of one- and two-mile races for purses ranging from $25 to $200. A formal course was also established behind Myrick's tavern, south of the city. By the early 1840s, as well, three cricket clubs sought competition with outlying communities. The formalization of leisure activities served notice of the different cultural perspectives between the early settlers and the eastern newcomers.[14]

Chicago continued to take on more urban, eastern, and commercial characteristics as migrants from New England and Europe arrived in the city. It was incorporated as a city in 1837, with New Yorker William B. Ogden, an 1835 arrival, as its first mayor. Canals had already opened western lands for speculation, and railroads brought more settlers over the next two decades. By 1845 the population numbered more than 12,000, including 1,056 Germans, 972 Irish, 531 Norwegians, and smaller numbers of other ethnic groups. During and after 1848, the social upheavals in Europe swelled the immigrant ranks, and within five years, 52 percent of the city's residents were foreign-born. Migrants from the American South dwindled to less than 2 percent of the 1850 total, while easterners comprised 21 percent of the city's population and New Yorkers, 13 percent.

It was this group of increasingly numerous easterners that imparted its own values to the economic and cultural face of Chicago. New Englanders, descended from the earliest colonial English migrants, came to Chicago intent on exploiting the area's natural resources and advantageous geographical location for commercial trade. In fact, more than 88 percent of the new settlers who arrived in Chicago from 1830-1840 came from the Northeast, and nine of the first ten mayors were from New England or New York. In 1846 the New England Society was formed to demonstrate their allegiance to their eastern birthplaces.[15]

As Chicago competed with its Midwestern rivals—St. Louis, Cincinnati, and Milwaukee—for the growing economic markets, its eastern settlers indelibly marked the city's early development by controlling political power and capital resources. Early businessmen such as William B. Ogden, John H. Kinzie, and Oliver Newberry assumed the reins of economic leadership and constructed elaborate canal and railroad systems to serve the vast economic hinterlands. They recognized the importance of good transportation to Chicago, and campaigned to raise funds for building projects throughout the 1840s. Ogden, Kinzie, and Newberry were not, of course, alone in changing the face of the region. In 1848 the Illinois and Michigan Canal opened the Mississippi River trade to Chicagoans, a year after Cyrus McCormick built his reaper works in the city, financed by Ogden. The first railroad, the Galena and Chicago Union, began operation in the same year. The Chicago and Northwestern Railroad then extended its track into Wisconsin, and the Illinois Central moved southwest. Other lines entered Iowa, Indiana, and Michigan; and Chicagoans could reach New York by rail in only thirty-six hours by 1852. By mid-decade, ten railroads served the city with 120 daily trains. The vast transportation network allowed its builders to preempt their rivals in making Chicago the major farm market of the Midwest. Merchants, such as Potter Palmer, John V. Farwell, Marshall Field, and Levi Leiter, established the city as a dry goods center, while a number of others processed the farmers' meat products. Such schemes brought a commercial economy to the region, transplanting the subsistence lifestyles and the barter system of the early settlers.[16]

As these entrepreneurs organized the economy along commercial lines, they also adopted eastern-style commercialized leisure structures. New Yorkers established the Jockey Club based on the constitution and bylaws of the Union course in their home state in August 1840. Four years later, when William B. Ogden served as president, the club owned a one-mile track, which was encircled by a larger four-mile oval laid out on the prairie near the Illinois and Michigan Canal. The group held a three-day inaugural event that year and in 1845 it arranged a week of harness racing for $400 in gold. A New York newspaper report of the undertaking exhibited an optimistic faith:

> We had some sport here and no mistake. I reckon, you and other old sportsmen may ridicule it all as children's play, as you probably will when you look for your Fashions, Peytonas and others of that like, among our performers: notwithstanding I shall stick to it that we had first rate sport...permit me to observe, that we out here are beginning just about these days to entertain considerable tall notions about ourselves. We have actually taken into our heads to look upon the result of our Fall meeting as a glorious consummation for Northern Illinois, the commencement of a new era in the history of the turf, and the Lord knows what else beside.[17]

The comparison to the East served as the standard by which the commercially minded measured themselves as well as their city.

Horse racing satisfied the interests of various constituencies during the early history of the city. The horse owners rationalized racing as an essential means of improving the breeding stock. For the frontiersmen and gamblers, the horse track, as well as the poolroom, was a place:

> where the "sporting" fringe of the upper class—the hedonists, and hell-raisers given to heavy drinking and gambling and whoring—could get together with the "sporting element" of the lower class and the lower middle-class to the exclusion of those who subscribed to "middle-class morality.[18]

Racing thus served a utilitarian function and presented a perception of social equality as it entertained the residents of the city.

The vast majority of the early Chicagoans were young adult males, who formed a bachelor subculture. Their daily activities revolved around their leisure practices—sport, drink, and womanizing. Although heterosexual, this group shunned marriage and preferred male companionship as it sought its pleasures in the poolhalls, saloons, and brothels. Such a bachelor subculture persisted in various forms into the twentieth century, but the preponderance of young adult males yielded to the influx of immigrant families in the decade prior to the Civil War. In the city census of 1843, adults constituted nearly 60 percent of the male population. By 1850 nearly 50 percent of the same group were children. Within ten more years the sexes had reached parity.[19]

As the social composition of the city changed dramatically in the 1850s, so did its sporting life. The bachelors' lifestyles often offended the Victorian sensibilities of many of the newcomers. They sought greater respectability and sophistication, and the carefree, autonomous bachelors faced greater regulation. The five bowling alleys that had been licensed by the city and the billiard parlors that had served as young male haunts were subjected to municipal gaming laws in 1851. Despite such restraints, the bachelors persisted in their behaviors, but the laws served notice of alternative value systems within the early society, as acceptable work and leisure practices became an issue.[20]

The Protestant morality of many easterners intruded upon the traditional practices in other ways, as well. Among the most extreme cases was that of Seth Paine, who established a "Christian" bank and refused to do business with smokers and drinkers, as well as competitors whom he judged to be unethical. This narrow view of "right" behavior transcended the worlds of work and leisure.[21]

However, a double standard existed in sport, as well as business. Horse racing, which was controlled by the Jockey Club and favored by the politically powerful, won acceptance. Gentlemen assumed that they had, for the most part, greater self-discipline in matters of morality and certainly more money with which they could afford such dalliances. They made the laws, presumably for the benefit of all. Yet, the restrictive legislation aimed to curtail the practices of those who were deemed less responsible, particularly the wage earners who had less expendable income.

As the political leaders attempted to regulate the leisure lives of others through legislation, they also pursued the commercial opportunities in sport. The Garden City track opened in 1854, and John Wentworth, later to become mayor, opened the Brighton Park Racetrack southwest of the city in 1855. Since thoroughbreds were in short supply, both courses accommodated harness racers.[22]

In emulating their eastern contemporaries, the transplanted Yankees introduced other cultural organizations and institutions in Chicago. Northwestern and Lake Forest Universities and the Young Men's Christian Association all were established during the 1850s. John C. Dore, a Bostonian, was hired as superintendent for the first public high school in 1856, following the pattern of public education in Massachusetts. Early park development, too, followed the model of the eastern landscaped pleasure grounds, often merging and rationalizing self-interests with the common good. Early park board members, such as Paul Cornell, were also real estate developers, and they often acted in their own behalf, acquiring and selling land to the city for landscaped parks modeled on the New York plan.[23]

European Influences

Before native Americans could fully establish their cultural dominance, large numbers of foreign immigrants poured into the city. By 1850, when Chicago had almost 30,000 residents, Irish refugees comprised more than 20 percent of the total, and Germans accounted for another 17 percent. In all, foreigners constituted over 52 percent of the population, and they, too, established numerous organizations. As early as 1844 Catholics founded St. Mary of the Lake University and by 1853 had a dozen parochial schools. By 1847 the small contingent of German-Jewish settlers organized a congregation and built the first synagogue at Clark Street and Quincy Avenue in 1851. Six years later they had established an independent B'nai B'rith organization (Ramah No. 33). The Danes, Swedes, and Norwegians had already founded the Chicago Scandinavian Union in 1854.[24]

These ethnic groups tried to maintain their particular lifestyles by living within segregated communities, adhering to European customs and languages, and practicing religious beliefs considered peculiar by the American Protestants. Some of them also actively resisted native actions intended to incorporate them within the native structure. When the Illinois legislature heeded the admonitions of temperance groups and prohibited nonmedical liquor sales in 1851, it faced opposition from a coalition of Germans and Irish. After mayor Levi D. Boone actually enforced the law and imposed excessive licensing fees, rioting ensued. Eventually, the nativist attempt to end consumption of the nondistilled alcoholic beverages preferred by the Germans resulted in the Lager Beer riots of 1855. After one death, several injuries, and the imposition of martial law, a political referendum overturned the prohibition law. The riots marked the first violent confrontation of natives and foreign-born residents over an issue related to leisure practices.[25]

Europeans and Americans temporarily assuaged the rift in the rapidly growing society when the Civil War broke out. Many of the European immigrants joined other Chicagoans in supporting the Union cause. The German Turner Union cadets supplied 105 enlistees to the 24th Illinois Regiment a week after the fall of Fort Sumter. Scots formed the Highland Brigade; a Scandinavian regiment and a French battalion that included French-Canadians, Belgians, and Swiss were organized; and another company of Hungarians, Bohemians, and Slavs formed to serve the Union cause.[26]

The onset of the Civil War produced more than an interlude in ethnic and nativist social frictions. It also altered commerce and industry and the competitiveness of Chicago in the national economic picture. The vastly enlarged population—by 1860 Chicago had 112,172 people and was the country's ninth largest city—spawned a growing industrial work force, which manned the granaries, tanneries, and food processing plants that served the Union war efforts.

This relatively cheap and abundant work force supported the commercial and industrial expansion of the city. More isolated from the fighting than its rivals, St. Louis and Cincinnati, Chicago consolidated its commercial leadership and emerged as an industrial center. By 1861 Chicago had become the nation's leading meat packer, surpassing Cincinnati. Meat packing became centralized in the city with the opening of the massive Union Stockyards in 1865, and Philip Armour and Gustavus Swift established other major meat processing plants in succeeding years. By the end of the war, too, Chicago's merchants were shipping more than 41 million bushels of grain, 50 million pounds of cured meats, 450 thousand barrels of beef and pork, and over 272 million feet of lumber, in addition to lesser amounts of clothing, hides, food products, iron, lead, and coal.[27]

The timely transport of such goods required greater efficiency and work discipline. Railroads, which dominated the transport network in Chicago, paid locomotive engineers as much as $5.65 per day in order to keep the goods moving in an orderly manner. The wage was more than four times the rate for artisans and skilled mechanics in the 1850s. Engineers were in short supply, and they benefitted from their specialized status. Railroad workers, in general, received better wages and bonuses compared to other workers; but with the increased income, workers lost a good measure of the autonomy that they had previously enjoyed. Efficient transport required the institution of fixed schedules, which, in turn, required greater work discipline. So railroad companies introduced rule books that prohibited smoking and drinking, defined specific responsibilities, and regulated working hours. Pinkerton detectives investigated suspect employees and intransigents were dismissed. Employers, rather than workers, began to dictate work rhythms.[28]

After the war, workers stayed on the job more than sixty hours per week, but weather and seasonal demands often caused fluctuations in their work and in their wages. Companies lowered other production costs by refusing to install expensive safety features. Workers responded by banning together and striking to insure their rights. A National Labor Union was organized in 1866 to secure an eight-hour day, and the Brotherhood of Locomotive Engineers initiated a life insurance program for its members in 1867. Illinois workers were the first to win the eight-hour day on March 5 of that same year, but employers soon learned to circumvent the law by offering hourly rather than day wages.[29]

Organized Leisure

One way for employers to increase productivity, efficiency, and profit was to attempt to regulate their laborers' leisure lives. Activities such as billiards, gambling, and drinking often resulted in "blue Mondays," which decreased workers' outputs and lowered profits. Therefore, temperance and the wholesome use of leisure became commercial as well as social interests. Employers and other moralists saw athletic sports as a worthy alternative to the traditional leisure practices of many young men, which often centered around the saloon. In an effort to change such practices, employers such as J.V. Farwell, Marshall Field, and Cyrus McCormick solicited and supported the evangelical work of Dwight L. Moody and the YMCA.[30]

Baseball, in particular, met with great popularity in Chicago after spreading westward from New York in the 1850s. The Union Base Ball Club was organized in 1856, and in 1858 the Chicago Base Ball Club adopted the rules of the Association and Congress of Base Ball Clubs of New York. With uniform rules, clubs soon proliferated. Three more organized by 1860, and a total of forty-five existed by 1867. In the same year the Board of Trade sponsored competing baseball teams, and the city boasted more than fifty company teams in local leagues by 1870.[31]

Businessmen and politicians fielded teams and served as leaders of the local leagues, helping to form the North Western Association of Baseball Clubs and the Illinois Association of Baseball Players in 1865. The firm of Marshall Field, Levi Leiter, and Potter Palmer sponsored a company league with five separate teams organized by department. Company, and even civic, pride were at stake when local champions took the field. In 1869 a Chicago Board of Trade team ventured to Milwaukee in search of supremacy; and the regional rivalries with St. Louis and Cincinnati led Chicago merchants to raise $15,000 in a joint stock company to support a professional team, the White Stockings. Potter Palmer, the club president, and prominent stockholders George Pullman and General Phil Sheridan must have beamed with pride as 100,000 Chicagoans welcomed the team home after its 157-1 defeat of Memphis in 1870.[32]

Early proponents of the game extolled its healthful nature and character-building qualities. Baseball, many argued, echoed and promoted the desired values of teamwork, efficiency, discipline, and self-sacrifice, while still allowing for individual achievement. The *Chicago Tribune* proclaimed baseball to be a wonderful form of exercise, devoid of the vulgarity of other sports. The *Chicago Times* described baseball players as noble and vigorous gentlemen who did not allow alcohol at their game sites, providing a "pleasing sobriety."[33]

In effect, baseball became a means to, and a symbol of, both a robust manhood and a vigorous economy. Chicagoans considered themselves to be "rich-blooded, strong-nerved, and large-brained...superior to the average American," and wholesome athletic endeavors could help them to retain such standing.[34]

The disastrous Chicago fire of 1871, which nearly leveled the city, only temporarily halted the city's most visible team, the White Stockings. The "phoenix" rapidly rebuilt as William Hulbert, a New Yorker by birth but now a member of the Chicago Board of Trade, succeeded Palmer as club president and enticed four stars from the Boston Red Stockings, including pitcher Albert Spalding, and Cap Anson from the Philadelphia Athletics to join. Hulbert balanced both the club and league presidencies precariously and in a high-handed manner amidst charges of conflicting interests. The *Chicago Tribune* came to his defense, retorting: "Who should boss the league if not Chicago?...What is good for baseball in Chicago is good for the league as a whole."[35]

With its usual aplomb, the *Tribune* had adequately characterized the presumptions of city leaders, who were emerging as principal players in many of the nation's enterprises. Such presumptions and self-assurance did not, however, produce widespread and lasting changes in the practices and values of the bachelor subculture, ethnic groups, and the working class in the postwar years. Remnants of the frontier society persisted in the leisure lifestyles of Chicago's bachelors, where ubiquitous gambling coincided with other activities deemed immoral by business and civic leaders.[36]

Gambling and the unabashed pursuit of male pleasures continued to be centered in the saloons, brothels, and poolhalls. Men congregated around bars, billiard tables, and bowling alleys to share drinks and camaraderie. They often refused paternal discipline and scandalized elders by speeding trotting horses past Sunday church services, along with their gambling activities that revolved around sporting events. Moreover, some members of the bachelor subculture gave horse racing an unsavory reputation. One such colorful character was professional gambler George Trussell, owner of the champion trotter, Dexter. Trussell, whose violent confrontations with his gambling rival, "Cap" Hyman, often erupted in gunfire on the city streets, met an untimely end. He was killed by his girlfriend, "Irish Mollie" Cosgriff, allegedly because he had paid greater attention to his horse than to her. Trussell's lifestyle, which revolved around gambling and saloon life, characterized the young "sports" that transcended class lines in the male haunts. Both middle class "dandies" and working class bachelors subscribed to similar values and practices within the cult of masculinity.[37]

In addition to horse racing, occasional boxing matches provided other opportunities for betting. The Prairie Queen, a State Street brothel, held dogfights and a weekly bare-knuckle fight, the winner of which received a house prostitute. A good fighter might also have earned as much as $500 for a single fight in the 1850s, a sum equal to a laborer's annual wage. Some laborers' sporting activities thus allowed them to circumvent the growing system of wage labor on an occasional basis, but at the risk of offending Victorian mores.[38]

The city leaders desired to bring about change in such practices, especially those that exhibited brutality or alleged wantonness. A particular boxing match aroused the ire of the *Tribune* when it stated that:

> Prize fights between men are beastly exhibitions, but there is an unutterable loathsomeness in the worse brutality of abandoned, wretched women beating each other almost to nudity, for the amusement of a group of blackguards, even lower in the scale of humanity than the women themselves.[39]

Physicality was an integral part of the working class lifestyle, but the violence, gambling, and the saloon life that accompanied some working class sporting practices affronted Victorian sensibilities and caused boxing to be outlawed in the state in 1869.

Such restrictions failed to deter promoters, who observed only the letter of the law when they did not actually defy it. Despite the ban, the Turner Hall on Clark Street hosted a fight between John Keenan and Jem Mace the next year by billing it as a music festival. Ethnic sport associations, such as the Turners, continued to operate within their own structures, while other promoters simply set the sites of their contests across the nearby Indiana state line to circumvent the prohibition.[40]

City officials continued to try to regulate such actions that they deemed immoral. By 1865 billiard tables were renting at a rate of $4,000 per day in the city, and city fathers enacted a $25 licensing fee for all billiard tables, bowling alleys, and shooting galleries the following year to curtail illicit practices. While such legal measures helped to increase the city's revenues, they did little to stop gambling. Thirty thousand dollars was bet on a single dogfight between a Chicago animal and its Boston counterpart in February of that year.[41]

In addition to the legal measures, private agencies such as the YMCA attempted to counteract such practices by providing moral guidance. Founded in England by George Williams in 1841, a Young Men's Christian Association was formally organized in Chicago in 1858. Led by evangelist Dwight L. Moody, the trustees consisted of merchants, manufacturers, and bankers who shared the belief in a temperate and Christian lifestyle, a lifestyle that was antithetical to the city's bachelor subculture. Businessman such as Samuel Dexter Ward and John V. Farwell served as early presidents; Cyrus McCormick, George Armour, George Pullman, Marshall Field,

John Crerar, and Martin Ryerson later served as trustees or provided large sums for financial support.

Intent on controlling the leisure habits of their work force, these employers worked closely with the YMCA to extend wholesome activities to their employees. The nonsectarian association clearly opposed saloon life. During the 1860s the YMCA surveyed the city and drew attention to the temperance issue. It reported the existence of 2,000 saloons and gambling houses, as well as an annual total consumption of 20 million gallons of liquor. Faced with such a phenomenon, the YMCA designed programs to create a more wholesome atmosphere and a more worthwhile use of leisure time. A library, religious instruction, and a clean living environment were offered to encourage young men to forego the carnal pleasures available in the city. In such efforts, the state backed the YMCA by granting it a thousand-year charter in 1861 and providing it with tax-exempt status in 1867.[42]

By 1871 the YMCA claimed success by virtue of its membership, counting 1,838 young and older enrollees. The success may have been either illusory or transitory, for two years later, membership had dropped to 1,011. By 1875, in an attempt to reverse its losses, the YMCA introduced games such as chess, specifically "to occupy so idleness will not cause temptation" and "to keep them from evil, to win them to be Christian gentlemen, industrious workmen, good citizens, loyal to their homes and the church."[43]

There is little evidence to suggest that such activities increased membership, and even when the YMCA added a gymnasium to its facilities "to attract and hold them,"[44] it experienced only a slight rise in enrollment.Throughout the 1870s and into the next decade, membership remained below the 2,000 mark. For some, it was the gym rather than the message that was attractive. Ed Morris, a member of the Pittsburgh National League team, found it necessary to reassure the sporting fraternity that although he had abstained from liquor and joined the YMCA, he had not "become religious, his object in joining the Association being to get the use of its gym."[45]

The difference in values and the pattern of stratified, commercialized leisure practices and organizations became quite evident by the 1870s. This pattern emerged under the guidance and leadership of the native-born easterners who had wrested control from the early pre-Anglo American residents and embarked upon work and leisure patterns characterized by a profit motive. The position of laborers within that system remained tenuous, however. Increasing industrialization relegated most to positions of wage labor and an unequal share of the commercial wealth.

The emerging exclusivity of leisure practices and the ostentatious displays of the wealthy accentuated and reinforced the social stratification inherent in the capitalist system. Leisure practices helped to define one's status within the society and wage labor limited the available choices. That particular sport forms remained unavailable to the masses thus reinforced the socioeconomic hierarchy.

The increasing numbers of European immigrants who arrived in the city in the latter half of the nineteenth century questioned and challenged this system. Although the Civil War had resolved the greatest national crisis, smaller, but no less significant crises affected Chicagoans in the postwar years. Industrial leaders had forged a commercial economy during the boom years that accompanied the city's rapid rise. They had gained a hold on the social ladder during the war, but many were self-made men intent on securing status and creating a system they controlled. They attempted to regulate and counteract practices that did not reflect their own values. Organizations such as the YMCA, and wholesome games such as baseball, were meant to induce the desired results; but native Americans had more to fear than their unruly sons.

Oppositional views between employers and employees over the nature of leisure and the perceived inequities of the wage labor system came to a head in the eight hour movement of the immediate postwar years. In the years that followed, the differences became more acute. Chicago became a seething cauldron of discontent, where tempers boiled and cultures clashed. The mixture of ideologies and lifestyles over the next half-century produced a volatile social blend and the most explosive urban center in the United States. The polarities between natives and ethnics and employers and employees were particularly evident in the organization of work and

Early Chicago

leisure practices throughout the remainder of the nineteenth century as competing lifestyles challenged those of the native guard.[46]

Notes

1. Lois Wille, *Forever Open, Clear and Free* (Chicago: Henry Regnery, 1972), 8; Jacqueline Peterson, "Wild Chicago: The Formation and Destruction of a Multicultural Community on the Midwestern Frontier, 1816-1837," in Melvin G. Holli and Peter d'A. Jones, eds., *The Ethnic Frontier* (Grand Rapids, MI: William B. Eerdmans, 1977), 27-61.

2. Harold McCracken, *George Catlin and the Old Frontier* (New York: Bonanza Books, 1959), 32, 123-4; George R. Lee, *The Beaubiens of Chicago* (Canton, MO: Culver-Stockton College, 1973), 45; Homer Hoyt, *One Hundred Years of Land Values in Chicago* (New York: Arno Press, 1970), 3, 19.

3. Lee, *The Beaubiens,* 9-21.

4. Ibid., 31.

5. Ibid., 33.

6. Ibid., 33-5, 38; Clarence W. Alvord, ed., *The Centennial History of Illinois* (Springfield: Illinois Centennial Commission, 1918), 153; Peterson, "Wild Chicago," 38-61.

7. McCracken, *George Catlin,* 166-7; Wille, *Forever Open, Clear and Free,* 12; Emmett Dedmon, *Fabulous Chicago* (New York: Random House, 1953), 6; Robert Cromie, *A Short History of Chicago* (San Francisco: Lexikos, 1984): 7, 32-3, 42. Bessie L. Pierce, *A History of Chicago* (New York: Alfred A. Knopf, 1937), 1: 207, 210-11, cites the *Chicago Democrat* and the *Chicago American* regarding horse racing purses ranging from $500-$1500; as well as the *Chicago Democrat* and *Chicago American* for dancing schools. She cites sailing parties in the *Chicago American* and the *Daily American.*

For a detailed description and the importance of physical prowess in a frontier society, see Elliot J. Gorn, "Gouge and Bite, Pull Hair and Scratch: The Social Significance of Fighting in the Southern Backcountry," *American Historical Review,* 90 (February 1985): 18-43.

8. Wille, *Forever Open, Clear and Free,* 12, 14; Francis M. Huston, *Financing an Empire: History of Banking in Illinois* (Chicago: S. J. Clarke, 1926), 536-7.

9. Lee, *The Beaubiens,* 39-40.

10. Ibid., 13, 14, 46-53, 75-8; Pierce, *A History of Chicago,* 1 (1937): 41; Louise Christopher, "Henry Whitehead, Circuit Rider," *Chicago History,* 5:1 (Spring 1976):2-11; Peterson, "Wild Chicago," 61.

11. Lee, *The Beaubiens,* 32, 78.

12. Wille, *Forever Open, Clear and Free,* 14-15, 17, 23; McCracken, *George Catlin,* 178-9 on treaty arrangements.

13. Pierce, *A History of Chicago,* 1 (1937): 206-08, and 215 n. 236 on the anti-gambling committee.

14. Ibid., 207; John Hervey, *Racing in America* (New York: Scribner Press, 1944), 2: 236-7; Alvord, ed., *Centennial History,* 411.

15. Pierce, *A History of Chicago,* 1 (1937): 173-9, 416; Dedmon, *Fabulous Chicago,* 14; Wille, *Forever Open, Clear and Free,* 20-1.
Frederic Cople Jaher and Jocelyn M. Grant, "Chicago Business Elite, 1830-1930," *Business History Review,* 50 (Autumn 1976): 288-328; Alvord, ed., *Centennial History,* 321.

16. Lawrence H. Larsen, "Chicago's Midwest Rivals: Cincinnati, St. Louis and Milwaukee," *Chicago History,* 5:3 (Fall 1976): 141; Hoyt: *One Hundred Years of Land Values,* 58; Dedmon, *Fabulous Chicago,* 14; and Pierce, *A History of Chicago,* 1 (1937): 105, 109, 114-170; Rodney O. Davis, "The People in Miniature," *Illinois Historical Journal,* 81 (Summer 1988): 95-108.

17. Hervey, *Racing in America,* 2: 236-8, who cites the *Turf Register* of October 1840 for the initial establishment of the Jockey Club.

18. Ned Polsky, *Hustlers, Beats and Others* (Chicago: Aldine, 1967), 28.

19. Pierce, *A History of Chicago,* 1 (1937): 415, gives the 1843 city census figures as 3,834 males, of which 2,364 (59 percent) were over the age of twenty-one. The demographic changes are discussed in detail in 1 (1937): 172-4. Statistics for 1850 and 1860 are also from 2 (1940): 5. The 1860 figures show 50.77 percent of the population as male and 49.23 percent as female.

20. Ibid., 215.

21. Huston, *Financing an Empire,* 145-6.

22. Arthur Todd, chairman, *Chicago Recreation Survey* (Chicago: Chicago Recreation Commission, 1937): 2: 53, 89; Glen E. Holt and

20 Early Chicago

Dominic A. Pacyga, *Chicago: A Historical Guide to the Neighborhoods* (Chicago Historical Society, 1979), 142.

23. Pierce, *A History of Chicago,* 2 (1940): 20, 390, 396-7, 418; Galen Cranz, *The Politics of Park Design: A History of Urban Parks in America* (Cambridge, MA: MIT Press, 1982), 160, 164, and 281 n. 13.

24. Louis Wirth, *The Ghetto* (1928; reprint, Chicago: University of Chicago Press, 1956), 153-64; and Edward Mazur, "Jewish Chicago: From Diversity to Community," in Holli and Jones, eds., *The Ethnic Frontier,* 264-83.

25. Pierce, *A History of Chicago,* 2 (1940): 436-8; and Mari Jo Buhle, *Women and American Socialism, 1870-1920* (Urbana: University of Illinois Press, 1981), 6, 20.

26. Pierce, *A History of Chicago,* 2 (1940): 258; Henry Metzner, *History of the American Turners* (1911; revised ed., Rochester, NY: National Council of American Turners, 1974), 19. Metzner offers an incomplete list of at least four Turner regiments. Stephen Longstreet, *Chicago, 1860-1919* (New York: David McKay, 1973), 39, states that the city sent 15,000 to the Union ranks, of whom only fifty-eight were draftees. Joseph Szeplaki, *The Hungarians in America, 1583-1974* (Dobbs Ferry, NY: Oceana Pub., 1975), 14.

27. Larsen, "Chicago's Midwest Rivals," 141; Clarence Danhof, *Change in Agriculture: The Northern United States, 1820-1870* (Cambridge, MA: Harvard University Press, 1969), 35-6. Shipping figures are derived from the *7th Annual Statement of the Chicago Board of Trade, 1864-1865,* cited in Pierce, *A History of Chicago,* 2 (1940): 496. Grain figures include barley, corn, oats, wheat, and flour.

28. Walter Licht, *Working for the Railroad: the Organization of Work in the Nineteenth Century* (Princeton, NJ: Princeton University Press, 1983), 61-9.

29. David Montgomery, *Beyond Equality: Labor and the Radical Republicans, 1862-1872* (New York: Alfred A. Knopf, 1967).

30. *Webster's Biographical Dictionary,* 1st ed., s.v. "Farwell, John V."

31. Pierce, *A History of Chicago,* 2 (1940): 470, who cites Smith and DuMoulin, *Directory, 1859-60,* in the Appendix: 1 to identify the early teams. In addition to the Union (1856,) they were the Atlantic, Columbia (1859), Excelsior, and Olympic clubs. Arthur R. Ahrens, an historian of Chicago baseball, adds the Eurekas, Ogdens, and Garden Cities in "How the Cubs Got Their Name," *Chicago History,* 5:1

(Spring 1976): 39-43. Company teams of the postwar years are discussed by Stephan Freedman, "The Baseball Fad in Chicago, 1865-1870," *Journal of Sport History,* 5 (Summer 1978): 52, 54; and Steven M. Gelber, "Their Hands Are All Out Playing: Business and Amateur Baseball, 1845-1917," ibid., 11 (Spring 1984): 5-27.

32. Cited in Freedman, "The Baseball Fad," 45; Pierce, *A History of Chicago,* 2 (1940): 470.

33. Freedman, "The Baseball Fad," 44.

34. Cited in ibid., 45.

35. Harold Seymour, *Baseball: The Early Years* (New York: Oxford University Press, 1960), 90; Peter Levine, *A.G. Spalding and the Rise of Baseball* (New York: Oxford University Press, 1985).

Joseph Medill's 1874 takeover of the *Chicago Tribune* would lead it on an increasingly conservative path. In succeeding years it blatantly espoused an ethnocentric bias, serving as the mouthpiece of the middle class, commercial, and nativist sentiments.

36. Jaher and Ghent, "Chicago's Business Elite," 307.

37. Richard Sennett, *Families Against the City: Middle Class Homes of Industrial Chicago, 1872-1890* (Cambridge, MA: Harvard University Press, 1970), 19; Dedmon, *Fabulous Chicago,* 77-9; Longstreet, *Chicago, 1860-1919,* 41-2; *The Sporting Life,* 9:52 (Nov. 25, 1882): 1, 4. Michael T. Isenberg, *John L. Sullivan and His America* (Urbana: University of Illinois Press, 1988), 39-59.

38. Pierce, *A History of Chicago,* 2 (1940): 468; Longstreet, *Chicago, 1860-1919,* 30, on the Prairie Queen, and Elliot J. Gorn, *The Manly Art* (Ithaca, NY: Cornell University Press, 1986), 105, on prize money.

39. Quoted in Pierce, *A History of Chicago,* 2(1940): 468.

40. Ibid.

41. Freedman, "The Baseball Fad," 49; Todd, *Chicago Recreation Survey,* 2: 53.

42. Paul Boyer, *Urban Masses and Moral Order in America, 1820-1920* (Cambridge, MA: Harvard University Press, 1978), 109, 113-19; Pierce, *A History of Chicago,* 2 (1940): 378; Edwin B. Smith, John C. Grant, and Horace M. Starkey, *Historical Sketch of the Young Men's Christian Association, 1858-1898* (Chicago: YMCA, 1898); Elizabeth Halsey, *The Development of Public Recreation in Metropolitan Chicago* (Chicago Recreation Commission, 1942) covers the interrelationships of the city's commercial leaders with the YMCA movement.

Among the major YMCA contributors were John V. Farwell, who donated $60,000 in land and cash, including the group's first building; John Crerar, $50,000; Joseph and Philip Armour, who endowed their mission with more than $100,000; and, later, Martin Hughitt, president of the Chicago and Northwestern Railroad, who gave $18,000.

43. Pierce, *A History of Chicago,* 2 (1940): 378; 3 (1957): 443 on membership; quotes from Smith, Grant, and Starkey, *Historical Sketch of the YMCA,* 24, 29.

44. Quoted in Smith, Grant, and Starkey, ibid., 32.

45. Ibid., 37. The quote is from *The Sporting and Theatrical Journal,* 11:7 (Dec. 24, 1887): 7.

46. Jaher and Ghent, "The Chicago Business Elite, 1830-1930," 288-328, analyzes the socioeconomic backgrounds of 1,186 Chicago business leaders. Of the 346 surveyed between 1830-1880, the vast majority were native-born northeasterners and Protestants. The authors characterize two-thirds of all those surveyed as self-made men on the basis of noninherited wealth, although less than 10 percent had working class origins and none were unskilled.

CHAPTER 2

The Clash of Cultures and Leisure Stratification

The processes of urbanization and industrialization affected American communities at uneven rates, but eastern towns and cities were able to address the accompanying problems and issues inherent in social and economic change over an extended period of time. In Chicago, the transformation from a frontier community to an industrial metropolis was largely condensed in a single generation. Wage labor dictated the amount and nature of leisure as employer-imposed work hours and earnings left little, if any, disposable income for recreation. The cohesive potential of sporting practices was largely lost as particular class-based sporting cultures accentuated the growing social division. The wealthy eventually retreated to palatial estates at a distance from the city, where they participated in sport forms unavailable to others. The growing middle class, too, distinguished itself from the laboring masses by forming exclusive clubs for their athletic interests. The largely immigrant working class spent its leisure within the ethnic neighborhoods, often in saloons; while others faced unwelcome leisure during long periods of unemployment. Displaced by mechanization or child labor and with limited access to resources, many questioned the nature of equality and freedom in America. Also, employers disputed workers' use of leisure, whether in the consumption of alcohol that affected their productivity, or in the organization of groups that promoted class and ethnic issues that threatened their hegemony. The questions were answered with emotion and intensity, and the responses included class warfare as natives, ethnics, employers, and employees tried to make sense of their rapidly changing lives in the generation that followed the Civil War.[1]

Inquiries by government agencies and private concerns regarding the causes of social unrest produced conflicting opinions and fueled both sides of the debate. Unbridled capitalism, however, gave many workers ample cause for complaint. A European immigrant claimed that he was recruited to work in America, then "swindled and driven into poverty by ruthless capitalists," who paid minimal wages, then dismissed him at Christmas in favor of cheaper labor.[2] A survey of Chicago's bakers found that they worked an average of almost sixteen hours a day, six days a week, not counting the additional two to three hours while they awaited the rising of the dough. Even then, bakers could not relax outside the shop, as workers began to conceive of leisure as "free time" to do as they wished. Skilled workers charged that employers dismantled their craft structure, demeaned their work, and segmented the labor force by hiring "helpers" who performed specialized tasks at a fraction of the tradesmen's wage scale. Only a minimal number of apprentices were hired to learn the trade. Moreover, workers faced dismissal for a variety of charges. In addition to alcohol usage, employers even forbid talking or walking around in some factories, and others labored under the watchful eyes of police guards. Unionized packing house workers lost their jobs for protesting the company's confiscation of their fund to help an injured co-worker. Laborers likened such employment to slavery without a whip, stating that "big business has become a curse, and a plague, promising want, destruction, and misery."[3] Employers countered that cultural differences and dissolute lifestyles led to self-destructive behaviors, poverty, and the conditions that despoiled the city. Different perceptions of work and leisure lay at the heart of the matter.

Initial Organization of Labor

A harbinger of Chicago's economically driven dissension appeared in the economic lapse that followed the Civil War. On May 1, 1867, 6,000-10,000 workers walked off the job as craftsmen and laborers hoisted flags and banners in a mile-long parade to demand an eight-hour day. Rioting and violence followed. Nine months later Chicago still had 25,000 unemployed workers and 19,000 charity cases. Rebuilding the city after the fire of 1871 temporarily eased the problem of unemployment; but in the aftermath of the Panic of 1873, Chicago's businessmen moved to safeguard their own interests. After unemployed railroad workers denounced the "aristocracy of wealth" in a demonstration at the 12th Street Turner Hall and 10,000 marched on City Hall, commercial interests formed the "Citizens Association" on July 24, 1874. Thereafter, employers moved to create a militia capable of responding to any threat from radical socialists and their largely ethnic leaders. The First Regiment became a reality a month later, three years before the enactment of a state militia law.[4]

Ethnic social-athletic organizations allied with labor unions often spearheaded the assault on the industrial system. Radical groups held their meetings at the Turner and Sokol (gymnastics) halls, and heavily armed ethnics posed a particular concern to the employers. The Bohemian Sharpshooters, a workers' militia, had maintained useful skills by holding regular shooting matches throughout the war years. The Sharpshooters alarmed employers, as did the German Turners, who responded to authoritarian measures by forming the Lehr und Wer Verein (education and defense society), another quasimilitary organization, in 1875. The Bohemian Turners hosted a socialist speaker that same year. Individual firebrands, such as August Spies and Albert Parsons, soon followed suit, espousing the violence that had already convulsed European industrial capitals. In the midst of a major economic depression, radical sentiments took hold among the increasing number of unemployed and those facing wage cuts, layoffs, or decreased work hours. By 1877, 30,000 Chicagoans, 18 percent of its work force, were unemployed.[5]

On July 17, 1877, strikes and rioting broke out in the face of wage reductions on eastern rail lines. Employers feared that the Illinois lines, which employed more than 68,000 railway workers and sustained countless others, would soon follow. In Chicago, Albert Parsons and the Workingmen's Party questioned the servile conditions, employers' greed, and even the right to private property, the foundation of the capitalist system. As radical speakers became more impassioned, Marshall Field and Levi Leiter armed their employees and the McCormick works doubled its guards. The nativist media charged that a civil war was at hand and vowed to put down any insurrection.[6]

Amid such agitation, Chicago's railway workers joined in the national strike without violence or demonstration, as urged by labor leaders. All business came to a halt, and melees pitting police against the congregations that filled the streets broke out. Some Bohemian women pelted the police with rocks, while others resupplied the hurlers by carrying the projectiles in their aprons. Although the riots produced less violence than did those in Baltimore and Pittsburgh, Chicago's mayor called for volunteers to serve as special police in helping the army to restore order. Papers proclaimed a "Red War" and "Reign of Terror," and rumors of slaughter excited emotions on both sides. At this point, then, the confrontations did become violent, with 30 killed and 200 reportedly injured, 50 of whom were policemen. One death resulted when the police invaded a peaceful labor meeting at the Germans' 12th Street Turner Hall. In response, laborers formed workers' militias that did not serve the employers. Within a year the Lehr und Wehr Verein counted a thousand members.[7]

In the wake of the Great Strike, employers sought to break unions in any way they could. They offered promotions, wage increases, and insurance benefits to entice some workers from their radical sentiments. The state legislature enacted a bill to curb the leisure activities of the workers' militias, but it failed to curb their parades. Employers used a cooptive strategy and governmental interdiction with recurring frequency in Chicago over the next two decades as various strains of socialist philosophy defined the class struggle more clearly for a growing number of workers.[8]

Both sides marshaled their forces for the impending struggle. Among the capitalists, Marshall Field and the Citizens Association purchased a Gatling gun, and the Board of Trade resolved to increase the military's strength to 100 regiments of a thousand men each. The German Turners, Scandinavian Turners, and Bohemian Sokols solidified bonds with the International Working People's Association. Women, who had formed the Working Women's Union in 1878, with Alzina Parsons Stevens as president, also joined.[9]

The women and ethnic groups within the movement often shared their leisure time in dances, masquerade balls, picnics, drama productions, and in choral groups which served as fund raisers for socialist causes. The gymnastic activities of the ethnic sport associations complemented the militaristic shows of strength by the rifle companies.[10]

Such cultural forms established rituals and symbols antithetical to the value systems of the dominant native culture. Whereas baseball teams reinforced commercialism, work discipline, and Americanism, leisure practices organized on a communal basis and designed to support socialist activities reinforced the Old World customs and presented a direct challenge to American individualism and capitalism. Labor groups conducted such affairs almost weekly. The twenty-six gymnastic groups held one or two festivals per month in addition to the dances. Picnics celebrated both American patriotism and European Socialist holidays and drew thousands of participants. An 1878 affair raised $7,000 from the estimated 15,000-30,000 people in attendance. Such affairs regaled the newfound freedom of expression found in America, but they also confronted the lack of freedom in the workplace and the increasing attempts to control workers' leisure time. The radicals felt that the unequal distribution of wealth and the privileges inherent in a stratified society violated the equality guaranteed by the U.S. Constitution. Their black flags symbolized hunger, and the Communist red ones instilled fears of bloodshed. They organized their "long red lines" on American holidays and paraded through upper class neighborhoods to the sound of martial music to demonstrate their collective power.[11]

The fund-raising leisure activities of the socialist groups also enabled them to spread their message through ethnic papers and garner new members, thereby increasing their strength. As early as 1878 the Socialist Party elected a state senator and three state representatives. In the municipal elections the next year, they won three city council seats. In March 1879, the Exposition Building on the lakefront was stretched beyond its 40,000 capacity as workers met to dance, meet the Socialist candidates, and celebrate the anniversaries of the Paris Communes of 1848 and 1871. One of the victorious candidates was Reinhold Lorenz, elected as alderman of the 14th ward, a German saloon keeper, and a member of the Lehr und Wehr Verein. Another was Dr. Ernst Schmidt, the Socialist mayoral candidate, who had garnered 12,000 votes, or 20 percent of those cast. Following that celebration the Citizens Association and the *Chicago Tribune* interceded with the authorities to deny the socialists the use of the facility.[12]

The number of socialist groups in Chicago had grown to twenty-six by 1886 and, when they were denied the use of public buildings, the Turners made their meeting halls available. In such a manner, the labor movement often brought together its various feuding elements in concerted, but too often isolated efforts. Thus, despite its internecine quarrels, the labor movement continued to instill fear among Chicago's elites.

The potential for unity among the disparate factions portended dire consequences for the city's capitalists and kept them on edge. Wage cuts set off an 1884 strike at the Pullman plant and walkouts at the McCormick Harvester Works in 1884 and 1885. Still, in July of that year, the Knights of Labor numbered only 104,066 members, with less than 2,000 in Chicago. After the Knights' phenomenal successes against the railroads owned by the powerful Jay Gould, however, membership rose in 1886 to 702,924, of whom 21,753 were Chicagoans. The Knights, in their acceptance of unskilled laborers and women, fashioned a broad-based foundation to oppose the excesses of capitalism.[13]

The Death Knell of the Radical Labor Movement

The cultural clash turned nasty once more in 1886. The Lehr und Wehr Verein had held a prize shooting the previous summer at Sharpshooters' Park on the North Side. Middle class fears caused the entire police force and two regiments of the national guard to be activated to forestall any possible uprising. In January 1886, the U.S. Supreme Court upheld the 1879 Illinois law enacted against paramilitary groups, although local judges had previously declared it unconstitutional. Armed marchers with bayonets protested the decision.[14]

When the McCormick Harvester Works locked out its employees over a labor dispute in February 1886, scabs replaced the workers, and the hated Pinkertons were brought in to assure their security. As tensions escalated, the press predicted a general uprising on May Day. It passed without violence, although 80,000 workers, led by Albert Parsons, marched on City Hall to demand the eight-hour day. On May 3, the police made a particularly brutal attack on strikers in the vicinity of the McCormick plant. August Spies, who had been addressing a disinterested group nearby, witnessed the event and called for revenge, an appeal that he later retracted. The media sensationalized the outburst, which heightened the sense of fear and imminent danger. The following day both Spies and Parsons were among the speakers at a laborers' gathering at Haymarket Square on Randolph, between Halsted and Des Plaines streets in the market area west of downtown. Mayor Carter Harrison attended the meeting, judged it to be of no consequence, and went home after informing the police of its moderate nature.

Despite the mayor's assessment, the police marched on the assembly and ordered it to disperse. An unknown assailant launched a bomb into the midst of the police, and the resultant blast took eight patrolmen's lives and wounded another sixty-six.[15]

The press labeled the disaster a massacre and irrevocably tied the labor movement to a subversive plot by foreigners to foment anarchy. Public hysteria ruled, and Chicago became a police state. Anyone even remotely suspected of complicity was rounded up without concern for civil rights or due process. Prominent businessmen joined in a secret association to counteract labor groups and raised $70,361 by August. Employers used Pinkerton agents and police to infiltrate labor organizations as spies and informants. Annual contributions from the employers over the next six years rewarded the police for their diligent suppression. The Commercial Club, led by Philip Armour, purchased a machine gun at a cost of more than

$2,000 for the First Infantry Regiment, which was quartered in Chicago.[16]

The ensuing trial was such a travesty of justice that it provoked a widespread clemency movement, to which even Potter Palmer subscribed. George Pullman, Philip Armour, Marshall Field, and Cyrus McCormick, Jr., on the other hand, were clearly pleased with the verdict. Six of the eight defendants were Germans, and all but one were condemned to death. Three were later granted pardons, one committed suicide in his cell, and four were hung on November 11, 1887. Albert Parsons and August Spies were among them. The Chicago Bar Association feted Judge Joseph E. Gary in a dinner afterward, although he had permitted a stacked jury and offended judicial protocol by allowing women to share his bench during the proceedings.

Class lines were clearly drawn. Pullman, Armour, and Field were among the 300 who raised over $100,000 to aid the investigation and police families. The Turners raised defense funds for the trial, while 7,000 supporters attended a gymnastic and choral performance by twenty clubs in January 1889, to aid widows and children of the convicted.

Socialists praised the convicted as martyrs, but the labor movement was clearly forced to take the defensive. In 1887, the state legislature passed a conspiracy bill to repress labor unions and increase police powers. An antiboycott law was also enacted and employers were allowed to implement convict labor despite an 1885 law prohibiting its use. The Commercial Club purchased 632 acres north of the city and donated it to the federal government with the stipulation that it provide a garrison of troops. The subsequent encampment became known as Fort Sheridan in 1888. The labor crises of the 1880s thus enabled the commercial interests to demonstrate their power to mobilize government forces in their own behalf to conserve the established order.[17]

The succeeding five years brought greater prosperity but little decline in labor ferment. Chicago had 300 labor unions by 1891 with an estimated 60,000 members. From January 1887 through June 1894, Chicago experienced 528 more strikes, involving 282,611 workers at a cost of almost $9 million in wages and $14.5 million to employers.[18]

As mechanization increasingly endangered the autonomy of the European craftsmen and wage labor subjected others to less freedom than they had expected, work issues continued to erupt into violent confrontations. Armed conflict, however, failed to overthrow the established capitalist system, nor did it win a clear-cut victory for the commercial interests. Such encounters did, however, invoke the judicial and legislative powers of the upper classes to maintain their status whenever threatened.

The labor "movement" remained a collection of groups, however, and the disparate factions at both the local and national levels failed to achieve unity. In Chicago, frustrated labor leaders increasingly turned to middle class liberals, such as Henry Demarest Lloyd, who championed their cause within the more acceptable forums while providing the necessary financial support in the wake of the Haymarket affair. However radical particular elements of the labor movement might become, the stigma of anarchy forced its leadership to seek acceptance within the boundaries of the established political-judicial system.[19]

As the fragmentation of the labor movement took place, the ethnic social-athletic associations that had been integral members of the socialist movement turned increasingly to nationalistic efforts to maintain their European traditions in the ensuing years. Others allied with the populist movement that included the middle class reformers. By 1895 Benno Koerner, one of the forty uniformed Turners who had valiantly guarded a workers' meeting against nativist interventions, opted for change within the established system as a candidate for alderman in the twenty-first ward. While most ethnics still clung to the fraternal and gymnastic associations that nourished social and nationalistic aims, the defection signaled a measure of accommodation, and political, ethnic, religious, and commercial leaders increasingly found sport a convenient vehicle for promoting their interests.[20]

Sport provided settings for political forums and allowed for more social contact between natives and ethnics, especially after the latter adopted some of the American sport forms. German and Irish players appeared on baseball diamonds in the postwar years, and eastern Europeans followed suit in the

1890s. Even labor unions sponsored baseball teams. By that time both native and ethnic businessmen competed in bowling leagues, while other immigrants contended for prizes in billiard tournaments and track meets. Such leisure practices and sport associations sometimes crossed class and ethnic boundaries, while others demonstrated and solidified the stature of particular groups.

Clubs of the Elite

Even before the Haymarket incident, the industrial process had contributed to the formation of associational leisure ties that created and reinforced a class-based sporting culture. Native businessmen formed social and commercial clubs, like the Dearborn Club, later renamed the Chicago Club in 1861, and the Commercial Club organized in 1877, limited to the city's sixty wealthiest citizens. Other socially elite organizations followed: the Calumet and Union Clubs in 1878 and the Union League in 1879.

In the aftermath of the Haymarket trial, Chicago's social leaders sought to solidify their positions of power and preeminence. For Chicago's elite, consolidation of the established social order became the critical goal. They realized it, in part, by forging intraclass networks through intermarriage, commerce, and leisure associations that excluded nonelites. By creating opportunities for private and exclusive leisure practices, the wealthy defined a distinctive lifestyle unavailable to the masses who were relegated to the public and commercial spaces. Upper-class pastimes such as yachting, coaching (4 horse tally-hos) and fox hunting, remained out of the question for all but the affluent and allowed socialites to maintain their distance.

Horse racing also continued to enjoy the favor of the wealthier residents, and a number of venues catered to their wants. In 1864, the Chicago Driving Park was established as a harness facility, and the Dexter Park Driving Association followed in 1871. The latter took a 10-year lease on Dexter Park Racetrack near the stockyards and took in more than $23,000 at the gate in its first meet. By 1873 the Chicago Driving Park offered a $45,000 purse. In 1879, the socially elite formed their own jockey and trotting club. In 1883, their Washington Park Jockey Club dedicated itself to thorough-bred racing, good fellowship, and entertainment. The elite racing clubs served several other functions as well.[21]

Upon the founding of the Washington Park Jockey Club, the *Sporting and Theatrical Journal* commented that "the General of the Army (Philip Sheridan) is the president of the club. Its members are all of the better class of citizens...."[22] The club's 500 members were also said to be worth $300 million. They each paid a $150 initiation fee and built a $50,000 clubhouse and a $40,000 grandstand. By 1892 the club counted 96 of Chicago's 278 millionaires as members. An interlocking network of the most prominent citizens served as directors and limited membership by requiring a unanimous vote of the executive council. The club's productions provided a showcase for elite patrons. Going to the racetrack was a gala affair for the city's socialites, and it was duly noted by the media. Women displayed their finery, while the men basked in the status accorded to the owners of racehorses. Races became more than just competitive ventures for good fellow-ship. They served as social events and grand spectacles given to ostentatious display, where elites defined their wealth, power, and privileged status in the face of labor upheavals.[23]

The clubs merged such symbolic entertainment with com-mercial enterprise. Race directors proposed Sunday matches with a low admission fee to attract laborers who worked during the week. They also encouraged paid spectatorship, even though club policies restricted workers from gambling, drinking, or entering the clubhouse. Although the track was located at some distance from the city, the Illinois Central ran directly to the park, and 8,000 attended a weekday race. Such careful planning meant to foster particular values and paid handsome dividends for the investors: the initial eight-day schedule earned $87,000 in 1884. The club's American Derby drew more than 10,000, and by 1887 the Driving Park in-creased its seating capacity to accommodate "multitudes" of spectators for a military exhibition and a marksmanship tournament unrelated to any horseracing purposes. While such commercialized leisure ventures earned profits, they proved especially attractive to the gamblers and the bachelor subculture, and the elites failed to impose their moral suasion.[24]

The elites embraced other leisure interests, such as boating, as well. They established the Chicago Yacht Club, which was even more exclusive than the Jockey Club. One required an invitation to even witness the races. The Farragut Boat Club, founded in 1872, limited its membership to 250; and the Iroquois Boat Club, organized in 1887, accepted only 300. The Catlin Boat Club enrolled considerably less. Its "elegant soiree" featured fifty couples dressed in white suits and sailor hats.[25] Four other yacht clubs followed, but the expenses of a yacht, prohibitive initiation fees, and membership covenants relegated the activity to only the most affluent, insuring more control than their horse racing ventures. The most select of the socialites banded together in national ventures. Marshall Field and other elite members of the Chicago Club joined New Yorkers J. P. Morgan, Pierre Lorillard, William K. Vanderbilt, and Joseph Pulitzer in buying Jekyll Island off the coast of Georgia, where they built a private winter resort in 1888. Such ventures and the social register characterized a hierarchy even within the ranks of the most elite.[26]

Commercial groups, such as the Merchants', Illinois, and Iroquois clubs, also restricted membership to the native monied class. Native organizations banned Jewish businessmen, even though they shared similar commercial values. Religious and cultural differences restricted social intercourse between the two groups to business matters. Jews consequently founded their own elite organization, the Standard Club, in 1869.

As was the case with yachting and horse racing, only the wealthy could afford to go coaching in their elaborate carriages or hunt foxes in Lake Forest, the site of elite residences along the lakeshore north of the city. The extension of rail lines allowed the wealthy to acquire palatial estates and leisure preserves at a distance from the city and still commute to their business affairs, and the Lake Michigan coastline north of Chicago became a haven for high society. Winnetka and Lake Forest residents established cricket clubs, while another select group formed the Chicago Polo Club.[27]

Another wealthy Chicagoan, Charles Blair MacDonald, reputedly introduced the game of golf to the city after developing an interest in it while studying at St. Andrew's, Scotland, in the 1870s. Along with fellow members of the Chicago Club, he built a seven-hole course on the Lake Forest estate of Senator John Farwell in 1892. The following year Chicago Club members subscribed $10 each for the purchase of farmland west of the city to build the first eighteen-hole course in America, which they incorporated as the Chicago Golf Club. In 1894, Marshall Field, Robert T. Lincoln, and their associates raised a sum of $28,000 to buy a Wheaton farm that more closely approximated St. Andrew's. The adjacent cornfields, however, necessitated the first out-of-bounds rule, as balls were lost amid the growing cornstalks. Caddies had to be quartered in the barn, while members enjoyed the privacy of the clubhouse. The distinct master-servant relationship became more clear when the boys rebelled against the measures of a harsh caddy master. Club officers acknowledged the legitimacy of their complaints but refused to sanction any mutiny. The caddies stole twenty-five watermelons from the club patch in retribution.[28]

Golf in elite country clubs allowed upper-class men to assert their position in the social hierarchy as it helped define gender relations. As a sport in which both men and women could participate, golf might allow for acceptable socializing between the sexes, but more often reinforced male dominance as men "permitted" women to use the facilities on days when they were not so engaged. Moreover, the game was readily adapted to the same gambling activities that they had enjoyed at the track. When scandals caused a ban on horse racing, the Washington Park racetrack was converted into a golf course. The jockey quarters became lockers, and a Scotch golf pro named Richard Leslie was imported from St. Andrew's to make clubs and teach the game. Other socialites, including the McCormicks, Palmers, Armours, Swifts, and Cudahys, established the Onwentsia Club in Lake Forest in 1895. It vied, bitterly at times, with the Chicago Golf Club for preeminence among the city's elites, as members jockeyed for leadership within the class.[29]

Socialites took great pains to gain membership in the few elite country clubs that held national, as well as local, status. Chicago's commercial leaders maintained their ties in the most select. Among the trustees and early presidents of the Chicago Golf Club were Potter Palmer, Jr., Norris B. Henrotin, Edward L. Ryerson, Robert S. McCormick, and Robert Todd Lincoln, son of the slain president. Membership was limited to 250, and applicants required a sponsor. One could be denied entrance by a single negative vote. Honorary members included President William Howard Taft and Judge Kenesaw Mountain Landis by 1909. The most prominent families often held multiple memberships to assure their prospects. With a limited number of memberships available, some of which were awarded honorarily to nationally powerful figures, the less affluent and marginal members held a tenuous grasp on their social status.[30]

Each of these organizations focused on leisure practices that served to cultivate and reinforce their social status. Ostentatious display, social isolation, and the exclusivity of one's social network marked one's place in the evolving social strata of the late nineteenth century. The clubs of the elite served to dissociate and insulate them from the rising middle class and the lowly laborers. In pursuit of such solitude, the upper class erected almost impenetrable social barriers.

Clubs of the Middle Class

As the elites attempted to achieve national prominence, a burgeoning middle class also struggled to define its identity and affirm its place in society. Like their social betters, the middle class formed restrictive clubs based on professional associations and leisure interests as a means of distinguishing and shielding themselves from the masses and confirming their social status. Such associations served not only the members' leisure interests but heralded a growing political strength as well.[31]

Middle class communities blossomed to the west and south of the city. In these sequestered suburbs, residents formed cricket clubs, similar to the five clubs that competed within the city's confines. Like golf, cricket's British roots exuded class distinctions that helped set the middle class apart from workers, and Anglos from ethnics. White uniforms, a deliberate pace, and a traditional etiquette distinguished the game and its players from the rowdiness that had come to characterize the "American" game of baseball.[32]

As had the elites, the emergent middle class embraced golf, and their practice of it became one of the defining aspects of the increasing numbers of suburban country clubs. Even city park officials responded with the introduction of courses to the park system in 1899. By 1900, 26 different golf clubs dotted the Chicago area, but the game's association with the crusty British and the expense involved relegated golf to the more socially mobile during its embryonic period.[33]

Even within the city limits, the game of golf held particular distinctions associated with social class. The West Parks Commission stated that "the class of people attracted by the golf course has been the very highest and most desired; the results have been most gratifying, both to the park board and the public."[34] The game clearly was not meant for the working class. Within five years the five public courses, located solely in middle class areas, were relegated to the socially mobile upstarts, while the more status-conscious played at the 55 private sites in outlying areas.[35]

In addition to golf, the middle rank readily adopted tennis. *Outing* magazine declared tennis suitable for ladies and "far too refined to attract lower orders of society."[36] Like the associations formed by the elites, tennis clubs signified a mark of status and recognition. Four private groups had already started play in 1884 at the Kenwood Lawn Tennis Club in the suburb of Hyde Park. Tennis courts had been laid out in the parks by 1886, but public courts were all too open, even to laborers from whom the middle class wanted to distance themselves. Consequently, when the Woodlawn Tennis Club experienced financial difficulties, it sought to ally itself with either the Kenwood or Wanderers tennis clubs rather than use public facilities or accept laborers as members.[37]

As did the upper class, the upwardly mobile middle class established its social network among peer groups. The Woodlawn Tennis Club limited its membership. Applicants required the endorsement of two club members and approval by the executive committee. Members who failed to comply with strict rules of decorum were promptly expelled.[38]

The clubs also sought matches with those of similar social standing and values. Members shared the Victorian values of the amateur ideal, deference to superiors, and propriety in one's relationship with the opposite sex. Any transgression of the ideal behaviors could be cause for the termination of membership. Acceptance into such clubs signaled a measure of success, for not all could afford the initiation fees, and only a few gained the necessary social acceptance of the membership boards. Waiting lists were long. Charles Hermann, a member of the Chicago Athletic Association, maintained that his club had a waiting list in excess of 3,000 and that the membership committee "took its pick" to insure a continuation of the high standards, and the club president urged "fearlessness in rejecting undesirable applicants."[39]

Ostensibly "athletic" clubs, such associations promised much more in terms of their social and commercial possibilities. The Chicago Athletic Association provided the judges of the United States District Court in Illinois with honorary memberships, and the Fort Dearborn Athletic Club was organized by commercial leaders "to meet leading executives of other cities."[40]

Middle class athletic clubs organized in later years extended membership to greater numbers, but they retained their exclusivity and ties to the amateur associations. The middle class thus formulated ideals and socially acceptable standards of behavior for itself within its own ranks.[41]

By the 1890s Chicago had 500 cycling clubs, each with its own colors and uniforms. United in a national association, the League of American Wheelmen, they possessed substantial political clout. The Chicago Cycling Club, founded in 1879, was the oldest and largest local organization. It hosted the national convention of the cyclists' league as early as 1882, and later reorganized itself as a stock company on a business format to advance its interests.[42]

Such organizations allowed cyclists to exert their collective power to promote their sporting objectives. The Viking Cycling Club alone claimed 1,800 votes, which they pledged to their favorite candidates. Political power enabled the cyclists to get a cycling ban in Lincoln Park removed as early as 1882. In the next decade cyclists had Jackson Street declared a boulevard for cycling and the streetcars were removed, while they obtained a speed track in Lincoln Park for the "scorchers." No longer were bicycle riders required to dismount in the presence of horses. After a Chicago cycling show drew 100,000 fans in the winter of 1896, mayoral candidate Carter Harrison II decided to launch his political campaign with a 100-mile one-day ride in 1897.[43]

Unable to afford the coaches and horses to transport them, middle class cyclists supplied their own power to escape the filth and stench of the city. Cycling clubs enjoyed outings similar to the coaching parties of their social betters with long group excursions into the countryside. Such activities defined the status of the rising middle class. For most laborers, however, bicycles costing as much as $100, or even $35 for used models, remained too expensive. Like the industrial process as a whole, the cost of particular sport forms fragmented society along class lines.[44]

Sporting practices and associations thus helped the emerging middle class to define itself in the latter part of the nineteenth century, but particular sport forms also provoked gender issues within the ranks. Like golf and tennis, cycling provided an acceptable means of socialization among the sexes, and women took to the sport readily. Yet controversy waged over the dress reforms that accompanied the cycling movement as women took to pants or bloomers in lieu of skirts, challenging the male hegemony.[45]

The expanding participation of women in the sporting culture signaled a transition from their passive and domestic roles of the past. In June 1895, the school board took exception to Gyda Stephenson, a teacher at the Humboldt School, cycling to class in her knickers, but the board was forced to relent. Women showed unity in their newfound freedom. When the town of Pullman forbid women to use its streets for cycling unless they were properly attired in skirts, Hilda S. Peterson invented a cycling clip to gather and hold the skirt in a fashion similar to pants, effectively circumventing the law. Moreover, women refused to stay at home and even eschewed chaperones while cycling. Males, such as Pullman town supervisors and the school board, failed to cow the women riders. For these middle class women, cycling allowed them to throw off the Victorian shackles of previous years and forsake the traditional domestic roles for the freedom of outdoor adventure.[46]

Unlike the sport forms of the upper classes, baseball increasingly transcended class lines. Since baseball was relatively inexpensive and required little equipment, businessmen, laborers, women, and street urchins played the game. Middle class organizers had formed the National Association of Base Ball Players in 1858, and the National Baseball League followed in 1876. Since the 1870s, baseball promoters had initiated business practices in attempts to maximize profits in a fashion similar to that of industrial employers. Owners instituted the reserve clause to bind players to a single team rather than allowing them to seek their value in a free-labor market. Employers restricted players' leisure pursuits to insure maximum productive capabilities. Albert Spalding of the White Stockings went so far as to require total abstinence from his players. He assigned detectives to assure compliance, and recalcitrant players were fined or sold. Like the industrialists, owners reasoned that if optimal performance was to be achieved, they had to insure themselves of a reliable and consistent work force.[47]

Such regulations imposed restrictions on the players who performed for the profit-oriented professional clubs. Such players became employees, like many of their brethren mired in the system of wage labor. As national representatives of particular urban centers who earned wages equal to or better than the middle class, employers expected deportment consistent with their own.

Spalding's attempts to infuse middle class values and a wholesome image met with limited success among players and fans. Players unionized and mutinied to form their own short-lived league (the Players League of 1890), but like their low-paid counterparts in the factories, the ballplayers proved no match for the more powerful owners. The demise of the "Brotherhood" league left players at the mercy of owners, and though they continued to earn handsome salaries, they did so under the aegis of a dominant form of administration.

The continuous rowdy nature of play also caused the game to lose its appeal among Chicago's elite. When Warren Beckwith, the White Stockings' pitcher, married the daughter of Robert Todd Lincoln in 1892, his father-in-law denounced him as a "baseball buffoon."[48] The union later ended in divorce. Bill Lange, the team centerfielder and a local idol of the 1890s, quit the game at the height of his career when his fiancee's father refused to let his daughter marry a "pro." Professionalism was a concept that transcended the ranks of the middle and laboring classes but apparently violated the socially acceptable code of conduct among the elites. Salaried players whose earnings matched educated professionals in other areas were expected to conform to middle class standards, even though many players maintained working class roots.[49]

The game still enjoyed widespread support among employers who saw it as a wholesome activity congruent with competitive commercial values and organized in accord with the business principles of efficiency, specialization, and productive teamwork. The middle class media even expounded that non-English speaking immigrants and city waifs might be exposed to such ideals as the game was played on city streets and vacant lots.

While athletic organization and ideals appealed to the middle class, success required the physical skills and prowess familiar to laborers. For both the organizers and players, baseball fueled visions of the American dream. The stockholders of Chicago's first professional team were members of the social elite, but one of its first stars, Albert Spalding, personified the Horatio Alger myth. His physical ability combined with business acumen to gain him the club presidency and league leadership en route to founding a sporting goods empire. Even marginal professional players' salaries far outstripped those of laborers. The potential for personal profit, though relatively unequal, proved attractive to all classes.[50]

Charles Radbourne's professional baseball career followed a pattern similar to that of Spalding. The son of immigrants, Radbourne could not write, but he gained acclaim as a pitcher for a local team in Bloomington, Illinois. He soon distinguished himself against barnstorming professionals, who signed him to a contract. He compared his new profession to his past work as a butcher by stating that "I get ten times the money I used to get for working sixteen hours swinging a twenty-five pound sledge by playing ball for two hours a day."[51] Radbourne retired in 1892 to open a poolhall and saloon in his hometown. For increasing numbers of ethnics and laborers, sport began to be perceived as a meritocracy and a vehicle for economic mobility.[52]

Others experienced similar success by pursuing business opportunities in sport. As the socialites became more insulated and concerned with cultural affairs, they abdicated entrepreneurial ventures in the commercialized leisure markets to others. Spalding continued to promote sport and his own business, but neither Spalding nor baseball had a monopoly on the sports trade. John M. Brunswick, a Swiss immigrant, built his first billiard table in Cincinnati in 1845 and opened a Chicago office in 1848. Aggressive marketing and trade wars led Brunswick and rival companies, such as Balke and Collender, to hire professional players who toured the country performing in sham tournaments with fraudulent, but well-publicized, purses that attracted spectators and newspaper coverage. Such ventures helped to bridge the gap between the middle class and the masses, who followed the exploits of local and national celebrities, whom they considered their own.[53]

Among the expert pool players was Tom Foley, a member of Chicago's professional baseball team. His pool expertise allowed him to finance a large billiard hall, and such prowess won him election to the city council as a member of the Workingmen's Party. Jake Schaefer, too, earned enough in side bets to open his own billiard establishment in the 1890s. Thus, while the billiard companies bickered and prospered, individual players found the means to help themselves.[54]

The billiard companies resolved the internecine quarrels by mergers, and by 1879 the rapidly growing firm of Brunswick-Balke-Collender turned its eyes to other lucrative ventures. The craftsmanship displayed in the company's billiard tables led to the more lucrative business of bar construction and ornamentation in the saloons. The elaborate and custom-made bars reduced the down-time of the company's craftsmen, thereby increasing efficiency and profit.[55]

Employing the same marketing techniques which had proved successful for billiards, Brunswick-Balke-Collender created a bowling market. The company installed bowling alleys and promoted the sport and its business by recruiting city and state champions for its traveling all-star team. The top players then toured the country, playing for large purses. Newspapers generated publicity and interest soared as if a circus were coming to town. Moreover, despite the widespread gambling and unsavory images that accompanied both bowling and billiards during the nineteenth century, the company eventually succeeded in promoting the sports among middle class businessmen. Advertisements and promotional ventures proved so successful that the game even became fashionable among the social elites, who chose to practice the game in venues other than the saloon, however. The upper classes played billiards within the privacy of their homes, where ornate tables served as status symbols. By World War I, socialites, including Mrs. John Astor, Mrs. George Pullman, and Mrs. Marshall Field, were holding billiard teas.[56]

Cross-class alliances of a different nature often found root in common causes based on leisure interests. Alcohol consumption was rooted in tradition and was particularly prevalent among laborers and those engaged in the "sporting life." Bowlers, billiard players, saloon owners, and equipment manufacturers banded together in opposition to the temperance movement, uniting aspects of both the commercial and street cultures in the clash over acceptable leisure practices.

The interrelationships generated by leisure issues often brought diverse groups together in a common purpose, and in the process, sporting practices became more homogenized in a two-way process. Native Americans tried to impart particular values to sporting practices, but they also adopted ethnic sports. Bowling was a good example. Predominantly a German sport practiced in saloons, bowling became fashionable among Chicago's middle class urbanites in the 1890s. Organized like the company baseball leagues, intratrade bowling associations, such as the Commercial and Businessmen's Leagues, increased social and business contacts in a convivial atmosphere, mixing natives with ethnics. The concomitant wagering often helped to focus attention on commercial rivals and enhanced company pride. By the turn of the century, merchants, clothiers, mechanics, bankers, jewelers, and others had banded together to compete with colleagues. Some team members earned enough revenue from their leisure activities to open their own business establishments. The Brunswick-Balke-Collender Company played an instrumental role in organizing such groups into a national association in 1895, the American Bowling Congress. Chicagoans would continue to dominate the leadership of the national organization up to World War II.[57]

An Elite Venture in Social Control

The labor turmoil that followed the Civil War demonstrated that the previous assumption of a quiescent and pliable work force was a faulty one. Labor issues led to violence, and some class-based sporting cultures further emphasized and reinforced the social divisions. Others, however, such as baseball, crossed class and ethnic lines, appealing to the workers' value of physical prowess and the hope for socioeconomic mobility.

The appeal of sport thus formed the basis to address some of the divisiveness in the society. As the baseball owners moved to secure their position against the rising tide of the labor movement, George Pullman fashioned a comprehensive recreation program to gain greater control over his own affairs. Pullman's business was particularly affected by the labor unrest that followed the Civil War. Like other industrialists, he saw a need for wholesome leisure practices that would deter workers from the radical elements and encourage the work habits necessary to increase productivity. After a study of English industrial communities, Pullman constructed an entire town in which to locate his railroad sleeping car manufactory and the families of his employees. Magnificent facilities allowed for almost any interest, and the athletic program enjoyed greater financial support than any other social agency. Company officers administered the organization, which provided facilities for track and field, rowing, tennis, cricket, baseball, football, ice skating, billiards, bowling, and shooting. Pullman's town, however, lacked a most popular amenity, the saloon. The lone bar, housed in the company hotel, was reserved for company officers and privileged guests.[58]

Pullman's objectives were clear. He wanted to make sure that "the disturbing conditions of strikes and other troubles that periodically convulse the world of labor would not be found here."[59] The Great Railroad Strike of 1877 had served as a lesson for the country, and it affected Chicago and Pullman's business in particular. With a work force composed mostly of skilled foreign craftsmen, many of whom were bachelors, Pullman was greatly concerned with the potential for discontent and misconduct. He reasoned that sport and abstinence would produce the desired outcomes. To that effect, he incorporated an athletic association to serve as a workers' athletic club. From the town's inception, the company sponsored athletic teams and promoted athletic spectacles that brought national attention to the facilities and, hence, to the company. Blue collar workers composed the majority of virtually all of the Pullman teams, indicating the widespread appeal of sport to the laboring class. In both scope and purpose, the Pullman Athletic Association conducted the first modern industrial recreation program.[60]

Pullman's benevolence was limited, however, and the absence of a workers' bar was only one of the impositions placed upon them. While employees enjoyed model housing and facilities, they were expected to pay for them. George Pullman was both employer and landlord, and company housing was "strictly a business proposition."[61] In addition to rent, athletic association members were required to pay dues to fund their activities. Workers also paid a $3 fee to use the library, but they were relegated to a back room rather than the elegant reading room reserved for company officers. Control of all forty organizations in the town, including the Pullman Athletic Association, rested in the hands of company officials. As if laborers could not be expected to exhibit the middle class values of temperance, piety, and prosperity without some guidance, a local branch of the YMCA was also installed to offer moral direction.[62]

Newspapers provided extensive coverage for Pullman's athletic spectacles, which attracted nationally prominent athletes. As the advertising value of successful company teams became more apparent, the Pullman Athletic Association hired professional coaches and top athletes found ready employment. D. R. Martin, a prominent oarsmen, was hired as the school principal, despite parental objections and an apparent lack of qualifications for the position.[63]

Despite its athletic successes, Pullman's alienated work force went out on strike over pay cuts, layoffs, and reduced working hours in 1894. Other issues included the lack of leisure time and restrictions upon leisure activities. Rents ran as high as one-third of workers' salaries, which were reduced from the monthly average of $51 in 1893 to $36.50 in 1894. The lack of saloons sent many to the nearby communities to seek their preferred leisure activities. The main street in Kensington featured more than forty bars with gaming tables and a Turner hall. Roseland provided another nine saloons, which were frequented by workers denied such rights in the company town.[64]

Labor solidarity and the threat of violence in the prolonged altercation were reminiscent of the horrors of the Haymarket episode. Despite the objections of Illinois Governor John P. Altgeld, President Cleveland sent federal troops to Chicago to restore order and train service, ostensibly because federal mail delivery had been disrupted. Eugene V. Debs, the socialist leader of the striking groups, became a symbolic martyr and a national political figure in the ensuing defeat of the labor forces.[65]

George Pullman died in 1897, and a Supreme Court decision forced the sale of his town the following year. Yet, despite his death and the labor problems, the company's employees maintained their interest in sport and retained the community athletic teams. They continued to compete in city leagues, park districts, and intercity matches while they frequented saloons in the adjoining areas.[66]

Pullman's venture proved an abortive one and, perhaps, reinforced the inclinations of his peers to seek social isolation from the masses. Financially secure, they retreated to palatial estates in various locations around the country and assumed ostentatious lifestyles consistent with their wealth among peers. Even as Pullman's experiment failed, the prospect of creating an efficient, orderly, and moral society continued to intrigue other Chicagoans—middle class Chicagoans—in the last decade of the nineteenth century. Allied with wealthy benefactors, this group of social reformers, known as the Progressives, moved to fashion a more homogeneous American society within the established framework. They sought to allay social discontent and the clash of cultures that bred ignorance, distrust, and violence. While particular class-based sporting cultures continued to accentuate differences, sports such as baseball and bowling mixed natives with ethnics, allowed the expression of both middle and working class values, and fostered the perception of sport as a meritocracy and a vehicle to social mobility.

To assuage the turmoil and factionalism of the late nineteenth century, reformers and their social agencies attempted to overcome the stratification of society by bringing their programs directly to immigrant and working class neighborhoods. They used supervised play and team games to teach particular values, rather than the elite activities that signaled division and alienation. Pullman's failure proved a lesson, and Progressive reformers assumed a more benevolent and more subtle approach as they attempted to move divergent cultures toward a greater degree of accommodation.

Notes

1. Hartmut Keil and John B. Jentz, eds., *German Workers in Industrial Chicago, 1850-1910* (DeKalb: Northern Illinois University Press, 1983); Keil and Jentz, eds., *German Workers in Chicago: A Documentary History of Working Class Culture from 1850 to World War I* (Urbana: University of Illinois Press, 1988), 53, 100, 109.

2. Johann Rosinger, letter to the editor of *Chicago Arbeiter-Zeitung,* Feb. 6, 1883, in Keil and Jentz, *German Workers in Chicago,* 50-1.

3. "Statistics on Chicago's Bakers," *Chicago Arbeiter-Zeitung,* June 10, 1881; "How Wages Are Depressed," ibid., Mar. 7, 1883, states that 172 carpenters at the Illinois Central Railroad plant had only four apprentices, while the one apprentice for the painters earned only $6.50 per month. All felt that they were overworked and underpaid.

48   The Clash of Cultures and Leisure Stratification

"A Word of Warning to the German Unions," ibid., Mar. 24, 1881, lists factory rules; "The Fowler Brothers, Million Dollar Thieves," *Fackel,* Nov. 23, 1884, details the dispute over guards and the injured worker. The above are cited in the anthology by Keil and Jentz, eds., *German Workers in Chicago,* 55-60, 72-4, 87-8. The quote is from "Occupational Extinction: 250 Casing Workers Replaced by Machines," *Chicagoer Arbeiter-Zeitung,* July 8, 1882, on pages 71-2. See David M. Gordon, et al., *Segmented Work, Divided Workers* (New York: Cambridge University Press, 1982), 1-39, 48-78; and Rex Burns, *Success in America* (Amherst: University of Massachusetts Press, 1976), Chapters 1-3, on the transformation of the labor force.

While the Civil War addressed race and slavery, free labor ideology continued to question class and moral issues thereafter. See Eric Foner, *Free Soil, Free Labor, Free Men, The Ideology of the Republican Party Before the Civil War* (London: Oxford University Press, 1970); and Foner, *Politics and Ideology in the Age of the Civil War* (New York: Oxford University Press, 1980); David Montgomery, *Beyond Equality: Labor and the Radical Republicans, 1862-1872;* Eugene D. Genovese and Elizabeth Fox-Genovese, *The Fruits of Merchant Capital* (Knoxville: University of Tennessee Press, 1983). For similar developments in the East, see Hardy, *How Boston Played;* Rosenzweig, *Eight Hours for What We Will;* and Daniel J. Walkowitz, *Worker City, Company Town: Iron and Cotton-Worker Protest in Troy and Cohoes, New York* (Urbana: University of Illinois Press, 1978).

4. Unemployment figures cited by Montgomery, *Beyond Equality,* 263. Chester McArthur Destler, *Henry Demarest Lloyd and the Empire of Reform* (Philadelphia: University of Pennsylvania Press, 1963), 80; Keil and Jentz, eds., *German Workers in Industrial Chicago,* 187. Pierce, *A History of Chicago,* 3 (1957): 245-53, states that Germans, Swedish, Polish, French and English speakers all addressed thousands of workers at the meeting.

See Keil and Jentz, eds., *German Workers in Chicago,* 160-67, for the role of the Aurora Turnvereine, and 254-7 in the May Day parade. See Goodman, *Choosing Sides,* 91, 93-6, on the eight-hour movement and May Day parades in New York.

5. David J. Hogan, *Class and Reform: School and Society in Chicago, 1880-1930* (Philadelphia: University of Pennsylvania Press, 1985), 7; Keil and Jentz, eds., *German Workers in Industrial Chicago,* 210, 213; Pierce, *A History of Chicago,* 3 (1957): 243; Bruce C. Nelson, "Culture and Conspiracy," Ph.D. Dissertation, Northern Illinois University, 1985: 110.

For analysis of ethnic athletic clubs, see Benjamin G. Rader, "The Quest for Subcommunities and the Rise of American Sport," *American Quarterly,* 29 (Fall 1977): 35-69.

6. Russell Lewis, ed., *Chicago History,* 15:2 (Summer 1986), 28; Nelson, "Anarchism," 14; Licht, *Working for the Railroad,* 272; Foner, *Politics and Ideology in the Age of the Civil War;* Alan Dawley, *Class and Community: The Industrial Revolution in Lynn* (Cambridge, MA: Harvard University Press, 1976); Boyer, *Urban Masses and Moral Order,* 125-6.

7. Keil and Jentz, eds., *German Workers in Chicago,* 164-5, 228-36, 239-41; Nelson, "Culture and Conspiracy," 393; Pierce, *A History of Chicago,* 3 (1957): 245-53. Spies was a member of the Aurora Turvereine.

Pierce, ibid., 3 (1957): 254, and Paul Avrich, *The Haymarket Tragedy* (Princeton, NJ: Princeton University Press, 1984), 45, state that the Lehr und Wehr Verein and the Bohemian Sharpshooters were joined by the Irish Labor Guards and the Jaeger Verein, uniformed and equipped with rifles and bayonets. The middle class siege mentality is also apparent in Richard Sennett, "Middle Class Families and Urban Violence," in Stephen Thernstrom and Richard Sennett, eds., *Nineteenth Century Cities* (New Haven, CT: Yale University Press, 1969), 386-420.

See Richard Schneirov, "Free Thought and Socialism in the Czech Community in Chicago, 1875-1887," in Dirk Hoerder, ed., *Struggle a Hard Battle* (De Kalb, IL: Northern Illinois University Press, 1986), 121-42, on the role of Czechs in labor upheavals.

8. Nelson, "Culture and Conspiracy," 304-5.

9. Daniel T. Rodgers, *The Work Ethic in Industrial America, 1850-1920* (Chicago: University of Chicago Press, 1978), 158; Bruce C. Nelson, *Beyond the Martyrs, A Social History of Chicago Anarchism, 1870-1900* (New Brunswick, NJ: Rutgers University Press, 1988), 184-6; Buhle, *Women and American Socialism,* 22.

10. Buhle, ibid., xiii; Avrich, *Haymarket Tragedy,* 147; Keil and Jentz, eds., *German Workers in Chicago,* 162-3, 263-70, 191-9. Among those tried in the Haymarket episode, August Spies, Michael Schwab, and Oscar Neebe participated in Turner Hall drama productions.

11. Nelson, *Beyond the Martyrs,* 139-41, 146-52; Avrich, *Haymarket Tragedy,* 136-49; Keil and Jentz, eds., *German Workers in Chicago,* 203-12, 240-91, 378. See Clark D. Halker, *For Democracy, Workers, and God: Labor Song-Poems and Labor Protest, 1865-95*

50   The Clash of Cultures and Leisure Stratification

(Urbana: University of Illinois Press, 1991) for additional insight into the movement culture.

12. L. Ahern, *The Political History of Chicago* (Chicago: Donahue and Henneberry, 1886), 85-6; Nelson, *Beyond the Martyrs,* 61-2; Pierce, *A History of Chicago,* 3 (1957): 254. Estimates of attendance at the affair range as high as 100,000. All accounts attest to an overflow crowd forced to participate at a distance along the lakefront.

13. Nelson, "Culture and Conspiracy," 171-2; Nelson, "Anarchism," 11; Pierce, *A History of Chicago,* 3 (1957): 263-4, 270, 273.

14. Nelson, *Beyond the Martyrs,* 139-41.

15. The official report, John Bonfield to Frederick Ebersold, Gen. Supt. of Police, June 9, 1886, fails to mention any role by the mayor. See Ahern, *Political History of Chicago,* 239-54.

16. Pierce, *A History of Chicago,* 3 (1957): 275-281, 292; Destler, *Henry Demarest Lloyd,* 157, 188; Nelson, *Beyond the Martyrs,* 184-90; Carl S. Smith, "Cataclysm and Cultural Consciousness: Chicago and the Haymarket Trial," *Chicago History,* 15:2 (Summer 1986): 36-53; Pierce, *A History of Chicago,* 2 (1940): 281, cites the *Supt. of Police Report, 1886,* 64-79, for a list of contributors to the fund, some of whom were: Potter Palmer, $1,000; Levi Leiter, $500; Cyrus McCormick, $250; the Board of Trade, $13,046; the Lumberman's Exchange, $7,780, and the Iroquois Club, $1,900.

Nelson, "Culture and Conspiracy," 515, in an analysis of the ethnic composition of the police department, alludes to the ethnic rivalries and nativism which colored labor disputes and enhanced the potential for violence. English speakers held at least 82 percent of the police jobs, although they were a minority in the city.

17. "Jerusalem and Chicago," *Der arme Teufel,* Oct. 30, 1886, compared Judge Gary to Pontius Pilate, in Keil and Jentz, eds., *German Workers in Chicago,* 314-16; Paul Avrich, *Anarchist Portraits* (Princeton, NJ: Princeton University Press, 1988), 164-5, 177, 182, maintains that the Haymarket affair increased converts to anarchism outside of Chicago. Michael H. Ebner, *Chicago's North Shore: A Suburban History* (Chicago: University of Chicago, 1988), 140-47, on Fort Sheridan. Hoare and Smith, eds., *Selections from the Prison Notebooks,* 170, 181-5, 195, 208.

18. Chester McArthur Destler, *American Radicalism, 1865-1901* (New London, CT: Connecticut College, 1946), 162; Pierce, *A History of Chicago,* 3 (1957): 289-91, 298 cites the *U.S. Commission on Labor Report* on strike statistics; Pierce, ibid., 3 (1957): 304, states that police salaries ranged from $720-$1,000 per year, but such figures

had remained stable from 1872-1892. The police force numbered about 1,000 in 1886, but was increased to 1,680 by 1890.

19. The cooptation of the radical movement by the middle class and its incorporation into the established political process is discussed in a number of works: in addition to Destler, *American Radicalism, 1865-1901* (New London, CT: Connecticut College, 1946); Destler, *Henry Demarest Lloyd*; see Lawrence Goodwyn, *Democratic Promise: The Populist Moment in America* (New York: Oxford University Press, 1976); and Norman Pollack, *The Populist Response in Industrial America* (Cambridge, MA: Harvard University Press, 1962); Nelson, *Beyond the Martyrs,* 202-3, suggests a lingering rebelliousness in Chicago.

20. Destler, *American Radicalism,* 241; on the dilution of German culture in the 1890s, see "German in America," *Vorbote,* July 18, 1894; "German Culture," ibid., Mar. 13, 1895, in Keil and Jentz, eds., *German Workers in Chicago,* 380-86.

See Steven Riess, *Touching Base: Professional Baseball and American Culture in the Progressive Era* (Westport, CT: Greenwood Press, 1980); and, Riess, *City Games,* 171-202, on the relationships of sport, politics, and crime.

21. Dexter Park program, Sept. 30-Oct. 3, 1873 (Chicago: National Printing Co.), n.p; Chicago Jockey and Trotting Club, Inaugural booklet, June 21-27, 1879; The Washington Park Club, Yearbook, 1883; Pierce, *A History of Chicago,* 2 (1940): 467; 3 (1957): 476; Alfred T. Andreas, *History of Chicago* (1886; reprint, New York: Arno Press, 1975), 3:674-6.

22. *The Sporting and Theatrical Journal,* 4:7 (June 28, 1884): 106; Holt and Pacyga, *Chicago: A Historical Guide,* 95.

23. *The American Jockey Club* (New York: Thitchener J. Glastaeter, 1867); Chicago Driving Park, 1882 program; Washington Park Club, yearbooks, 1883, 1884; Harold M. Mayer and Richard C. Wade, *Chicago: Growth of a Metropolis* (Chicago: University of Chicago Press, 1969), 149; Pierce, *A History of Chicago,* 3 (1957): 476, and Dedmon, *Fabulous Chicago,* 118-22.

See Riess, *City Games,* 54-5, for comparisons with elite governance at eastern tracks.

24. *The Sporting and Theatrical Journal,* 4:1 (May 17, 1884): 10; and 4:5 (June 14, 1884): 74, 106; 4:8 (July 5, 1884): 122; Chicago Driving Park, official programs, 1883, 1887; Lionel A. Weeks, manuscript at Chicago Historical Society, on "Multitudes" and commercial events; Lloyd Wendt and Herman Kogan, *Lords of the Levee: The*

Story of Bathhouse John and Hinky Dink (New York; Garden City, 1944), 21, 26-9.

25. Andreas, *History of Chicago,* 3:676-80, on boat clubs; *Sporting and Theatrical Journal,* 4:1 (May 17, 1884): 10; 4:10 (July 19, 1884): 153, attests to the exclusivity of the yacht races; and 4:2 (May 24, 1884): 25, provides a list of Polo Club members.

26. Frederic Cople Jaher, *The Urban Establishment: Upper Strata in Boston, New York, Charleston, Chicago, and Los Angeles* (Urbana: University of Illinois Press, 1982), 531.

Wille, *Forever Open, Clear and Free,* 1972, 92-3. As late as 1944 the Chicago Yacht Club still banned Jews from membership. Even after the Stock Market Crash of 1929, the Chicago Yacht Club retained its exclusivity. Individual membership fees totaled $1,000, and three negative votes might deny applicants, in *By-Laws of the Club and Rules of the Yacht Owners Association* (Chicago Yacht Club, 1930), 1-2.

Charles Monaghan, "Readings," *Islands,* 9:3 (May-June 1989): 34-7. Members of the Union Club of New York initiated the Jekyll Island Club with fifty-three charter members.

27. *Chicago Tribune,* Sept. 1, 1890, 3; Sept. 2, 1890, 2; Kenneth T. Jackson, *Crabgrass Frontier: The Surburbanization of the United States* (New York: Oxford University Press, 1985), 92-3. By 1873 the extension of rail lines accounted for 100 suburban communities around Chicago with a population of 50,000.

Richard Wettan and Joe Willis, "Social Stratification in the New York Athletic Club, " *Canadian Journal of the History of Sport,* (Spring 1976): 45-63.

Thorstein Veblen, *The Theory of the Leisure Class* (New York: Macmillian, 1899); Harold L. Platt, "Samuel Insull and the Electric City," *Chicago History,* 15:1 (Spring 1986): 20-35, states that although electricity was more expensive than gas, wealthy Chicagoans had it installed in their homes as a status symbol during the 1880s. They were more cost conscious about their businesses, where the transition did not occur until after 1900.

J.P. Craig, *Tally Ho! Coaching Through Chicago's Parks and Boulevards* (Chicago: J.P. Craig Pub., 1888); Todd, *Chicago Recreation Survey,* 3:125, on cricket.

28. Herbert Warren Wind, "Golfing in and Around Chicago," *Chicago History,* 4:4 (Winter 1975-76): 244-50.

Chicago Tribune, August 26, 1900, 17. See ibid., July 13, 1930, part 2, 6, on the history of the Chicago Golf Club. Margaret Abbott, a member of the Chicago Golf Club, became the first female gold

medal winner when she won the golf competition at the 1900 Olympics during a sojourn in Paris.

29. Hardy, *How Boston Played,* 140-2, 144-6, Richard Lindberg,
Chicago Ragtime: Another Look at Chicago, 1880-1920 (South Bend,
IN: Icarus Press, 1985), 75-6, 177-80; *Chicago Tribune,* April 1, 1930,
23; *Chicago Golf Club* (Wheaton, IL: 1909), 17, 19; Wendt and Kogan,
Lords of the Levee, 28-9, 50-8; John Landesco, *Organized Crime in
Chicago* (1929; reprinted, Chicago: University of Chicago Press,
1968), 45-85; Riess, *City Games,* 58-9, 184. Scandals included undue
political influence, takeover by gamblers, and murders.

30. Charles H. Hermann, *Recollections of Life and Doings in
Chicago* (Chicago: Normandie House, 1945), 177, states that he
belonged to four Chicago-area golf clubs as well as two more in
Wisconsin; *Chicago Golf Club* (Wheaton, IL: 1909), 6-7, 10-12, 17-18,
38-43. Despite the stock market crash of 1929, the Onwentsia Club
built a $1million clubhouse the next year; see *Chicago Tribune,* April
1, 1930, 23. The founding of an elite resort within the city is detailed
by Aubrey O. Cookman, "Chicago's Exclusive Playground: The South
Shore Country Club," *Chicago History,* 5:2 (Summer 1976): 66-74.
When residents of the area protested the usurpation of land, the
seventeen bankers who were promoting the project threatened to
withhold financial services to the community. Among the members
were the Palmers, McCormicks, Armours, Swifts, Charles A.
Stevens, Mrs. George Pullman, and Harry I. Miller, head of the
Illinois Central Railroad, who used his company workers to complete
the landscaping in seven days. See Ebner, *Chicago's North Shore,*
71-2, 47-8, 196, 210-11, 219-24, 229, 232-40, on suburban country
clubs; and Hardy, *How Boston Played,* 140-5, on clubs and social
networks in the East.

31. Benjamin G. Rader, *American Sports: From the Age of Folk
Games to the Age of Spectators* (Englewood Cliffs, NJ: Prentice-Hall,
1983), 49-68, on sport and status. See Hardy, *How Boston Played,*
127-46, on clubs in that city. Burton Bledstein, *The Culture of
Professionalism* (New York: W. W. Norton & Co., 1978). Local professionalization movements are evident in *The Grocer's Bulletin,* Aug.
5 - Nov. 25, 1881; and the *High School Weekly,* 1:1 (June 12, 1893).

32. Andreas, *History of Chicago,* 3:681-2, states that the Chicago
Cricket Club, organized in 1876 by Canadians, had 150 members,
headed by Dr. E. J. Ogden, in 1885. Wilma J. Pesavento and Lisa C.
Raymond, "Men Must Play: Men Will Play: Occupations of Pullman
Athletes, 1880 to 1900," *Journal of Sport History,* 12:3 (Winter 1985):
233-51, found eight of eleven identifiable cricketeers to be white

collar workers. My own survey of cricket players, gleaned from rosters in the *Chicago Tribune* during 1890 and positively identified in the *1890 Lakeside Chicago City Directory*, showed two skilled craftsmen and fifteen white collar players. *Chicago Tribune*, Sept. 9, 1900, 18, indicated that all but one player on the Wanderers team were Anglos.

Kirsch, *The Creation of American Team Sports: Baseball and Cricket*, and Adelman, *A Sporting Time*, 110-17, on the rivalry between the two. On the ideology and social significance of cricket, see Richard Cashman, "Symbols of Unity: Anglo-Australian Cricketeers, 1877-1900," *International Journal of the History of Sport*, 7:1 (May 1990): 97-110; and Richard D. E. Burton, "Cricket, Carnival, and Street Culture in the Caribbean," in Grant Jarvie, ed., *Sport, Racism, and Ethnicity*, 7-29; J. Thomas Jable, "Social Class and the Sport of Cricket in Philadelphia, 1850-1880," *Journal of Sport History*, 18:2 (Summer 1991): 205-223. See Hardy, *How Boston Played*, 131, on Boston cricket teams.

33. *The Annual Report of the South Park Commissioners, 1899-1900* (Chicago: Cameron, Amberg & Co., 1900), 7; *West Parks and Boulevards of Chicago* (Chicago: Board of West Chicago Park Commissioners, 1913), n.p., in the Chicago Cultural Center, Neighborhood History Collection, Box EGPA, file 1/4; Reiss, *City Games*, 62.

34. *West Parks and Boulevards of Chicago*, 1913, n.p.

35. Harvey C. Carbaugh, ed., *Human Welfare Work in Chicago* (Chicago: A. C. McClurg & Co., 1917), 95-6; Hermann, *Recollections of Life*, 181-2, attests to the selection process of "hand picking" applicants to insure the status of clubs.

36. *Outing Magazine*, 1881, cited in Thomas Goodale and Geoffrey Godbey, *The Evolution of Leisure* (State College, PA: Venture Pub., 1988), 236.

Clarence E. Rainwater, *The Play Movement in the United States* (Washington, DC: McGrath Pub. Co., 1922), 17; Elizabeth Halsey, *The Development of Public Recreation in Metropolitan Chicago* (Chicago: Recreation Commission, 1940), 114, also cites the *South Park Commission Annual Report, 1886*, 11; Pierce, *A History of Chicago*, 3 (1957): 481.

37. Woodlawn Tennis Club, minutes of March 31, 1904 meeting; minutes of Apr. 3, 1907 meeting; and letter to members from Sec. A. B. Hall in file 7/3, Box WCC of CCC, NHC.

38. Woodlawn Tennis Club, *Constitution and By-laws, 1896*, 1; (revised edition, 1902) 3, 5, 58; minutes of March 31, 1904 meeting,

45; minutes of April 3, 1907 meeting, 107-8. The Chicago Cultural Center, Neighborhood History Collection, Box WCC, file 7/3 contains meeting minutes of July 19, 1897 and correspondence from the secretary, Harry G. Hurd, regarding the expulsion of R. A. Hume for improper conduct.

39. Hermann, *Recollections of Life,* 67; Everett C. Brown, *1910 Annual Report of the Chicago Athletic Association* (Chicago, 1911), 7.

40. George B. Dryden, *1922 Annual Report of the Chicago Athletic Association* (Chicago, 1923), 15; J. Frank King, "The Fort Dearborn Athletic Club," *The Greater Chicago Magazine,* 2:1 (Feb. 1927): 30-3; Rader, *American Sports,* 224-28.

41. Webb Drum, ed., *The Illinois Athletic Club Magazine,* 2:2 (July 1912); L. E. Torrey, ed., ibid., 2:12 (May 1913); *Chicago Athletic Association Annual Reports, 1910-1922.*

John G. Hemmer and W. J. Kenna, eds., *Western Bowlers' Journal, Bowling Encyclopedia* (Chicago: 1904), attests to the fact that the distinction between amateur and professional was cloudy. Many of the "amateur" athletic club members gambled extensively at bowling, billiards, and baseball.

42. *Chicago Tribune,* January 8, 1900, 10, on the reorganization of the Chicago Cycling Club.

43. Bushnell, "When Chicago Was Wheel Crazy," *Chicago History,* 4:3 (Fall 1975): 172-3; *Associated Cycling Clubs of Chicago Directory, 1896* (NHRC 59, Box ECC, file 2/1); *The Chicago Bicycle Directory* (Chicago: Carr & Martin, 1896); *Chicago Cyclers' Guide for 1896* (Chicago: Chicago Cyclers' Guide, 1896). Longstreet, *Chicago, 1860-1919,* 223, places the Viking voters at only 1,500.

Halsey, *The Development of Public Recreation,* 114; Bushnell, "When Chicago Was Wheel Crazy," 174-5. The speedtrack and thousands of parading cyclists are featured in *Lincoln Park Souvenir* (Chicago: Illinois Engraving Co., 1896), 70. I. J. Bryan, *A History of Lincoln Park and the Annual Report of the Commissioners* (Chicago: Lincoln Park Commission, 1899), 88, states that speeding cyclists accounted for 132 arrests in 1898. The *Report of the South Park Commissioners, 1896-1897* (Chicago: Cameron, Amberg & Co., 1898), 16, indicated that the practice was even more prevalent in that area, as "scorchers" accounted for 889 of the 1,004 arrests made that year. Undoubtedly, many more were not caught. *The Sporting and Theatrical Journal,* 4:19 (Sept. 20, 1884): 317, carried a copy of the constitution of the League of American Wheelmen, which was organized in 1880.

44. Perry Duis, "The Saloon in a Changing Chicago," *Chicago History,* 4:4 (Winter 1975-76): 214-24. Lindberg, *Chicago Ragtime,* 76, contends that bicycles could be purchased on credit with $20 down and $1 per week. *Dziennik Chicagoski,* March 12, 1894, stated that the Polish Cycling Club was able to rent vehicles for $1 per day, still beyond the means of laborers.

David Nasaw, *Children of the City: At Work and At Play* (Garden City, NY: Anchor Press, 1985).

45. Richard Harmond, "Progress and Flight: An Interpretation of the American Cycle Craze of the 1890s," *Journal of Social History,* 5 (Winter 1971): 235-57; Patricia Vertinsky, "Body Shapes," in James A. Mangan and Roberta Park, eds., *From Fair Sex to Feminism* (Totowa, NJ: F. Cass, 1987); Bushnell, "When Chicago Was Wheel Crazy," 167-75. Longstreet, Chicago, 1860-1919, 218, 223; and Pierce, *A History of Chicago,* 3 (1957): 480.

46. Marguerite Merington, "Women and the Bicycle," in *Athletic Sports* (New York: Chas. Scribner's Sons, 1897), 209-219; Bushnell, "When Chicago Was Wheel Crazy," 170; Lindberg, *Chicago Ragtime,* 77-8; *Roseland Review,* 7:19 (May 18, 1895) clipping in Box CRCC, file 4/31 of the Neighborhood History Collection at the Chicago Cultural Center. Similar conditions prevailed in New York. See Goodman, *Choosing Sides,* 125, on the arrest of Eleanor Penrose for wearing slacks.

47. Harold Seymour, *Baseball: The Early Years* (New York: Oxford University Press, 1960), 128; Seymour, *Baseball: The People's Game* (New York: Oxford University Press, 1990), 214, 221, 443-527; Peter G. Levine, *A.G. Spalding and the Rise of Baseball* (New York: Oxford University Press, 1985); Louis C. Wade, *Chicago's Pride: The Stockyards, Packingtown, and Environs in the Nineteenth Century* (Urbana: University of Illinois, 1987), 292.

48. David Q. Voigt, *American Baseball: From Gentlemen's Sport to the Commissioners System* (Norman: University of Oklahoma Press, 1966), 74, 103, 282-3, and especially Chapter 12. Voigt quotes the *Sporting Life,* May 14, 1892, for the Beckwith story. Riess, *City Games,* 225-27, on unruly fans.

49. *The Sporting and Theatrical Journal* regularly reported dismissals of players for excessive drinking; admittedly favoring the players. It likened their working lives to slavery in the issue of March 15, 1884, 286; David L. Porter, ed., *Biographical Dictionary of American Sports: Baseball* (Westport, CT: Greenwood Press, 1987), 324.

See Goldstein, *Playing for Keeps,* on the sometimes conflicting ideologies of baseball.

50. Levine, *A. G. Spalding and the Rise of Baseball.*

51. David L. Holst, "Charles G. Radbourne: The Greatest Pitcher of the Nineteenth Century," *Illinois Historical Journal,* 81:4 (Winter 1988): 263.

52. Ibid., 255-68.

53. By 1884 the *Sporting and Theatrical Journal,* 3:23 (April 19, 1884): 373, listed at least seven billiard halls making $500 a day in the city. Rick Kogan, *Brunswick* (Skokie, IL: Brunswick Corp., 1985); *Sporting and Theatrical Journal,* 3:17 (Mar. 8, 1884): 270; 3:21 (Apr. 5, 1884): 334; 3:23 (Apr. 19, 1884): 373; and *The Sporting Life,* 10:1 (Dec. 9, 1882): 4.

Stephen Hardy, "Adopted by All the Leading Clubs: Sporting Goods and the Shaping of Leisure, 1800-1900," in Richard Butsch, ed., *For Fun and Profit: The Transformation of Leisure into Consumption* (Philadelphia: Temple University, 1990), 71-101; and Riess, *City Games,* 171-222, on sports entrepreneurs. See Francis Couvares, "The Triumph of Commerce: Class Culture and Mass Culture in Pittsburgh," in Michael H. Frisch and Daniel J. Walkowitz, eds., *Working Class America* (Urbana: University of Illinois Press, 1983), 123-52, for elites' concerns in that city.

54. Hermann, *Recollections of Life,* 42; *The Sporting and Theatrical Journal,* 3:21 (Apr. 5, 1884): 340; and Ted Vincent, *Mudville's Revenge* (New York: Seaview Books, 1981), 26 on Foley.

Sporting and Theatrical Journal, 3:23 (Apr. 19, 1884): 373; 4:1 (May 17, 1884): 9; 4:4 (June 7, 1884): 1, on Schaefer. Adelman, *A Sporting Time,* 221-9; Hardy, "Adopted by All the Leading Clubs," 77, on Phelan.

Challenge matches and billiard tournaments provided similar opportunities well into the twentieth century; Patrick Chelland, *One for the Gipper: George Gipp, Knute Rockne and Notre Dame* (Chicago: Regnery, 1973), 106; and the personal papers of Frank Di Benedetto on the Oliva family, city billiard champions whose winnings provided capital for entrepreneurial ventures.

55. Kogan, *Brunswick;* Andreas, *History of Chicago,* 682-3.

56. Kogan, *Brunswick,* 45; *Sporting and Theatrical Journal,* 6:6 (June 20, 1885): 9, and 3:23 (Apr. 19, 1884): 373, report the cancellation of a pool tournament due to the objections of the Citizens' League.

58   The Clash of Cultures and Leisure Stratification

New York Times, Feb. 14, 1915, Sec. 4:2, cited in Virginia Evans, "Status of American Women in Sport, 1912-1932," Ph.D. Dissertation, University of Massachusetts, 1982, 90; see Ebner, *Chicago's North Shore,* 63, on bowling among socialites.

57. The formation of the American Bowling Congress is covered in detail by American Bowling Congress, *Constitution, By-Laws, Rules and Regulations of the American Bowling Congress* (Chicago: J.M.W. Jones Stationery & Printing Co., 1903). John G. Hemmer and W.J. Kenna, eds., *The Western Bowlers' Journal Bowling Encyclopedia: A History of Bowling,* is explicit on the interrelationships among bowlers, and its biographical sketches indicate the extent of middle class and non-German participation. My own survey of team rosters suggests that 70 percent of 230 bowlers were non-German. League listings are found in the *Chicago Tribune,* Jan. 1, 1900, 9; Jan. 6, 1900, 7; Sept. 9, 1900, 19; Hemmer and Kenna, eds., *Western Bowlers' Journal,* 144; American Bowling Congress, *Constitution;* and American Bowling Congress, *First Fifty Years, 1895-1945* (ABC: 1945). Frank L. Pasdeloup, a city official, served the ABC as treasurer for thirty-five years; and Adrian "Cap" Anson, former White Stockings' player and manager, was a second vice-president. The Executive Committee included Godfrey Langhenry, another Chicagoan, who also served as the president in 1901-02. Judge Howard was president for two terms, from 1912-1914.

58. Wilma J. Pesavento, "Sport and Recreation in the Pullman Experiment, 1880-1900," *Journal of Sport History,* 9:12 (Summer 1982): 38-62.

59. Stanley Buder, *Pullman: An Experiment in Industrial Order and Community Planning, 1880-1930* (New York: Oxford University Press, 1968), viii.

60. Pesavento, "Sport and Recreation"; Pesavento and Raymond, "Men Must Play," identified 329 of 530 athletes and found the cricket, riflery, and football teams to be predominantly white collar workers; half of cyclists were blue collar, and 60-75 percent of track, rowing, baseball, and soccer athletes were blue collar.

61. Buder, *Pullman,* 44.

62. Ibid., 44, 79, gives the average age of males in 1885 as 29; 53.4 percent of residents were foreigners. By 1892 only 28 percent were native Americans. Chicago Cultural Center, Neighborhood History Collection, Box HPC, file 8/14, contains the original state certificate of incorporation for the Pullman Athletic Association, dated October 18, 1882, with a list of stockholders. The association had a capital

stock of $10,000, offered at $10 a share. File 8/7 contains a Pullman Demographic Questionnaire, c. 1885, describing the extent of the facilities. File 8/14 contains early Field Day programs (1887, 1904) indicating the comprehensive nature of activities and participants. Early team photos are contained in the audiovisual collection, Box HPC: 1.75; 1.76; 1.77.

63. Ibid., 125; and Pesavento, "Sport and Recreation in the Pullman Experiment, 1880-1900," 38-62. Extensive references to Pullman sporting activities are covered in the Chicago newspapers throughout the period.

64. Buder, *Pullman,* 87-8, 121-2, 125.

65. Ibid., 81-4, 98-9, 121-5; Richard L. (sic) Ely, "Pullman: A Social Study," *Harper's Monthly,* 70, 1885: 452-466; Charles H. Eaton, "Pullman: A Social Experiment," *To-Day,* January, 1895. High rental rates caused the work force to assume a transient nature within a decade of the town's founding. The average length of residence by 1892 was four and a half years. Many other Pullman workers sought opportunities for home ownership and leisure in the nearby communities of Kensington and Roseland.

Nick Salvatore, *Eugene V. Debs* (Urbana: University of Illinois Press, 1982); Clayton D. Laurie, "Antilabor Mercenaries or Defenders of Public Order?," *Chicago History,* 20:3-4 (Fall-Winter, 1991-92): 4-31; Janice L. Reiff, "Manufacturing a Community: Pullman Workers and Their Towns," presented at American Historical Association Convention, Chicago, Dec. 1991.

66. The *Chicago Tribune* lists the Pullman teams throughout the period; see Apr. 4, 1910, 10; Apr. 11, 1910, 12; Nov. 22, 1920, 19; Chicago Cultural Center, Neighborhood History Collection, Box CRC, file 4/31; the *Pullman Standard Carworker,* Sept. 20, 1946; May 2, 1947; Feb. 4, 1949; May 6, 1949; July 1, 1949; and clippings and interviews from Box HPC, file 8/1.

CHAPTER 3

The Progressive Vision

Progressive reformers began the process of restructuring American society in the late nineteenth century. Often allied with and supported by commercial interests, they moved to shape, direct, and organize urban centers in accord with their own visions of order, efficiency, and morality. With the decline of the radical labor movement, progressives believed that they had the opportunity, resources, and zeal to fashion a more homogeneous society by bridging class and cultural divisions as they addressed urban ills. Reformers situated settlement houses within the teeming ethnic neighborhoods to bring their programs directly to dissimilar groups. They especially made a concerted effort to "Americanize" the immigrant offspring. They did so in a systematic fashion, removing them from the work force through the passage of child labor laws and enacting compulsory education statutes. Reformers also shaped the city spaces to create parks and playgrounds, attracting others who sidestepped the formal educational process. In schools and playgrounds, trained instructors taught the values of democracy, teamwork, and competition under the guise of sports and games. Chicago's cultural leaders not only shared such a vision, they embraced it, assuming leadership roles in the national movement and offering their city as a grand experiment in social engineering.

By the early 1890s the middle and upper class Chicagoans who had been furiously rebuilding the city since the great fire of 1871 were ready to display it to the world. The Columbian Exposition, the World's Fair of 1893, the rights to which Chicago had won in a competition against New York, served as that display. A congressional commission that had awarded the event to the city understood the various messages put forth by the emissaries from the "Windy City." It recognized the dynamic growth of the urban center as well as the pretentious attitude of its leaders. It appreciated the commercial, industrial, and financial capabilities created by the Chicagoans. Finally, the commission realized that such capabilities might well enable Chicago to wrest cultural dominance of the nation from New York![1]

Social leaders also hoped to upgrade the lifestyles of the immigrants and laboring class by introducing the high culture that they esteemed. The elites structured the city and its other cultural offerings to accentuate the aesthetic. City making became, in itself, an art form. Skyscrapers began to dominate Chicago's downtown skyline in the late nineteenth century, and they symbolized the commercial power of "the Loop." Carl Smith, in *Chicago and the Literary Imagination,* referred to the city's architects as "poets in stone" who assisted cultural leaders in their attempt to transform the city's image from one of an industrial center to that of a national cultural leader.[2]

Art and education also became objects of the city makers. Potter Palmer, Marshall Field, Levi Leiter, and Charles Yerkes tried to establish Chicago as a preeminent art center by fostering, acquiring, and displaying the works of prominent artists. John D. Rockefeller, on the other hand, funded the construction of a new University of Chicago to enhance the educational offerings. Others hoped to refine plebeian tastes by introducing a symphony orchestra.[3]

These concerned Chicagoans who produced the World's Fair spectacle concurred in a particular vision of a cooperative, orderly, and efficient society that became the theme of the exposition. They chose to portray a white city as a symbol of the real life they sought to create. Classical architecture symbolized the order, harmony, grandeur, and idealism of the organizers' social vision. True to the Social Darwinian perspective of the planners, three distinct models of the world's nations—savage, semi-civilized, and civilized—would be presented. In keeping with the organizers' moral and educational mission, the *Columbian Exposition Album* "hoped the Dahomans would take back the influence of civilization to West Africa."[4] Such ethnocentric bias characterized the planners' assumptions of cultural superiority and the values that they intended to impart.

The fair also stressed American technological and industrial might. Various engines in the Machinery Hall, elevators in the Transportation Building, and the widespread use of electricity gave fair goers visible proof of the progress of American culture. Such progress, the planners believed, had enabled the young nation to assume its place among the imperial powers on the international stage. America and Chicago had come of age, and the fair was meant to serve notice to the world.[5]

For visitors, the fair offered something for everybody. The Midway Mall of Jackson Park became the amusement center for the expo, where middle class pursuits such as classical music, educational and technological exhibits took their place alongside commercial amusements such as the giant ferris wheel, belly dancers, and vendors that provided a circus environment appealing to the masses. Boating, swimming races, and the American game of baseball provided respite for spectators and reinforced the merits of competition and commercialized leisure.[6]

In addition to its exhibits and amusements, the exposition offered numerous services that made it appear as a discrete, and autonomous, city within a city. An electrical power plant supplied the grounds with state-of-the-art systems in transportation and energy. The White City even had its own fire and police departments. The Columbian Guards gave helpful advice and directions, and, contrary to laborers' views of police as antagonistic oppressors, they augmented order and efficiency rather than just imposing it. True to the fair's design, the guards were another cog in a great social utopia, whose fundamental lesson to the world was to be what could be accomplished through a "progressive" vision.[7]

While the Columbian Exposition proved a resounding success in many ways, it failed to achieve many of its social goals. By January 1894, the buildings had been pillaged for souvenirs, and, in the aftermath of the financial panic of 1893, the White City became a haven for unemployed tramps. Fires started by the new residents destroyed many of the magnificent structures, while others were set ablaze by Pullman strikers on July 5, 1894, as they opposed federal troops.[8]

In effect, the image of a social utopia displayed at the 1893 World's Fair stood in stark contrast to the reality of life that occurred around it. The orderliness, efficiency, and harmony of the "White City" were sorely lacking in real-life Chicago. A malodorous stench stifled the environs of the stockyards district, and a thick layer of grease coated the Chicago River, courtesy of the factories and tanneries that lined its shores. Industrial plants emitted a dense stream of smoke into the surrounding air and contributed to the waste and garbage that littered the city's grimy streets. In the commercial downtown district, skyscrapers had begun to blot out the sunlight; horse-drawn wagons, carriages, streetcars, and pedestrian traffic clogged the streets. Railway engines belched throughout the city, adding to the pollution and congestion by disgorging cargo and thousands of passengers at their appointed stops.

The deleterious products of this mass of human, animal, and mechanical processes paled in comparison to the degradation of the neighborhood slums. People crowded ten to a room and thousands to the block in the shabby tenement districts. With industrial plants operating around the clock, three men often shared the same bed, alternating according to their work shifts. Children, too, lived and played amid the filth of the streets and alleys while cows, pigs, and goats inhabited the small parcels of open space remaining on homeowners' lots.[9]

Within the ever-growing metropolis, one could even find elements of the old frontier town or rural community, and some visitors described the city with phrases from the past. George Ade, a local writer, characterized it as a "mining camp five stories high."[10] Joseph Cook, a Boston preacher, cautioned visitors to the World's Fair about the "harlotry, drunkenness, gambling, robbery, murder, anarchy, greed and Sunday desecration" that would confront them in Chicago; while W. T. Stead, an evangelical reformer and author of *If Christ Came to Chicago,* assured his readers that the city was the wickedest place on earth.[11]

The Chicago that these observers decried lacked virtually everything that the Columbian Exposition defined as desirable and beneficial. It was filthy, steamy, and depressing; it was inefficient and disorderly. If the progressive vision was to be achieved, greater order would have to be imposed in the organization of the public spaces and in the education of those who did not share the progressive viewpoint.

The progressive movement assumed national proportions in its attempt to refashion government, redistribute power, address urban ills and the social hierarchy. A loose coalition of cross-class alliances worked for particular issues but promoted a largely Protestant, middle class agenda that included more direct participation in the electoral process, tax revision, antitrust laws, greater regulation of industry and work conditions, social welfare programs, the "Americanization" of immigrants, and legislation to impose particular standards of morality. Despite its liberal tone, the movement meant to uphold, rather than challenge, the capitalist system. Its scope and nature have since led to various historical interpretations.[12]

Chicagoans, particularly Jane Addams and her Hull House associates and Graham Taylor, a clergyman, took on national leadership roles. Within the local movement, business interests stressed greater commercial and technical education so that they, and their employees, could compete with European industrial powers and overcome the social blight of poverty and unemployment. Political reformers, in particular the academics at the newly founded University of Chicago, advocated civil service reform to terminate the administrative inefficiency and corruption that plagued government. Social scientists at both Chicago and Northwestern Universities called for objective analysis, efficient organization, and charity to combat health concerns and industrial issues. However, despite their different messages, all three groups, as well as others, agreed on a common means of approaching the lack of progress: amelioration through education to incorporate the wayward and unenlightened masses into their particular social vision in the 1890s and later. If reformers hoped to bring order, efficiency, and unity to the culture under their guidance and maintain the native hegemony, they would have to systematically get children out of the factories, off the streets, and into the schools where they could be inculcated with the desired values. They would not, however, find the going easy.[13]

Schools

In order to gain control of the schools and Americanize immigrant youth, reformers first had to wrest administrative power from alternative interest groups, particularly ethnics who had been active in school affairs since the antebellum period. Although a central high school served more affluent patrons by 1856, neighborhood councils administered the elementary schools and a largely ethnic clientele. By 1884, Adolph Kraus, a German-Jew, headed the school board, and reformers' attempts to centralize the bureaucracy, standardize the curriculum, and assume control of extracurricular activities met with opposition from politicans, teachers, and students.

As relatively early immigrants, whose numbers provided significant political power, the Germans were particularly active in shaping local schools. They introduced their own teachers, language, and the German kindergarten practices. The Turners also initiated their exercise system, which emphasized fitness, strength, and discipline, into the schools as early as 1866.[14]

By 1885, through the efforts of Louis Nettlehorst, president of the Chicago Turngemeinde, the board of education had appointed a committee to consider formal physical education in the schools. The board decided to adopt the Turner system of gymnastics and apparatus work and hired Henry Suder, a German Turner, to supervise the program. The next year administrators hired eight more teachers, including Friedrich Ludwig Jahn, grandson of the Turners' founder, to initiate the system. Chicago thus became the first American city to adopt a formal program of physical education in its public school curriculum. The informal and unregulated leisure practices of the students, however, circumvented such discipline.[15]

Students organized their own extracurricular athletic activities as early as the 1860s. In 1884, the students at Hyde Park, North Division, and Lake View high schools banded together to form their own baseball teams. Lake View formed a tennis club as well. The following year student officers met with the football clubs from other schools to form a league. Interest in league games ran high, but teachers feared that students were neglecting their lessons in favor of the new-found competition.[16]

Probably the most profound and consistent student interest and effort continued to be generated by football, where defeat tarnished school pride and elicited lament. A student reporter to the *High School Journal* explained, "Who can hope for success in Foot-Ball when most of the players are weighed down daily by a long Cicero lesson, or some other mark of tyranny of 'the powers that be?'" [17] Like the laborers, students viewed their leisure time as their own. Their extracurricular activities allowed them to define and control certain aspects of their lives, and, like the laborers, they resented the restrictions and regulations imposed by the school administrators.

Despite its apparent popularity, football generated a host of responses. Injuries, parental objections, rule differences, and the hiring of professional coaches in quest of victory brought students' leisure practices into question. Reformers questioned a growing commercialization and professionalism adopted from collegiate models. Following the lead of high school alumni who organized the Chicago Foot Ball League, representatives from six schools met to form a high school version in 1886. North Division High School called for a pennant to be given to the champion in lieu of a money prize. Other representatives focused on the issues of professionalism and eligibility.[18]

The interscholastic sport programs soon expanded and diversified. By 1887, at least seven high schools fielded teams as boys competed in five different sports, and girls soon formed their own athletic association at Lake View and West Division high schools. Calls also went out for a high school baseball league to match the interscholastic competition in football. Informal scheduling and the lack of eligibility rules, however, allowed widespread abuse and elements of the street culture to intrude upon the sports programs.

Both football and baseball teams competed against adults, which resulted in a West Division football victory over Lake

Forest College, despite the fact that Lake Forest used three professors on its team. Boys at West Division also took up boxing and bet on the sparring matches. They soon issued challenges to other schools. Despite growing concerns about the nature of such practices, businessmen, who valued the inculcation of competition, offered trophies and medals to winners of athletic contests and field day events. The latter included activities for both boys and girls in track and field, cycling, baseball, and football.[19]

The interest in physical training and competition mounted, and students raised considerable sums of money to serve their leisure needs. Commercial interests, such as Spalding's sporting goods firm, took note and began advertising their wares in school publications. Company representatives attended league organizational meetings, offering advice, awards, and their own "official" products as they attempted to gain control of lucrative new markets.[20]

Improvising teachers found ways to incorporate students' athletic interests into the formal curriculum. Englewood High School hired Frank Pecival as its physical education director in 1889. Physical training up to that time had consisted of calisthenics and formal drill, and "the surplus energy of the boys was often expended against teachers and freshmen...in order to steer this energy into the right direction, the faculty put their heads together and decided to try out this new idea of a gymnasium."[21] Pecival added games for both boys and girls, as well as intramural competition, in the hopes of deterring the frequent pranks and mischief. Within a year, school officials approved physical education for the high schools and spent about $15,500 for the program in 1890. Northwest Division High School added a gymnasium to its facilities in 1892. It was the first indoor public school gym in the country and led to a demand for others. Further, the school board was besieged by requests to transfer to schools with gyms and physical education facilities. Administrators had discovered the means to gain some control over student activities by incorporating them within the school. The process of fully subordinating native sons would take another two dozen years, as reformers faced more pressing concerns as the children of ethnic immigrants overwhelmed the school system. [22]

The Politics of Education

Reformers considered control of the educational process to be essential if they were to Americanize foreign youth, address alternative values, and incorporate ethnics into their vision of society. Most ethnic groups, however, did not fully embrace the dominant society's schools. Many ethnics perceived different values in the educational process, and they saw education as a means of retaining their own cultures. Socialists, atheists, Jews, and Catholics supported their own schools in opposition to the perceived Protestant Christianity of city schools. Such alternative institutions drew the ire of social reformers and nativists who saw them as obstacles to assimilation.[23]

In the local public school districts, residents chose their own teachers and initiated language courses to preserve their native tongues. Poles saw American public schools as secular institutions that inculcated values opposed to their traditional lifestyle. Working class Slavs and Italians also saw school as a nuisance when children could be working and making a more practical contribution to the family's needs. In Europe, child labor contributed to family income in the hope of securing a home of one's own. Southern and eastern European peasants thus had little use for classrooms and easily circumvented child labor laws. Twelve-year-old girls operated sewing machines in Chicago's sweatshops, and children remained employed in factories as messengers and in department stores, where they composed 14 percent of the work force in the seven largest firms in 1897. By 1900, 50 percent of ten- to twelve-year-olds worked, with immigrant children being five times more likely to be employed than natives.[24]

Most ethnics who complied with the law sent their children to church-related schools to avoid the Protestant influences of the public educational system. The parochial school system provided separate yet parallel organizational structures that allowed ethnics to protect and preserve their religious differences. By 1890 Catholics had established 62 elementary schools with 31,053 students in the city, another 1,571 in the suburbs, and 1,348 in Catholic high schools. Under Archbishop Feehan, administrator of the Chicago Archdiocese from 1880-1902, ethnic parishes grew and prospered. Irish and Polish independence movements, supported and often headed by Old World immigrant clergy, operated within the church as nationalism and religion remained enmeshed. The widespread parochial school system fostered not only Catholicism, but cultural pluralism, rather than the cohesion sought by the reform groups.[25]

Given the cultural differences, the truancy law of 1889, designed to get children to school, met with widespread ethnic opposition. After successive Republican losses at the polls in 1890 and 1892, the law was repealed. The authorities persisted, however, and, as in the labor disputes, found governmental support. A more stringent 1897 statute required education and allowed the state to assume parental rights by way of the doctrine of *parens patriae* for violators. In 1898 the city established a reformatory with 1,300 boys as inmates, more than 25 percent of them for truancy violations.

Theodore J. Bluthardt, the city supervisor for compulsory education, stated:

> We should rightfully have the power to arrest all these little beggars, loafers and vagabonds that infest our city, take them from the streets and place them in schools where they are compelled to receive education and learn moral principles....measures cannot be taken any too soon...which will make the control of this class easier of solution.[26]

Truancy officers were subsequently increased from fifteen in 1898 to fifty-three by 1914. Street life thus became subject to government control and middle-class standards of decorum.

Chicago established the first juvenile court in the United States in 1900. It interpreted delinquency broadly, including such offenses as immorality, profanitiy, begging, peddling, and street singing. Fifty percent of its cases addressed disorderly conduct, and dependent children, delinquents, and truants were sent to the new parental school, founded in 1902 through anonymous donations. With the apparatus of enforcement then in place, the legislature passed a more effective child labor act on July 1, 1903, and schools became the primary caretakers of children. The legislation and its enforcement proved effective. By 1900 Chicago's high schools overflowed with more than 10,000 students.[27]

Reformers also moved to centralize the educational bureaucracy and thereby reduce ethnic and political influences. In 1899 the Bureau of Education issued the Harper Report, chaired by the University of Chicago president, ostensibly to identify administrative inefficiency, graft, corruption, and political influence on the board of education. The report recommended reducing the board membership to eleven members, who would serve a four-year term by appointment of the mayor. Such a move would negate popular control of the board and limit autonomy in local school districts.[28]

In other statements, the Harper Report recommended manual training for all grades, increased physical culture, citizenship training, and the inculcation of patriotism in lower grades before students had the opportunity to leave school. To reach more students, 94 percent of whom left school before the age of fourteen, the report advocated vacation schools to continue education during the summer months and the use of schoolyards as playgrounds. The latter items recognized the limited abilities of the schools and urged incursion into the leisure sphere to inculcate the desired values.[29]

Such changes would cement commercial control over educational policy, particularly in high schools that did not fall under the purview of local boards. Businessmen had long wanted a switch from classical to vocational education to meet their industrial needs. Using the former Central High School building, the Commercial Club incorporated an independent manual training school in 1883, with such members as George Pullman and Marshall Field serving as trustees. Unlike the traditional grammar school classes where female teachers taught basic skills, vocational classes, with the direction and support of businessmen, trained workers. Male teachers instructed students in the operation of machinery, reading and measuring technical materials, and how to respond to authority under conditions similar to those found in the workplace, thus reinforcing an hierarchical male hegemony. Labor leaders roundly denounced such schools as an alternative to the union apprentice system.[30]

Superintendent Albert G. Lane brought manual training to the public high schools in 1895. The Civic Federation opened the Medill School for Manual Training as the first vacation school the next year, where sponsors treated attendees to summer excursions. There were 122 such educational sites by 1901. Immigrant children composed 93 percent of the enrollment. Two years later the board of education opened the Crane Technical High School, and all Chicago high schools offered a two-year manual training course. Thus, the commercial agenda was nearly complete.[31]

In the districts where ethnics did not predominate, public school curricula came to be designed to "Americanize" immigrant children. In 1888 Victor F. Lawson, owner-publisher of the *Daily News,* offered medals for patriotic essays and induced the board of education to enact his plan by offering the interest on $10,000 each year as a gift. Superintendent Lane added U.S. history to the curriculum in 1894 to cultivate patriotism and a high regard for American institutions, in opposition to "immigrant thoughts, politics, and beliefs antagonistic to American institutions."[32]

The report also proposed higher salaries for male teachers to attract men to teaching positions in the elementary grades, implicitly reinforcing the dominant class and sex roles. Up to that time, teachers generally had come from the working class, were mostly Irish, and either served an apprenticeship similar to craftsmen or attended a two-year normal training school. The Harper Report referred to teachers as uncouth and uncultured and recommended a college degree as a teaching requirement and a demonstration of cultural attainment which might fit them better to inculcate moral teachings.[33]

Such reforms met with less than uniform acceptance. Ethnic leaders opposed manual training classes as early as 1886. In her 1897 address to the National Education Association in Chicago, Jane Addams also criticized the American educational practices for failing to meet immigrants' needs. The competitive nature and worklike environment of the school, she said, was due to the fact that control lay in the hands of businessmen. School, like work, was dull and laborious. It exhibited an ethnocentric bias that failed to educate children and merely trained them to become obedient, prompt, unquestioning laborers and clerks. The process of inculcating such habits as obedience, discipline, patriotism, and respect for authority started in kindergarten and progressed through the manual training and Americanization classes that implicitly denigrated ethnic cultures.[34]

The Harper Report generated a backlash from the Chicago Teachers' Federation that was immediate and effective. Formed in 1897 to safeguard teachers' rights, provide job security, and improve working conditions, the federation's membership proved strong enough to defeat the Harper Bill. When Superintendent Andrews attempted to implement the provisions of the Harper Bill by fiat, he was forced to resign in March 1900.[35]

Edwin G. Cooley replaced Andrews, but he continued Andrews's work of centralizing the bureaucracy and assuming greater control over appointments and retention, effectively limiting ethnic and working class power, except at the voting booths. Teachers fought back, and the battle for control of the school system developed along class lines. When the board threatened teachers with salary cuts in 1900, the educators filed suit against tax evaders, among whom were five utility companies owing more than $2 million. Despite the teachers' victory in 1901 and payment of the taxes, the board reneged on salary payments; instead, it disbursed the money to increase buildings, kindergartens, and janitorial services. The Teachers' Federation then joined the Chicago Federation of Labor, despite vehement protestations from the board in 1902.[36]

Progressives had hoped to avert the overt class conflict of the 1870s and 1880s by assuming control of the educational process. The assumption of a passive and pliable clientele proved faulty, however, as control of education was hotly contested by native, ethnic, and class factions. The political power of the ethnics and the laboring class retarded middle class goals as district councils reversed the centralization process, more women were hired as superintendents, and teachers regained a measure of their lost freedom. But Cooley remained as head of the system, and the confrontation continued along ethnic and class lines throughout the succeeding administrations. Unable to fully implement their reforms in the school, the progressives turned to alternative means of education, which ultimately proved more successful.

Focusing on students' interest in extracurricular and physical activities, the Harper Report addressed the need to install American teachers to teach American values. The commission rationalized that the great influence of the German Turners might be reduced and physical training might be less expensive if regular teachers, not specialists, taught the physical culture classes. Trained instructors, using schoolyards as playgrounds, might teach American games and American values, drawing youth away from the street life and the ethnic athletic clubs that had fomented radicalism in the past. The middle class reformers thus promulgated a definite plan for the assimilation of the diverse ethnic groups and the dismantling of the organizational structure that had perpetuated the alternative cultures.[37]

The broad-based reform movement reached beyond the schools into the streets and ethnic neighborhoods, as private agencies buttressed the efforts made in the schools. Universities, commercial organizations, and private individuals sponsored agencies designed to study and change the society. They brought their programs directly to ethnic communities, providing an alternative means of education. The process, however, was not a unilateral one, as the reformers often learned as much as they taught. The imposition of cultural values in the schools gave way to adaptation and accommodation in the neighborhoods.

Settlement Houses

Among the private agencies that tried to address the myriad social concerns in Chicago was Hull House. Founded by Jane Addams, the daughter of a small-town banker, it served the teeming immigrant community of the 19th Ward on the West Side. Hull House became a symbol of the progressive reform efforts, and Jane Addams became a national, even an international, figure through her work. Hull House served as the headquarters for an international network of social reformers who embodied the humanitarian concerns of middle class progressives as well as their ethnocentric and class biases.[38]

Some social activists, particularly the women engaged in settlement work, held social and humanitarian concerns consistent with the feminine role of nurturance and moral guidance of the Victorian era. As one of the first generation of American college women, Jane Addams bridged the traditional female domestic role of nurturer with newer professional roles of teacher and nurse. A woman of some means, she had toured Europe, where she was introduced to the abject poverty of the slums and became familiar with the social reform endeavors of contemporaries in London. In 1889 she returned to the United States and, along with her college friend Ellen Gates Starr, settled in Chicago to begin her life's work. They opened Hull House, a former mansion in disrepair and wholly encircled by an immigrant ghetto, on September 18, 1889.[39]

Typical of the settlements, Hull House served as the scene for the merger of divergent cultures, and Addams used her extensive social contacts to acquire funding for her charitable works, social causes, and programs aimed at assimilating ethnic groups. Early attempts to bring high culture to the community proved a major disappointment. The kindergarten provided for more practical needs and met with success, offering much-needed child care. The kindergarten was financed and run by Jenny Dow, the daughter of a wealthy Chicagoan. In 1893 Louise de Koven Bowen, one of the city's most prominent socialites, became a member of the Hull House Women's Club and a Hull House trustee. She provided much of its financial support throughout her long life. John Dewey, the eminent philosopher and University of Chicago professor, also became a trustee in 1897. With Hull House serving as a social laboratory, his pragmatic philosophy found great application in settlement work.[40]

Through such contacts, Addams and Starr produced a web of support groups for their enterprises. They engaged other special interests, which often crossed paths on educational, social, political, and economic issues, to create a network of public and private organizations, agencies, and associations to address their concerns. These groups differed in their individual objectives, but they shared the belief that an orderly, efficient, and homogeneous society was a better one for all. The progressives exhibited a distinctly homogeneous social profile as well. Stephen Diner analyzed 215 reformers active in Chicago from 1892-1919, many of whom were associated with the Hull House network. The vast majority were middle class, well-educated professionals, and Protestant businessmen. Most lived within three-quarters of a mile of the University of Chicago, or in the Gold Coast area along the lakefront north of downtown, and both men and women held membership in upper class clubs. The profile exhibited a distinct group of middle class associates imbued with the values of a competitive and commercial system, as well as a broad spectrum of social concerns.[41]

With such support, settlement houses soon proliferated in the immigrant districts. Unlike the European models, they professed to be secular in nature in order to appeal to both Catholics and Jews. Between 1895 and 1917, social agencies founded sixty-eight settlement houses in Chicago, with programs designed to bring the progressive vision to the neighborhoods.[42]

The setting in which Hull House operated was also typical of the settlement environment. It drew clientele from a surrounding area populated by 70,000, representing eighteen different nationalities. The average weekly income was $5, and the average family in slum areas had five members living in less than three rooms. Work was irregular, so the 295 saloons in the district and the pool rooms of the 19th Ward, which comprised one square mile, did a thriving business.[43]

Children filled the grimy streets, and rampant unemployment caused enforced leisure among adults, so play and games figured prominently in the "Americanization" programs of the settlements. When William Kent, a Chicago businessman of inherited wealth and later a California congressman, donated three-quarters of an acre to Hull House for a playground, it proved a major attraction to the local children. To the sandlot were added swings, seesaws, a giant stride, and building blocks. Such facilities achieved their purpose of attracting children to the grounds and away from the unhealthy and hazardous streets. The Chicago Commons

Settlement opened its playground in 1896, and the University of Chicago offered a supervised playground, as well as an indoor gym for use by youths and adults, in June 1898. By that time the public schools had also adopted the playground concept and embarked upon a program of sports and games to train youth. Jane Addams asserted that "I believe sports will be the only agency powerful enough to break into this unwholesome life...(on the playground) a rude sort of justice prevails; which may become the basis for a new citizenship and will overthrow the gang leader and the corrupt politician."[44]

Hull House provided facilities and fielded teams for both males and females in several sports. The success of such teams, which often contended for city championships, enhanced the reputation of Hull House and continued to attract youth to its doors throughout its long history. Participants, however, often adapted such programs to their own purposes, and Addams warned against the development of gambling and professionalism. Heeding her suggestion for proper supervision, such competitive activities became a mainstay of progressive reform efforts in both public and private agencies thereafter.[45]

In addition to the programs directed at youth, settlements often served as liaisons with the labor movement. Settlement workers fashioned the agencies that addressed laborers' concerns within the established political-judicial system, thus abating the violent confrontations of the past by serving an advocacy role. For these reformers, political activism on behalf of, or in conjunction with, ethnic and labor groups stemmed from moral convictions as well as knowledge gained from their interactions in the urban ghettoes. Such interrelationships brought the realization of the need to restructure not only the society, but the physical space that it inhabited. Once again, the process brought conflict.

Parks

From its inception, the city spaces served as a commodity for speculators in search of profit. Aesthetics and leisure had long been a concern of the cultural leaders in Chicago, who valued a more genteel culture. The city's park system began when the U.S. Congress provided the state with land to develop the Illinois and Michigan Canal in 1827. The federal government had also ceded a block of land on the lakefront in 1839, which became Dearborn Park, Chicago's first. By 1837 part of the original grant served as a combined cemetery and recreational site. Administrators took heed of such needs and consolidated the congressional allotment as Lincoln Park, the city's largest, in 1842. City officials created Washington (commonly known as Bughouse) Square and began to acquire additional tracts in succeeding years.[46]

By 1851 the state legislature had agreed to the levying of taxes for the acquisition of park land. Civic leaders favored the passive European style, which they planned to install around Lake Michigan in a crescent shape. An 1851 ordinance forbid ball playing in such parks, and aesthetic improvements enabled city leaders to promote urban amenities and dispel the images of a frontier community.[47]

By 1864 the city council approved a swamp reclamation project to increase the Lincoln Park acreage. Throughout the 1860s, real estate developers led by Paul Cornell and John S. Wright lobbied the state legislature to increase taxes for landscaped parks that would enhance particular areas and increase their land values. By 1869 they succeeded in establishing a belt of parks on the city's perimeter, to be interconnected by a system of boulevards based on the plan of Cornell's previous home in New York. The plan allowed for a parks commission independent of the city council with the ability to levy taxes, issue bonds, and buy land. Cornell earned handsome profits by selling his own land south of the city for incorporation in the plan. On February 24, 1869, the Illinois legislature passed a parks bill, establishing three independent governing boards for each area of the city—the South Parks, West Parks, and Lincoln Park on the north side. Both the Lincoln and the West Parks boards were to be appointed by the governor, while the South Park commissioners would be appointed by the circuit court. In actuality, Leverett B. Sidway, an early park administrator, had free rein to handpick the commission, which he financed through his own Illinois Trust and Savings Bank.[48]

In 1869 Chicago city officials followed the lead of New York's Central Park and hired Frederick Law Olmsted and Calvert Vaux to landscape the South Park District, a year after they constructed the planned suburban community of Riverside, west of Chicago, with money from eastern investors. They were followed by Ossian C. Simonds, whose long tenure in Chicago (1878-1931), and Jens Jensen, a Danish immigrant who rose from laborer to creator of Columbus Park, established the Chicago School of Landscape Architecture.[49]

In addition to the large landscape parks, Chicago established thirty-four smaller parks in the 1860s and 1870s. Charles Wicker donated land for a park along Milwaukee Avenue, and Douglas Park was partitioned from a portion of Senator Stephen Douglas's estate. With such acquisitions and the extension of Lincoln Park, Chicago ranked second in park acreage per capita in the nation, following only Philadelphia. Chicago provided one acre of park land for each 252 residents in 1880. However, the European masses that flooded the city after that time and the annexation of suburban areas had changed the ratio to 1:725 by 1900, causing Chicago to drop to thirty-second among American cities.[50]

As the city and its population grew at a rapid rate, overcrowding caused health concerns. The proper use of the city's remaining open spaces for healthful purposes engendered debate over the nature and function of its parks. City leaders expressed concern for the aesthetic appearance of the growing metropolis, but laborers wanted areas in which to play during their leisure hours. Park administrators did little to encourage such activities. The active use of the parks was slow in coming and, to a degree, dependent upon the initiatives of special interests.[51]

Among the special interests, ethnic and fraternal groups had always found the parks a convenient location for picnics. Sunday crowds numbered as many as 30,000 in Lincoln Park by the 1870s. Other special interest groups, such as ball players, cyclists, horse racers, ice skaters, and tennis players, all defied the ban on active use of the parks. After 1870 the Lincoln Park Commission began to develop Lake Shore Drive, which soon became a popular raceway for horse drivers. The sport became so popular, in fact, that both the Lincoln and

South Park commissions were forced to establish schedules to limit the racing, allowing the use of Grand Boulevard for two hours on Wednesday evenings and Lake Shore Drive for another five hours on Fridays.[52]

The Lincoln Park police force was organized in 1872, with particular responsibilities that included the regulation of speeding cyclists. The Washington Park meadow was finally opened to team games by 1876; a decade later business teams required permits for their games, indicating that active users faced greater regulation in their use of the parks. Up to that point, administrators had focused on aesthetic concerns. The *Twelfth Annual Report, 1887* stated that "the appropriations...have been largely sufficient to pay for...beauty spots...adorned with flowers and shrubbery, and no effort spared to make them attractive to the eye and pleasant to visit." [53] Itemized expenses in the accounts, such as the need for earth-filling and reseeding, suggest that park users did more than just visit.

Other special interests were quick to realize the potential of parks and shoreline. In 1852 the Illinois Central Railroad acquired shoreline rights and refused to relinquish them, despite intense litigation, until reaching a compromise with the South Park Commission in 1912. Private interests developed the harbor for commercial purposes as early as 1868. [54]

When Potter Palmer moved his residence from Prairie Avenue on the South Side to Lake Shore Drive on the north in 1882, Chicago's wealthy soon followed, structuring city spaces along distinct class lines. The wealthy had garbage dumped in the lake to serve as landfill, thus creating Oak Street Beach. Any subsequent residences built along the exclusive "Gold Coast" were required to exceed $15,000 in cost. Palmer erected a seawall in conjunction with the Lincoln Park board and sold his reclaimed lots only to his peers, such as the McCormicks and Robert T. Lincoln, who constructed similar mansions. Rents for apartments in the area skyrocketed to $1,500 annually, well beyond the means of most and three times the average annual salary of common workers. When beaches along the lakefront were opened for public use after 1895, swimmers were required to wear attire that conformed to the mores of the area's exclusive residents, whose windows faced the lakefront across Lake Shore Drive. The enforced decorum contrasted sharply with New York, where boys swam in the East River clad only in their underwear or nothing at all. Litigation by local residents and even the state's attorney general against the private development were summarily dismissed, and the area continues to retain its exclusive nature to this day.[55]

When Chicago's elites attempted to bring institutions of high culture to the area, they were met with additional protests. Henry Magee, in his 1884 broadside, *A Protest, Dearborn Park: Shall It Be Surrendered?*, stated that commercial interests had already taken a former playground, and they intended to breach a promise made by the U.S. government that the land would remain a park in perpetuity. Nevertheless, in 1892 the sponsors usurped Dearborn Park for the construction of a public library and later erected an Art Institute. A zoo was also built in Lincoln Park with donations from wealthy Chicagoans and their New York friends.[56]

One who championed the workers' cause was Aaron Montgomery Ward, the mail order magnate who had gotten his business start as a clerk for Marshall Field and Levi Leiter. Ward conducted a twenty-year fight to keep the lakefront free of all buildings, winning four state supreme court decisions to that effect. Ward stated that he did not think it right for the area to become a showground for the educated rich. His efforts earned ostracism from the social circles of the elite, but failed to deter Ward, who foiled the construction of Marshall Field's museum until his death in 1913.[57]

Unlike Ward, other Chicago leaders subscribed to the Harper Report, which called for the use of playgrounds to educate youth. Commercial interests saw particular merit in the concept. Edgar A. Bancroft, president of the Merchants' Club, stated in the *Tribune,* on November 12, 1899, that "Businessmen have the roots of their strength and business in the centers of population. It is...a mere matter of intelligent selfishness, of prudence, of wisdom to recognize that they should be interested in improving a city's condition."[58] Regarding the parks, he stated that "the city is asked to do something not out of the goodness of its heart, but out of the soundness of its head...a matter of business, of sound economy, of self-protection."[59] Mayor Carter Harrison II responded by appointing a special parks commission the following month.

The commission consisted of nine aldermen and six citizens, all professionals. Its mission was to secure sites for play space by philanthropy or legislation. Parks and playgrounds, including schoolyards since 1898, thus took on the double responsibility of improving health and social reform. The composition of the commission membership and financial support for such projects indicated that the ensuing programs would be directed at, rather than formulated with, groups that they considered subordinate.[60]

The masses resorted to the electoral process to meet their own needs. On July 1, 1895, the Illinois legislature passed a General Enabling Act that allowed any 100 voters of a district to petition a county judge for a new park district. Citizens got their play spaces by badgering ward bosses and threatening to withhold votes for aldermen. For once, both the reformers and those they expected to reform agreed on an issue. Between 1900 and 1917, Chicagoans created over 90 new parks and more than 100 playgrounds, with 56 different park governments in 22 separate and autonomous park districts by 1934. In 1900 the city government consisted of 8 major and 30 minor governing bodies. Cook County had a total of 3,000 precincts. Such a disjointed infrastructure allowed for a wide dispersal of power. Even as the progressives worked for greater centralization of the bureaucracy, park districts remained a haven of ethnicity and patronage. Political activism provided ethnic and working class groups with a measure of control in the park districts and allowed for pluralistic values rather than the assimilation envisioned by the reformers.[61]

As Americans entered the twentieth century, the progressives moved to consolidate their power and policies at both the national and local levels. In Chicago, however, they met with opposition to educational and moral reforms as they tried to restructure the schools and public spaces to impose their particular cultural values. Unable to re-create the White City of the Columbian Exposition and thwarted in their initial attempts to convert the working class and its largely ethnic constituents, the reformers embarked upon more concerted efforts to reach the immigrants' offspring through alternative means in the schools, parks, and playgrounds. It was largely within the realm of leisure practices that such divergent groups managed to reach an uneasy and, at times, fragile accommodation. Commercialized leisure and competitive sport would play a prominent part in the cultural interchange that transpired thereafter.[62]

Notes

1. Reid Badger, *Great American Fair* (Chicago: Nelson Hall, 1979), 47-52; Michael Kammen, *Distant Chords of Memory: The Transformation of Tradition in American Culture* (New York: Alfred A. Knopf, 1991), 141, 271, on local pride; and Robert Rydell, *All the World's a Fair: Visions of Empire at American International Expositions, 1876-1916* (Chicago: University of Chicago Press, 1984), 40-3, on intercity rivalry.

2. Carl S. Smith, *Chicago and the American Literary Imagination, 1880-1920* (Chicago: University of Chicago Press, 1984), 122-4. See Couvares, "The Triumph of Commerce: Class Culture and Mass Culture in Pittsburgh," for a similar movement in that city.

3. Helen L. Horowitz, *Culture and the City* (Lexington: University Press of Kentucky, 1976); Laurence W. Levine, *Highbrow/Lowbrow: The Emergence of Cultural Hierarchy in America* (Cambridge, MA: Harvard University Press, 1988), 116-18, 131, 208.

Carol Baldridge and Alan Willis, "The Business of Culture," *Chicago History,* 19:1-2 (Spring-Summer 1990): 33-51; Stefan Germer, "Pictures At an Exhibition," ibid., 16:1 (Spring 1987): 4-21; and Sarah J. Moore, "On the Frontier of Culture," ibid., 16:2 (Summer 1987): 4-13, which details the Chicagoans' attempts to supercede New York in such importance.

4. Allen F. Davis, *Spearheads for Reform: The Social Settlements and the Progressive Movement, 1890-1914* (New York: Oxford University Press, 1967): 187-9; Trachtenburg, *The Incorporation of America,* 208-16; Burton Benedict, *The Anthropology of World's Fairs* (Berkeley, CA: Scolar Press, 1983), 16-17, 21, 32-4, 45, 50; Rydell, *All the World's a Fair,* 48-68, for an extended discussion on racial comparisons.

Svornost, April 8, 1890; Feb. 2, 1892; Feb. 4, 1892, Works Progress Administration, Foreign Language Press Survey (1942), hereafter abbreviated as FLPS; *Columbian Exposition Album* (Chicago: 1893),

98, cited in Larzer Ziff, *The American 1890s,* (New York: Viking Press, 1973 ed.), 3-4; Badger, *The Great American Fair,* 10, 58-9, 71, 80, 105. See Louisiana Exposition Co., *The Greatest of Expositions* (St. Louis, MO, 1904) on comparative anthropological exhibits designed to demonstrate Anglo superiority.

5. Maurice F. Neufeld, "The Contribution of the World's Columbian Exposition of 1893 to the Idea of a Planned Society in the United States," Ph.D. Dissertation, University of Wisconsin, 1935; Rydell, *All the World's a Fair,* 47, 52, 64, 67; Badger, *The Great American Fair,* 91-2, 104, 120-3; Ziff, *The American 1890s,* 20; Benedict, *Anthropology of World's Fairs,* 6-12, on the rearrangement of status hierarchies.

6. Badger, *The Great American Fair,* 107-09; Benedict, *Anthropology of World's Fairs,* 5, 49, 53-4, 57, 59; Rydell, *All the World's a Fair,* 40-1, 60-8.

7. Badger, *The Great American Fair,* 90-2; Neufeld, "The Contribution of the Columbian Exposition"; Rydell, *All the World's a Fair,* 69-71; Boyer, *Urban Masses and Moral Order,* 182-4.

8. Smith, *Chicago and the American Literary Imagination,* 146-7; Badger, *The Great American Fair,* 130; Trachtenberg, *The Incorporation of America,* 223-5.

9. Hoyt, *One Hundred and Twenty-Five Photographic Views of Chicago* (Chicago: Rand McNally & Co., 1911); Larry A. Viskochil, *Chicago at the Turn of the Century in Photographs* (New York: Dover Publications, 1984).

10. Ade cited in Ziff, *The American 1890s,* 158.

11. Badger, *The Great American Fair,* 39, 96; Boyer, *Urban Masses and Moral Order,* 184-7.

12. Jane Addams, *Twenty Years at Hull House* (New York: Macmillan, 1930); Graham Taylor, *Chicago Commons through Forty Years* (Chicago: John F. Cuneo, 1936); William G. Domhoff, *The Powers that Be: Processes of Ruling Class Domination in America* (New York: Random House, 1978), 96-100, 198; Goodman, *Choosing Sides,* 100-08; Rosenzweig, *Eight Hours for What We Will,* 139, 142-6; Hofstadter, *The Age of Reform;* Wiebe, *The Search for Order;* Arthur Mann, ed., *The Progressive Era* (New York: Holt, Rinehart, and Winston, 1963); Alan Dawley, *Struggles for Justice: Social Responsibility and the Liberal State* (Cambridge, MA: Harvard University Press, 1991), 98-171; Robert M. Crunden, *Ministers of Reform: The Progressive Achievement in American Civilization, 1889-1920* (New York: Basic Books, 1982).

13. Addams, *Twenty Years at Hull House;* Carson, *Settlement Folk,* 14-16, 57, 63-4, 109-19; Hilda Satt Polacheck, *I Came a Stranger: The Story of a Hull House Girl* (Chicago: University of Illinois Press, 1989); Rivka Shpak Lissak, *Pluralism and Progressives: Hull House and the New Immigrants, 1890-1919* (Chicago: University of Chicago Press, 1989); Steven J. Diner, *A City and Its Universities: Public Policy in Chicago, 1892-1919* (Chapel Hill: University of North Carolina Press, 1980); Cavallo, *Muscles and Morals,* 1-11, 65-7.

14. A survey of the *Manual, Board of Education, City of Chicago, 1870-71; Manual of the Public Schools of the City of Chicago, 1873-74, 1874-75, 1875-76;* and *A Manual for the Use of Teachers, 1878,* indicate that German influences in curriculum were already firmly entrenched in the postwar years. Other ethnic concerns are evident in Mary F. McWhorter, "Irish History in the Parochial Schools," *New World,* July 3, 1909: 6; and "German Culture," *Vorbote,* Mar. 13, 1895.

David J. Hogan, *Class and Reform: School and Society in Chicago, 1880-1930* (Philadelphia: University of Pennsylvania Press, 1985), 79-82; William J. Reese, *Power and the Promise of School Reform: Grassroots Movements During the Progressive Era* (Boston: Routledge & Kegan Paul, 1986); Mazur, *Minyans for a Prairie City,* 126; Wade, *Chicago's Pride,* 155-9, on Irish and German demands.

Wilma J. Pesavento, "A Historical Study of the Development of Physical Education in the Chicago Public Schools, 1860 to 1965," Ph.D. Dissertation, Northwestern University, 1966, 9-10, 15, 16, 21, 25; Todd, *Chicago Recreation Survey,* 1 (1937): 20, places the introduction of the Turner system between 1863-1864.

15. A national conference was held in Boston in 1889 to discuss the adoption of competing German, French, Swedish, and American systems in the public schools. The conference failed to reach agreement. See Isabel Barrows, ed., *Physical Training, A Full Report of the Papers and Discussion of the Conference in Boston in November, 1889* (Boston: George H. Ellis, 1890).

16. John W. Bell, "The Development of the Public High School in Chicago," Master's Thesis, University of Chicago, 1939, 159; W.E. Mellinger, ed., *High School Journal,* 2:1 (October 1884): 2, 6; 4:2 (November 1885): 5; 4:3 (December 1885): 4-5, 8; Archie Oboler, ed., *The Oski-Wow-Wow: A History of Hyde Park Athletics* (Chicago: Hyde Park High School, 1924), 1.

17. Edwin L. Shuman, ed., *High School Journal,* 6:2 (October 1886): 5; quote is from 6:4 (December 1886): n.p.

See Joel Spring, "Mass Culture and School Sports," *History of Education Quarterly,* 14 (Winter 1974): 483-500; Timothy P. O'Hanlon, "Interscholastic Athletics, 1900-1940," *Educational Theory,* 30 (Spring 1980): 89-103; Jeffrey Mirel, "From Student Control to Institutional Control of High School Athletics: Three Michigan Cities, 1883-1905," *Journal of Social History,* 16:2 (Winter 1982): 83-100; and J. Thomas Jable, "The Public Schools Athletic League of New York City: Organized Athletics for City School Children, 1903-1914," in *Sport and American Education: History and Perspective* (Washington, DC: American Alliance for Health, Physical Education, Recreation, and Dance, 1979), Chapter 1.

18. Shuman, ed., *High School Journal,* 6:3 (November, 1886): 1, 5; and 6:2 (October 1886): 5.

Addams, *Twenty Years at Hull House,* 443; Donald J. Mrozek, "Sport in American Life: From National Health to Personal Fulfillment, 1890-1940," in Kathryn Grover, ed., *Fitness in American Culture: Images of Health, Sport, and the Body, 1830-1940* (Amherst: University of Massachusetts Press, 1989), 18-46; Larry Fielding, "The Battle over Athletic Priorities in the Louisville YMCA, 1892-1912," presented at North American Society for Sport History Conference, May 28, 1989, Clemson, SC.

19. The *High School Journal,* 1885-1887, indicated that boys competed in football, baseball, track, tennis, and boxing. Shuman, ed., ibid., 7:4 (December 1887): 63-6; 7:7 (March 1888): 107-9; 8:4 (December 1888): 27-32; John J. Nutt, ed., ibid., 8:8 (April 1889): 61-8. Politicians and businessmen moved even more quickly after the turn of the century to capitalize on the playground movement by providing land, money, and even instructors.

20. E. Mellinger, ed., ibid., 4:5 (February 1886): 5; 1:1 (May 1886): 1, 3. Cook County High School Indoor Baseball League Records, 1895-99; Meeting minutes, Jan. 2, 1896, 25, at CHS.

See Stephen Hardy, "Adopted by All the Leading Clubs," and Hardy, "Entrepreneurs, Structures, and the Sportgeist: Old Tensions in a Modern Industry," in Donald G. Kyle and Gary O. Stark, eds., *Essays in Sport History and Sport Mythology* (College Station, TX: Texas A & M Press, 1990).

21. Laura Bergquist, et al., *History of Englewood High School* (Chicago: Chief Printing Co., 1935), 111-2, in Box EHS, file 1/1 of the Neighborhood History Collection, Chicago Cultural Center.

22. *Mayor's Annual Message and 15th Annual Report, 1890, xviii; Mayor's Annual Message and 16th Annual Report of the Department of Public Works, 1891* (Chicago: Cameron, Amberg & Co., 1892), xviii; *Mayor's Annual Message and 17th Annual Report of the Department of Public Works, 1892* (Chicago: Cameron, Amberg & Co., 1893), xxvi;

Todd, *Chicago Recreation Survey,* 1 (1937), 20; Bell, "The Development of the Public High School," 159-160; Pesavento, "A Historical Study of the Development of Physical Education," 22-7; Robert Pruter, "The Rise of Interscholastic Athletics in the Chicago Area: The Cook County League, 1889-1913," presented at the North American Society for Sport History Convention, May 27, 1991.

23. *Svornost,* October 8, 1878; February 27, 1880; May 2, 1880; June 29, 1881; September 10, 1885 (FLPS); Krzywonos, ed., *Poles of Chicago,* 124-7; Richard T. Ely, ed., *Hull House Maps and Papers* (New York: Thomas Y. Crowell, 1970), 105; Keil and Jentz, eds., *German Workers in Chicago,* 371-2; David Tyack, *The One Best System: A History of Urban American Education* (Cambridge, MA: Harvard University Press, 1974), 105.

24. *Svornost,* January 8, 1890; *Dziennik Chicagoski,* July 22, 1892, 4; August 27, 1892; and *Zgoda,* November 14, 1894, 4; January 19, 1899, 6; *Dziennik Chicagoski,* June 6, 1896 and September 1, 1908 (FLPS); Pacyga, *Polish Immigrants and Industrial Chicago,* 55-9.

Hogan, *Class and Reform,* 55-8, 100, 102; *Chicago Tribune,* Mar. 26, 1890; Mar. 27, 189; Tyack, *The One Best System,* 36-9, 106-9, 177-9.

See Steven Seidman, "Substantive Debates: Moral Order and Social Crises—Perspectives on Modern Culture," and Peter Berger, "Social Sources of Secularization," in Jeffrey C. Alexander and Steven Seidman, eds., *Culture and Society: Contemporary Debates* (New York: Cambridge University Press, 1990), 217-35 and 239-48, respectively, for discussion of the secularization process.

25. Hogan, *Class and Reform,* 125-127; Pierce, *A History of Chicago,* 3 (1957): 389, estimates the 1890 figure at 38,000.

See Pacyga, *Polish Immigrants and Industrial Chicago,* 146-8, on Polish schools.

26. Anthony Platt, *The Child Savers: The Invention of Delinquency* (Chicago: University of Chicago Press, 1977), 129-41.

William R. Harper, chairman, *Report of the Educational Commission of the City of Chicago* (Chicago: 1899). The Bluthardt quote is on pages 163-4 of the report. See Ahern, *Political History of Chicago,* 271-2, on Bluthardt's political career.

27. "The Sweat Shops," from Bureau of Labor Statistics, *Illinois 7th Biennial Report* (Springfield, 1893), 357-99, cited in Diamond, ed., *The Nation Transformed,* 221; Pierce, *History of Chicago,* 3 (1957): 294-5; Cantor, ed., *American Working Class Culture,* 335; Hogan, *Class and Reform,* 55-8, 60-3, 100, 105, 127-8, 132, n. 34, 268,

n. 46, 270; Tyack, *The One Best System,* 70-1, 177-9; David L. Angus, "Conflict, Class, and the Nineteenth Century Public High School in the Cities of the Midwest," *Curriculum Inquiry,* 18:1 (Spring 1988): 7-31.

28. David Nasaw, *Schooled to Order: A Social History of Pubic Schooling in the United States* (New York: Oxford University Press, 1979), 106-112; Hogan, *Class and Reform,* 57-8, 195-8. The Harper Commission had no teachers, no women, and no labor leaders among its members.

29. Harper, *Report of the Educational Commission,* 133, 135, 174.

30. E. Mellinger, ed., *High School Journal,* 1:4 (July 1884): 3; and 10:7 (March 1897): 102.

Stanley Aronowitz, *False Promises: The Shaping of the American Working Class Consciousness* (New York: McGraw-Hill, 1973), 72-5; Nasaw, *Schooled to Order,* 138, 145, 153.

Chicago Board of Education, *23rd Annual Report,* 1877, 51-3, 55-6, 63-5, cited in Hogan, *Class and Reform,* 138. Domhoff, *The Powers that Be,* 198, charges that industrialists feared a system that might produce intellectual radicals, but favored the education of technicians, who served their own needs. When the Board of Education was reluctant to initiate the industrial education courses suggested by business leaders, the labor conflict of the late nineteenth century spurred the commercial interests to pursue independent efforts.

Charles H. Thurber, "Is the Present High School Course a Satisfactory Preparation for Business? If Not, How Should it be Modified?," *Journal of Proceedings and Addresses, National Education Association* (Chicago: 1897): 808-18, in Diamond, ed., *The Nation Transformed,* 411-19. See Edwin G. Cooley, "The Need for Vocational Schools," and John Dewey, "An Undemocratic Proposal," in Marvin Lazerson and W. Norton Grubb, eds., *American Education and Vocationalism: A Documentary History* (New York: Columbia Teachers College Press, 1974), 141-7, for oppositional views on the issue.

31. Harper, *Report of the Educational Commission,* 221-2; Nasaw, *Schooled to Order,* 122, 153.

Domhoff, *The Powers that Be,* 96-100, charges that the Chicago Civic Federation, which influenced legislation favorable to business interests, served as a model for the national organization.

32. Hogan, *Class and Reform,* 60, 156; Pierce, *History of Chicago,* 3 (1957): 388; Robert Bellah, "Civil Religion in America," in Alexander and Seidman, eds., *Culture and Society,* 262-72; and Tyack, *The*

One Best System, 229-55, on the process of Americanization in other urban school systems.

33. *Report, Showing Results of 15 Years of Organization to the Teachers of Chicago* (Chicago Teachers' Federation, December 1, 1908) stresses the lack of freedom, subserviency, the autocracy of the school system, pay cuts and unfair merit testing. Harper, *Report of the Educational Commission,* 60; Hogan, *Class and Reform,* 196-8; Tyack, *The One Best System,* 59, 66, 170, 257, 268. Margaret Haley, president of the CTF, charged that Harper hoped to gain a monopoly on the teacher education program at the University of Chicago, just as his benefactor, John D. Rockefeller, had with Standard Oil.

34. Hogan, *Class and Reform,* 79-82, 153; Jane Addams, "Foreign Born Children in the Primary Grades," *Journal of Proceedings and Addresses, NEA* (Chicago: 1897): 104-12, in Diamond, ed., *The Nation Transformed,* 420-6; "German Instruction," *Chicagoer Arbeiter Zeitung,* Oct. 31, 1900, in Keil and Jentz, *German Workers in Chicago,* 376-7.

35. Robert L. Reid, ed., *The Autobioigraphy of Margaret A. Haley* (Urbana: University of Illinois Press, 1982); Hogan, *Class and Reform,* 97-8; Addams, *Twenty Years at Hull House,* 328-39.

36. Tyack, *The One Best System,* 168-82, 257-68; Hogan, *Class and Reform,* 199-203, 207; and Julia Wrigley, *Class, Politics and the Public Schools: Chicago, 1900-1950* (New Brunswick, NJ: Rutgers University Press, 1982), 62-127 on Cooley, 34-5, 512, on the Chicago Federation of Labor. The Chicago Federation of Labor supported coursework in music, drawing and foreign language, and a liberal education in general. Business leaders opposed such courses and favored increased manual training in all grades, although they provided such private classical instruction for their own children.

City of Chicago, *Proceedings of the Board of Education, July 6, 1904 - June 21, 1905* (Chicago: Barnard and Miller, 1905), 785-6, on reference to the board's opposition to the teachers' union affiliation. After a twenty-year battle, including four electoral defeats of the Harper Bill, centralization became a reality when teachers gained tenure.

37. *Harper Report,* 155, 180; Riess, *City Games,* 133-40, 151-2; Hardy, *How Boston Played,* 85-8, 98-101, 106; Rosenzweig, *Eight Hours for What We Will,* 143-8; Cavallo, *Muscles and Morals,* 49-72; Rader, *American Sports,* 159-60.

38. Addams, *Twenty Years at Hull House;* ibid., *The Second Twenty Years at Hull House* (New York: Macmillan, 1930); Taylor, *Chicago*

Commons; Richard Hofstadter, *The Age of Reform* (New York: Alfred A. Knopf, 1977 ed.), 208; Dominick Cavallo, *Muscles and Morals,* 125-46; Boyer, *Urban Masses and Moral Order,* 155-61; Allen F. Davis, *American Heroine: The Life and Legend of Jane Addams* (New York: Oxford University Press, 1973); T. J. Jackson Lears, *No Place of Grace: Antimodernism and the Transformation of American Culture, 1880-1920* (New York: Pantheon Books, 1981); Robert M. Crunden, *Ministers of Reform.*

39. Addams, *Twenty Years at Hull House,* 201-07, 222-3, 310-11; Mina Carson, *Settlement Folk: Social Thought and the American Settlement Movement* (Chicago: University of Chicago Press, 1990), 54-6, 71-2, 77-82, 89-92, 110, 125, 130-1, 176-7; Davis, *American Heroine.*

40. Addams, *Twenty Years at Hull House,* 89-112, 236-7; ibid., *The Second Twenty Years,* 348-50; Crunden, *Ministers of Reform,* 52-61; Carson, *Settlement Folk,* 118-19.

In addition to Dow, and Bowen, who died in 1953, many local and national leaders frequented Hull House, while others received their training there. Among them were Henry Demarest Lloyd, Governor John Peter Altgeld, and historian Charles Beard.

Allen F. Davis, *Spearheads for Reform: The Social Settlements and the Progressive Movement, 1890-1914* (New York: Oxford University Press, 1967), 33-40, states that more than 80 percent of settlement workers had a B.A. degree, and more than half did graduate work. Most were young and unmarried, and many were teachers who saw the settlements as an alternative form of education with a broader scope than the institutionalized school systems.

41. Steven Diner, *A City and Its Universities: Public Policy in Chicago, 1892-1919* (Chapel Hill: University of North Carolina Press, 1980), 56-8, 187-207; Horowitz, *Culture and the City,* 56, 246-7; Mann, *The Progressive Era,* 4-30; Hofstadter, *Age of Reform,* 131-9.

42. On the nature of European settlement houses see Davis, *Spearheads for Reform,* 16; and Mina Carson, *Settlement Folk,* 1-9, 31-5.

Harvey C. Carbaugh, ed., *Human Welfare Work in Chicago* (Chicago: A. C. McClurg, 1917), 148; Pierce, *A History of Chicago,* 3 (1957): 466; Graham Taylor, *Chicago Commons,* xii; Philpott, *The Slum and the Ghetto,* 283.

43. Richard T. Ely, ed., *Hull House Maps and Papers* (1895; reprint, 1970), 17-21; McCarthy, "Politics and the Parks," 159; Carson, *Settlement Folk,* 61; Philpott, *The Slum and the Ghetto,* 23, 67,

73-4, counts twenty-six or more nationalities within a three-block area of Hull House by the late 1890s.

44. Addams, *The Second Twenty Years,* 366-7 (quote); ibid., *Twenty Years at Hull House,* 442-4.

45. Ibid., *Twenty Years at Hull House,* 105, 442-4; *Hull House Bulletin,* 2:5 (June 1897): 5; Ely, ed., *Hull House Maps and Papers,* 106; McCarthy, "Politics and the Parks," 160; Rainwater, *The Play Movement,* 56; Taylor, *Chicago Commons,* xii; Riess, *City Games,* 125, 164-7. See Rosenzweig, *Eight Hours for What We Will,* 127-52; Hardy, *How Boston Played,* 56, 95-6; Goodman, *Choosing Sides,* 33-58, on playgrounds and the settlement movement in the East. Cavallo, *Muscles and Morals,* for an extended discussion of the play movement.

46. Dwight H. Perkins, *Report of the Special Park Commission to the City of Chicago* (Chicago: W. J. Hartman, 1904); Malcolm Collier, "Jens Jensen and Columbus Park," *Chicago History,* 4:4 (Winter 1975-76): 225-32; Halsey, *The Development of Public Recreatio,* 10.

47. Collier, "Jens Jensen and Columbus Park," 227.

48. Ibid., 225-7; Halsey, *Development of Public Recreation,* 1, 9, 10; Hoyt, *One Hundred Years of Land Values in Chicago,* 1970, 99; Todd, *Chicago Recreation Survey,* 1:14; Wille, *Forever Open, Clear and Free,* 27, 45-6; Cranz, *The Politics of Park Design,* 160, 164-5. The election that approved the parks commission was wrought with charges of fraud, but the called-for recount never occurred. Separate park boards operated until the consolidation of 1934.

49. Halsey, *The Development of Public Recreation,* 16-17, cites *Public Parks* (Griegs & Co., 1869); Collier, "Jens Jensen and Columbus Park," 227; CHS, "Prairie in the City: Naturalism in Chicago's Parks, 1870-1940," July 1-Oct. 27, 1991. Simonds was the architect of Graceland Cemetery, Lincoln Park, Morton Arboretum, and the University of Chicago Quadrangles. See Riess, *City Games,* 44-6; Boyer, *Urban Masses and Moral Order,* 231-42; Hardy, *How Boston Played,* 65-84, and Rosenzweig, *Eight Hours for What We Will,* 128-36, on the nature of park development, and Olmsted's role in Boston, New York, and Worcester.

50. Perkins, *Report of the Special Park Commission, 1901,* 23, 36, offers 1870 as the date for attainment of the number 2 ranking; Todd, *Chicago Recreation Survey,* 1:14, states that Chicago dropped to number 32 as early as 1890 when the population reached 1,099,850. *Mayor's Annual Message and 14th Annual Report of the Department of Public Works, 1889* (Chicago: Cameron, Amberg & Co., 1890), vi,

xv; *Mayor's Annual Message and 15th Annual Report of the Department of Public Works, 1890* (Chicago: Cameron, Amberg & Co., 1891), v-vi; Riess, *City Games,* 136-8.

See Rosenzweig, *Eight Hours for What We Will,* 134-6, 146-7, on the role of commercial interests in the parks movement in Worcester.

51. *Tenth Annual Report of the Department of Public Works to the City Council of the City of Chicago, 1885* (Chicago: Cameron, Amberg & Co., 1886), 81, 213; *Eighteenth Annual Report of the Department of Public Works, 1893* (Chicago: Cameron, Amberg & Co., 1894), 29; Rosenzweig, *Eight Hours for What We Will,* 127-68; Hardy, *How Boston Played,* 65-106; Riess, *City Games,* 132; Harold Seymour, *Baseball: The People's Game* (New York: Oxford University Press), 44-5.

52. Halsey, *Development of Public Recreation,* 19, cites the *Chicago Tribune,* Aug. 10, 1873, in regard to the crowd size; 20, on trotting schedules; Pierce, *A History of Chicago,* 3 (1957): 316, 318. See Riess, *City Games,* 131, for similar, though less successful, developments in New York.

Annual Reports of the West Chicago Park Commission, 1919-1920 (Chicago: 1920), 18, and *1926-1927* (Chicago: 1927), 40, assert that Chicago's first public swimming pool, in Douglas Park in 1895, was attained through the efforts of the German Turners.

53. Rainwater, *The Play Movement,* 17; *Twelfth Annual Report of the Department of Public Works* (Chicago: Cameron, Amberg & Co., 1888), 72.

54. Wille, *Forever Open, Clear, and Free,* 25, 80, Perry Duis, "Yesterday's City," *Chicago History,* 15:4 (Winter 1986-87): 66-9.

55. Halsey, *Development of Public Recreation,* 49; John W. Stamper, "Shaping Chicago's Shoreline," *Chicago History,* 14:4 (Winter 1985-86): 44-55; *L'Italia,* July 15, 1911. See Riess, *City Games,* 127, on swimming in New York.

56. Magee, *A Protest,* 3; Perry R. Duis, "Yesterday's City," 66-9.
Francis G. Couvares, "The Triumph of Commerce: Class Culture and Mass Culture in Pittsburgh," 123-52, analyzes the movement toward high culture in that city.

57. Wille, *Forever Open, Clear and Free,* 72-80.

58. Harper, *Report of the Educational Commission,* 180; McCarthy, "Politics and the Parks," 158-72. The *Tribune,* November 12, 1899, 2, cited in McCarthy, 161.

59. Hogan, *Class and Reform*, 71 also cites the *Tribune*, November 12, 1899.

60. *Mayor's Annual Message and 24th Annual Report, Department of Public Works* (Chicago: 1899), 11. The six citizens on the commission were listed as: architect, engineer, physician, landscaper, lawyer, and sanitary engineer. *Mayor's Annual Message and 21st Annual Report of the Department of Public Works* (Chicago: Cameron, Amberg & Co., 1896), xlii. *Mayor's Annual Message and 25th Annual Report of the Department of Public Works, 1900* (Chicago: P. F. Pettibone & Co., 1901), ix, on the mission of the Special Parks Commission.

Harper, *Report of the Educational Commission,* 222, reports that six schools began serving as playgrounds in 1898 upon a $1,000 appropriation from the city council and $750 in private donations. Todd, *Chicago Recreation Survey,* 1:19.

61. My conclusions are consistent with those found in studies of the parks movement in eastern cities. See Rosenzweig, *Eight Hours for What We Will,* 134-40; Hardy, *How Boston Played,* 67-79; Riess, *City Games,* 129-38.

Todd, *Chicago Recreation Survey,* 1: 22, 25; Philpott, *The Slum and the Ghetto,* 95; Hogan, *Class and Reform,* 259, n. 153.

62. Patricia Burgess, "Idealism and Arrogance: The White City and Planning Theory," presented at the 106th Annual Meeting of the American Historical Assn., Dec. 30, 1991; Cavallo, *Muscles and Morals,* 92-106; Boyer, *Urban Masses and Moral Order,* 265-76.

CHAPTER 4

The Interplay of Commercialism and Popular Culture

The first part of the progressive plan—to attract children to the schools, settlements, parks, and playgrounds, where they could be educated as good Americans—proved almost too successful. Play spaces overflowed, and city planners could not accommodate the demand. Within the structured parks and enclosed playgrounds, children had limited choices, as trained instructors tried to regulate activities and provide the proper moral guidance as they supervised their charges. But the educational process proved neither unidirectional nor passive, as youth imposed their own values—often at odds with those of the reformers. Other groups, such as the interscholastic teams, ethnic athletic clubs, and independent teams, often operated outside the pale of such supervision.[1]

Structured play took on the characteristics of work and commercialized forms of leisure, but still failed to fulfill the progressives' dream of a more cooperative and moral society. Commercialized sport fostered a growing professionalism that undermined the values of supervised play. Unable to wholly eradicate the street culture, ethnic differences, and the working class lifestyle, particularly the use of alcohol, reformers waged an ongoing battle to assimilate such groups in the schools, parks, playgrounds, and workplaces until the U.S. entry into World War I.[2]

The initial confrontation to the progressive vision presented itself from within its own ranks, as elements of the street life intruded across class lines within the newer forms of commercialized leisure. The proliferation of vice dens, movie houses, dance halls, and gambling attracted both ethnics and natives. Wagering accompanied even the games of youths, demonstrating the need for an even broader scope of control. With few ethnics in attendance in the city's secondary schools, the largely native, middle class students followed the lead of the colleges in the organization of their activities. While school administrators and reformist critics wrestled with the issues of curricular reform, students continued to pursue and organize their own sporting ventures. Age group, community, and club teams proliferated, and challenge matches provided ready competition throughout the city. Beyond the jurisdiction of school authorities, nominal school teams were often composed of both students and nonstudents. Interscholastic games and matches with alumni and other community teams often involved gambling and the use of "ringers" in the quest for victory. Such practices eventually prompted school administrators and social reform advocates to effect greater control over and provide proper guidance for student teams, based upon middle class perceptions of morality.[3]

Interscholastic Athletics

In September 1890, eight high school representatives met to formalize the Cook County High School Foot Ball League, initiated five years earlier. The representatives organized official schedules, assigned sites for play, and imposed a $5 entry fee, with $25 from the total used to pay for a championship banner. The remainder of the money, after expenses, was to go to the second-place team.

Visible symbols of success—banners, trophies, or media publicity—built school spirit and communal pride. Student publications lauded the achievements of the athletes, local businesses honored them, and fellow students feted them at banquets. Other students and teachers provided financial support for the teams.[4]

Students often measured their school's success and the virility of its male students in athletic competition. New schools gained immediate recognition with victories over established institutions. South Division extolled its newfound athletic success in 1891, due to the questionable use of "specials"— part-time students—some of whom were already college grads attending the school for single courses in music or drawing. The South Division football captain admitted using four such players on his team, and Manual Training protested that it was the only school using its own players. Such abuses plagued school sports throughout the country.[5]

German gymnastics prevailed in the formal physical education curriculum, but the interest in team games led authorities to include football and basketball by 1898 and baseball five years later. The change failed to curtail students' extracurricular activities, and the abuses continued unabated. Schoolboys continued to follow the commercialized model of the colleges that charged admission and the professional teams that played for money, but the administrators who increasingly sought to control their extracurricular activities adhered to the amateur ideology. Amateur athletic groups began forming separate associations in the post-Civil War years to safeguard and instill their particular value systems. The Chicago Amateur Athletic Association counted 300 members by March 1887, and the national AAU was founded the following year. As Ron Smith has argued, the class-based ideology of amateurism derived from British schools conflicted with American ideals of freedom and opportunity in a classless society.[6]

Some clubs bridged the amateur-professional gap in creative ways by providing "expense money," pawnable objects, or jobs to athletes in order to maintain their amateur status while still accumulating victories for the club. In 1892, Yale All-American Pudge Heffelfinger quit a railroad job in Omaha to play football "for expenses" with the Chicago Athletic Association. The team had split from the Chicago University Club team a year earlier over the reimbursement issue. While expense money paid to athletes was allowable under AAU rules, such a system created a corps of itinerant athletes at both secondary and collegiate levels who capitalized on their abilities in a free market. The faculty at Northwestern University in Evanston refused to allow its team to play against the Chicago "professionals."[7]

Interscholastic field days increased regularly scheduled track and field competition between schools after the University of Illinois invited high school teams to its athletic meet in June 1893. The university entertained more than 200 athletes and heightened the sense of spectacle with activities that included track and field, cycling, a baseball throw, and a football kick. There a university representative unveiled a draft of the constitution for an Interscholastic Athletic Association of Illinois that detailed specific regulations for eligibility and an executive role for the university. Despite objections by Chicago schools, the plan passed. The newly founded University of Chicago also augmented its own sponsorship of attractive interscholastic competitions, further increasing adult control over high school activities.[8]

The number of schools involved and the types of sports multiplied throughout the 1890s as interest grew among both boys and girls. Basketball and indoor baseball were especially popular. In 1896 boys inaugurated an indoor baseball league with city and suburban teams, a year after the girls began basketball play. However, the student-run organizations continued to struggle with issues of eligibility and sportsmanship, and a changing image of femininity fueled the rapid expansion of girls' sports, causing even greater concern among authorities.[9]

Commercial interests quickly realized the potential for profit in such student associations. Representatives of the Spalding Company attended the league meetings and offered balls, publicity, and playing sites in return for the adoption of its equipment and rules.[10]

Like the businessmen, school administrators took greater interest in student affairs, and adults gradually managed to assert even greater control over the student-initiated extracurricular activities. By early 1898 faculty members formed a Board of Control to administer and regulate school sports. Within four years they succeeded in removing all student representation, and the adults moved quickly to standardize rules, eligibility requirements, and eliminate money prizes and unsportsmanlike conduct. By 1904 the board controlled student activities in twenty schools, and it scheduled competition under adult supervision at approved sites such as school gyms, YMCA's, or settlement houses.[11]

The students at Medill High School credited their subsequent athletic success to faculty intervention, the use of school facilities, and the Board of Control decision to organize divisions within the athletic league based on size and weight. Whereas in previous years students had not been "forced to be on time or reprimanded" by peers, and exhibited a selfish attitude, faculty coaches instituted habits of time discipline and the work ethic.[12]

Most students, however, did not welcome such regulation. *The Review,* a student paper at Northwest Division High School, commented that "many of our Chicago high schools are hampered in their athletic work by the interference of their principal and faculty, even when there is no deficiency in lessons."[13] A later edition informed students that alumni football games were not governed by the Board of Control rules, and they need not bring written permission from parents to participate.[14]

When the board of education denied students the right to charge admission fees to their athletic contests, a high school principal petitioned the board on their behalf, stating

that it was necessary to raise funds to pay the expenses of these games and that if the power to raise these necessary funds was taken from the pupils by insisting upon the school halls being opened to all the students in the schools, athletic games would be carried on in public halls outside of the control of the schools, where rowdyism and other undesirable conduct would be indulged in, greatly to the detriment of athletics and of the schools.[15]

The late intervention of school administrators relegated them to a reactive rather than a proactive role. A student culture had already been established in the schools, including secret societies and ethnic social clubs. The antagonism between students and adults erupted into open rebellion over the athletic issues. As Stephen Hardy found in his study of Boston's interscholastic teams, sport fostered school spirit and a sense of community, but in Chicago the student culture opposed and resisted the intrusion of adult administrators.[16]

Athletics were of particular importance to the students. The Hyde Parkers even asserted that although schools "intended to train minds...athletics provided the larger half of their education."[17]

In 1902, when the Board of Control ruled Hyde Park athletes ineligible for spring sports, thereby costing them sure city and state championships, the students decided to "avoid all future involvement with the board and intended to organize their own league with other schools." [18] Superintendent Cooley thwarted a second revolt by suspending recalcitrant students over the next two years, and the Board of Control passed more stringent regulations, even requiring the athletes to return the uniforms that marked their status and symbolized their masculinity. Students continued to resist. When the board of education intended to honor local and national leaders by choosing new names at three schools, the students refused to adopt them.[19]

High school teams often engaged in interstate competition, and Chicagoans drew national recognition when they defeated New York schools 105-0 and 76-0 in successive years. Such affairs, billed as "national football championships," showcased athletic rather than academic excellence. They also provided politicians with a convenient forum and ready readers for the newspapers, who featured daily football reports and special sporting editions. Both groups extended their support to capitalize on such spectacles in the ensuing years, but the Board of Control faced more immediate frustrations from colleges and professional teams, whose recruitment of high school athletes frustated board efforts to regulate unauthorized play.[20]

The "value in attracting athletes to the university had been throughly proven." [21] From the school's inception, University of Chicago president William Rainey Harper had determined to use athletics as both a public relations and recruiting tool, and Amos Alonzo Stagg became the first coach accorded faculty rank. Football, in particular, became a profitable venture, and colleges entered the sphere of commercialized leisure with the construction of huge stadiums. Wisconsin entertained the high school athletes "royally," and was even accused of kidnapping a star Chicagoan.[22]

Michigan too coveted the Chicago athletes, and Superintendent Cooley met with representatives of the midwestern conference, then known as the Big Nine. They acknowledged that his concerns were well-founded, but did little to alleviate matters. When both the AAU and the Board of Control declared Walter Eckersall of Hyde Park an ineligible professional, Stagg campaigned for the retention of his amateur status, and the Big Nine concurred. Eckersall subsequently led the Chicago teams to remarkable success while gaining All-American honors.[23]

Stagg drew the particular ire of Cooley for proselytizing high school athletes. Stagg allowed local teams to use the university facilities and provided personal tutelage to the athletes. In addition to scheduling practice games with the local high schools, he initiated an annual interscholastic track meet that drew participants from Chicago and nearby states. Such events allowed Stagg to identify and cultivate the most promising talent, demonstrating his largesse by funding trips to other intercity competitions. By 1905 eight of the eleven players on the championship football team came from local schools. He later sponsored a basketball tournament that drew as many as thirty state champions. Despite inadequate coursework, the institutions of higher education admitted prize athletes, some of whom left high school before graduation.[24]

Just as the board failed to exert an influence over the colleges, it had limited effect on its own students. Gambling, professionalism, and foul play continued over the next decade. Administrators considered abolishing football and basketball. In 1911 no baseball title was awarded when the board discovered that six of eight contenders had violated the rules, including the use of five professional players. Twenty others played for other unauthorized teams. Despite the abuses, the interest in sport grew and the league offered students competitive opportunities in nine sports. Competition even attracted the ethnic and Catholic factions in "championship" matches, as partisans united behind their local favorites. If the reformers had not fully achieved their goals, they had at least transferred student energies, and that of their fans, to more acceptable diversions. The Cook County Athletic League dissolved in 1913 and reorganized as the Chicago Public Schools Athletic League, administered by school authorities and private sponsors. Similar to its New York counterpart in its commercial support, it differed in the more overtly religious objectives promoted by Luther Gulick, co-founder of the eastern organization. The formal alliance of commercial interests and educational reformers marked an ongoing relationship designed to reach ethnic and working class youth in the parks and playgrounds.[25]

Playgrounds

Interscholastic athletics reached only a small fraction of the youth who stayed in school. To develop the positive aspects of sports, such as healthy exercise and community spirit, reformers had to extend their programs beyond the formal educational institutions. As they slowly gained control of extracurricular activities in the schools, they also attempted to transform the perceived anarchy of the street culture into a more homogeneous social order by extending the supervised play concept to include the training of adolescents. American team games, taught, administered, and supervised by adults, could addresss health concerns and juvenile delinquency while promoting moral reform and the assimilation of ethnics. Such concerns led to concerted efforts to supply wholesome play spaces within the congested neighborhoods.

The playground or small parks movement at the turn of the century aspired to such goals. Reformers and city planners employed architects to structure public spaces in a particular manner for working class usage. The field house concept was designed to attract users on a year-round basis, with indoor facilities for winter use. Activities, however, were carefully segregated by gender and often reinforced traditional roles. Cary Goodman, in his study of New York playgrounds, emphasized the importance of fencing in the separation of boys and girls, not only from each other, but from undesirable elements as well. Within such spaces, instructors might hold a captive audience.[26]

The Chicago City Council allotted $11,500 for five playgrounds in 1900, but with the blessing and support of the commercial leaders, $6.5 million had been appropriated for new parks by 1903. The new playgrounds seemed to be attracting children, as the sponsors had hoped. In 1903, 734,693 were recorded as using the facilities. A year later the figure rose to over a million. Other cities followed suit, with 246 establishing supervised playgrounds by 1910.[27]

To facilitate its programs, each playground had a trained director and a park policeman or assistant director. Women conducted kindergartens in the summer and taught raffia weaving to the girls. The athletic director was a professional coach hired to instruct the older boys in sport skills. The parks commission reported that "this feature of the playground work has saved many a young man, by drawing him away from bad companions and the vicious atmosphere of saloons and dance halls."[28]

Park directors believed that corner gangs were at least becoming athletic gangs. In addition to developing their physical skills, they were learning to respect property rights, particularly safeguarding their own. Playground directors maintained that they were "laying the foundations for good citizenship and respect for law and order," as they brought the street culture under the regulation of middle class authorities.[29]

Insofar as the parks reduced delinquency and trained youth to become good Americans, business interests were willing to lend their support. Individuals, companies, and commercial organizations donated large amounts of land, money, and even instructors. A national organization, the Playground Association of America, was formed to realize the moral and social goals stated by Jane Addams in 1907. The group aimed to "replace the theaters, dance halls, saloons, gambling, and vice with parks, playgrounds, recreation centers, and festivals to increase socialization, decrease class, ethnicity and age barriers."[30] Clarence Rainwater, a director of Chicago's playgrounds, believed that the playground movement allowed the "opportunity to gain control of 80 percent of the population during the 64 hours per week when even laborers are at leisure." [31] Graham Taylor described the atmosphere of play and festival at the Playground Association's 1907 national convention as "Chicago as it is to be."[32] The statement was indicative of the progressives' optimistic faith in their ability to create change. Leisure activities in the public recreational facilities were carefully directed to achieve the desired results. In fact, the playground association stated that it was "almost better not to have a playground than one without careful direction."[33] E. B. DeGroot, a former Hull House resident and Director of Gymnastics and Athletics for the South Park District, instructed his staff to "...bring about order and esprit de corps, to teach obedience to authority and instant execution of orders."[34] Such an hierarchical relationship under careful direction and supervision, akin to the industrialization of the work force, served employers well.

A 1908 study by sociologist Allen T. Burns concluded that such work was immensely effective in combating delinquency. The Burns study stated that the South parks had reduced delinquency rates by more than 28 percent, and he predicted figures as high as 70 percent. The study exemplified the fascination with sociological statistics, faith in the progressive vision, and a belief in human ability to structure the environment and society. In reality it suggested a narrow sociological perspective and a case of middle class reformers seeing what they wanted to see. There was no doubt that play and games in the schools, playgrounds, and parks attracted both children and adults; neighborhoods had been clamoring for such spaces for two decades. But use of the parks did not guarantee acceptance of their programs, and even Burns acknowledged that prevention was not the same as reformation.[35]

Despite the optimistic reports, other accounts indicate that the reformers' regulations were often breached, and the participants adapted programs to suit their own needs. Individual and team sports were more popular than formal class exercises, which proved especially unpopular with the working boys. Older boys were allowed to choose their own activities, foregoing the guidance of playground directors. At Webster Field in 1903, football games had to be discontinued due to the "prairie football tactics" employed. Such coping mechanisms, congruent with, and essential to, the street culture, were considered cheating in the middle class value system, and nonconformity with the established middle class regulations brought reprisals, such as suspension from play or facility usage.[36]

Supervisors expected to improve conditions by imposing new regulations, increasing the park police force, and installing wooden railings to confine the thousands of fans in 1904. Local teams drew approximately 50,000 fans for the twelve Sundays during the season. Similar numbers supported their baseball teams, and Saturdays featured track competition between teams of working boys and high school students. The other playgrounds offered similar but separate competition for boys and girls, and both the Merchants' and Commercial Clubs donated hundreds of dollars for prizes and thousands more in order to build another playground site in the latter's name. The competitive programs of the park districts and playgrounds continued to enjoy considerable financial support from the Commercial Club and other business interests in the ensuing years.[37]

By 1907, however, it was becoming more evident that the boys and young men were reproducing the street culture in the parks and playgrounds. The athletic gangs were still gangs. They adopted sports, but used them as an extension of their illegal activities, primarily gambling. Parks and playgrounds became outdoor clubhouses, and political ties allowed the gangs a good deal of protection from prosecution. Politicians organized the gangs into athletic clubs, sponsoring their teams, and often paying the rent for club headquarters. The alliance often paid dividends, particularly to the Democratic Party, on election day. The Goldenrod Athletic Club, 100 Irish-American men, ranging in age from twenty to thirty years old, became a regular part of machine politics from 1905-1920. Sociologists of the time concluded that such gangs not only "served as vocational schools for politicians...but that they exercised considerably greater influence on the character of boys than the churches, schools, or any other communal agency."[38]

One of these gang clubs, Ragen's Colts from the Stockyards district, gained infamy through their exploits. Originally the Morgan Athletic Club, with headquarters at 5528 South Halsted, they assumed a new name when Frank Ragen, a future county commissioner, became president of the club in 1908.

Although they fielded athletic teams, they also served as henchmen for powerful interests. In the 1900-1913 newspaper wars, they were employed by the Annenberg brothers, circulation managers for William Randolph Hearst's *Chicago American,* to intimidate the opposition. The Colts achieved lasting notoriety in 1919 for their belligerent role in Chicago's worst race riot. By the 1920s the Colts ruled the area around Sherman Park, terrorizing the neighborhood with impunity.[39]

The Ragen Colts were only one of the more than a thousand gangs in the city. In an extensive study of 1,313 Chicago gangs, Frederic Thrasher recognized that recreation was not a panacea for delinquency. Particular sports held attractions for the boys. Team victories demonstrated group superiority, and individual sports such as boxing or wrestling, which determined prowess and constructed a social hierarchy based on physical domination, were particularly esteemed. The toughest boy became the leader, with the right or prerogative to fashion his own dictatorship. Thrasher stated that "about one-fourth of the membership of the WWW's (a Jewish gang from Roosevelt Road on the West Side) is composed of professional prize fighters, and more than once this gang has struck terror into the hearts of overaggressive Polish groups." Consequently, rather than assimilating ethnic groups in a homogeneous community, sports allowed such factions to play out the traditional hostilities that lingered beyond arrival in America.[40]

Ethnic hostilities paled in comparison to the displays of outright racial bigotry. In a mixed neighborhood near Comiskey Park, Buetner Playground witnessed violence between black and white groups as early as 1903. The Annual Report of the Special Parks Commission probably understated the case in acknowledging that white children had made blacks feel unwelcome at the parks in 1907. Coercion gave way to pitched battles for facilities and attempted drownings at pools. The report recommended separate playgrounds for blacks. By the onset of World War I, a *de facto* system of segregation in the parks and separate YMCAs ensued.[41]

Racial bigotry, as well as financial considerations, led the working class youth to safeguard their own interests. Pride encouraged athletic gangs to seek instruction from park coaches. Much money, in addition to club pride, often rested on the outcome of a contest with a rival gang. When a park director expelled eight boys from a park for gambling at baseball, twelve friends also quit the environs. They formed a club of 100 members that supported a baseball team at $100 per game.[42]

Territoriality also became an issue as gangs safeguarded their park space or built private facilities unrestricted by authorities. The Eclipse team, organized in 1900 by the Roseland YMCA as a club for thirteen- and fourteen-year-olds, evolved into a top semipro unit under the guidance of Gene Vollmer after 1904. They contended with other local teams in a series of matches for the rights to Palmer Park and the field at 107th and Indiana Avenue. Scavenging old railroad materials allowed the Eclipse to construct a fenced park with seating. Independent of the public park administrators, the team entered the business of commercialized leisure on its own terms.[43]

Most teams lacked the resources or physical space available to the Eclipse, and thus were dependent upon the public facilities. In December 1910, the board of education appropriated $10,000 to open school facilities for working youth two times per week as a "moral safeguard...to protect them against the temptations which frequently are associated with places of public resort."[44] J. Frank Foster, director of playgrounds and gymnasiums for the South parks, recognized the importance of sport in educating the masses. He stated that it was necessary to use physical activity to assimilate working class youth through "the law of suggestion" because they failed to read the middle class publications. Foster believed that the community centers might re-create, at least approximately, the rural values and social relations of the past. Competitive games might also foster physical and social development, as well as obedience to authority, and allow immigrant children to interpret the American culture for their parents.[45]

The centers were to be allowed local autonomy in their management and programming, and school principals expressed surprise at the youngsters' ability to regulate and control themselves. They attributed such capabilities to the influence and assistance offered by the Juvenile Protective Association, Women's Aid, and the YMCA. In reality, the children of the streets and the subculture of the gangs had already established an internal hierarchy. By 1912 gyms were operating at capacity. Intercenter athletic competition was planned to "provide an incentive to regular and systematic practice, and give more direct and definite organization to activities."[46]

Playground administrators introduced athletic efficiency tests in 1911, with prizes given for successful completion. But in keeping with the habits of work discipline, daily attendance was required. Supervisors remarked that "although the button has no intrinsic value, the desire to possess one greatly increases the number taking part in the various competitive sports."[47] The awards, supplied by commercial organizations, symbolized a badge of prowess, a characteristic esteemed by working class youth.

By 1912 the city operated eighteen playgrounds, but street cultures often prevailed. Despite careful direction and supervision, directors suspended 1,082 boys and girls from the grounds, 293 more than the previous year. The authorities stated that

> this increase was due to the temporary withdrawal of the
> police officers for several months during the spring because
> of strikes. If the police officers were permanently removed
> from service at the playgrounds as threatened, it would
> have a disastrous effect on the discipline.[48]

When police became unavailable for playground supervision, the city hired women as assistant directors "to elevate the moral tone."[49] Despite the added supervision, arrests continued and suspensions increased. Directors admitted a "bad boy" problem and requested the assignment of more police to playground duty.[50]

Contributions from business organizations and women's clubs allowed many more schools to be used as community centers and playgrounds. By 1916 the city managed 73 small parks, 70 playgrounds, 63 of which were in schoolyards, 3 beaches, and 4 public pools. Clarendon Beach, the nation's newest and largest, opened on July 1 with floodlights for nighttime use. Swimsuit, towel, and locker rented for ten cents. The beaches garnered $30,000 in revenue, on attendance of 1,238,000. Like the playgrounds, such facilities had a moral purpose as well.[51]

Despite the apparent success of the beaches and natatoriums, administrators imposed new rules disallowing white or flesh-colored suits and imposing fines on those who exposed too much skin. Users of the public facilities thus paid the price of conformity to the dominant group values.[52]

Playground programs also stressed team play to develop cooperation, loyalty, and self-sacrifice. Playground tournaments and city championships were organized in baseball, track, wrestling, skating, and playground ball, a version of softball. The Commercial Club supplied prizes, and Albert G. Spalding offered a trophy for the baseball championship. Three playgrounds—Hamlin, Wrightwood, and Buetner—also had enough space for football games, where "match games were played every Saturday and Sunday, under strict supervision...insuring clean, sportsmanlike conduct...and enjoyable entertainment for the thousands of spectators...." [53] The popularity of such games between teams from all over the city required teams to apply to the park district to reserve the fields, a practice that increased contact with and regulation by the middle class bureaucracy.[54]

The programs of the parks and playgrounds thus brought groups into closer contact with the dominant culture, but they also brought concessions and accommodations from both sides. Middle class organizers sponsored and designed other programs, such as play days, festivals, and patriotic celebrations, to assimilate diverse and divergent groups, yet the entertainment often reflected ethnic tastes and attractions. As much as they celebrated American patriotism and values, they also commemorated and reinforced ethnic customs. The 1911 July 4th festival, held in Lincoln Park in cooperation with the Sane Fourth Association of Chicago, opened with a flag raising and the singing of "America." Thereafter, however, the majority of the festival was devoted to ethnic sports and dances. Thousands attended these festivals that featured lectures, concerts, and patriotic speeches, and such "Americanization" activities provided some ethnics with a sense of shared community and inclusion in the society. Holiday celebrations in particular invented and ritualized pageants that extolled common ideals of freedom within the American melting pot.[55]

The planned competition in the public spaces, however, failed to assimilate the diverse groups in a homogeneous society. In describing the contest for supremacy in track and field, the 1912 Report of the Special Parks Commission noted that "the Moseley playground, with a team consisting entirely of colored boys, for the third consecutive year, won the championship. Great rivalry and keen competition resulted in the futile attempt to wrest the athletic honors from the colored boys."[56] The issues of supremacy inherent in athletic competition were not limited to racial confrontations, but crossed class and ethnic lines as well.

Among the immigrants, Czech soccer clubs used the parks to play against other ethnic teams, such as the Swedes, Germans, Hungarians, Norwegians, Danes, Scots, English, Jews, and Yugoslavs in the Illinois Soccer League, the Chicago Football League, and the International League. Sokols started, in 1913, "to foster the sport of soccer which they had played even in the old homeland."[57] Introduced into the schools as early as 1908, the high school leagues operated by 1913 with competition that included park district and church teams. The playgrounds initiated soccer play in 1915, but despite such accommodation, the Czechs had enough teams to form their own league in 1917. The Sparta club reinforced such separatism by adopting the Czech national colors for its team.[58]

The athletic competition brought ethnic factions together under less hostile circumstances, but resurrected some European animosities. In 1915, when the Slavic team lost the Olsen Cup, a symbol of the Chicago Football League championship, there were charges of bribery, corruption, and mismanagement. When the Western Electric Company team recruited three players from the Hibernian Club to defeat Slavia, a protest was issued. After the complaint went unheeded, Slavia and four other teams in the sixteen-team league resigned amid charges of bigotry. While common sporting interests brought heterogeneous groups together, the emphasis on winning fractured the fragile coalitions.[59]

The ethnic interest in sport carried over to American sport forms. *Svornost,* a Czech paper, had commented upon the growing ethnic interest in baseball as early as 1890. By 1901 at least three Chicago Bohemians were playing professional baseball, and Bohemian groups soon sponsored leagues. In 1911 the *Denni Hlasatel* declared that "Soon there will not be a team in the National or the American Baseball League, in which there will not be a Czech."[60]

The Sokol groups also competed against natives and other ethnic groups in gymnastics and track and field. The Pilsen Sokol, a perennial power in gymnastics, joined the Amateur Athletic Federation and the International Gymnastics Union in 1910. In 1914 the American Sports Club, dedicated to developing an interest in all sports, solicited the Sokols as members for their gymnastic prowess. The Amateur Athletic Federation, formed in 1908 to address professionalism on local teams, also moved to incorporate the ethnic clubs under its auspices. Such inclusion served a dual purpose. It fostered ethnic pride as it gradually undermined ethnic isolation and brought previously antagonistic groups closer to the mainstream.[61]

The ethnic teams and their fans formed a mutual support system with politicians. Among the Czechs, Anton Cermak, a member of the Sokol board of directors, provided sponsorship and playing fields for local teams and won election to numerous offices, eventually becoming mayor. Local athletic hero Henry Smidl, national gymnastic champion, also helped to bridge cultural differences in his various roles as athletic director at Lindblom High School and Big Ten official.[62]

Such middle class sponsors, promoters, or managers—who shared some of the commercial values of the native merchants and operated within institutionalized American structures—often brought the ethnic athletic clubs and their fans into contact with the mainstream culture. August J. Kowalski, a Polish saloon keeper, founded the Polish Saloon Keepers Association in 1886. Two years later he became the first Polish alderman and organized a Polish football team at St. Stanislaus Kostka parish in 1900. With Kowalski at quarterback, the team went undefeated for three years, confusing opponents by calling signals in Polish. The Polish baseball team changed its name to the Kosciuszko Colts in 1906, and by the early years of the century, Poles too were counted among the professional players. Like the Czechs, Polish Catholics formed their own baseball league in 1915. Such actions allowed for the adaptation of Americanized interests without adoption of secular influences.[63]

In addition to baseball, bowling crossed class and ethnic lines. Poles established both men's and women's league play early in the century. Although organized by middle class participants, playing sites remained closely tied to the saloon trade. Bowling alleys provided a place where the drinking, gambling, and noise of the street culture were the norms. For some, bowling provided even more than a psychological benefit. George M. Rozczynialski became a national bowling champ and later was elected alderman. Other aldermen, many of whom were also tavern owners, sponsored bowling teams, just as Cermak had done among the Czechs. Some Poles, particularly city champs Frank "Fat" Kafora and Felix Gajewski, also became local bowling heros. Casimir Wronski, born in Poland in 1888, speculated in real estate and owned the bowling alleys that hosted the newspaper, industrial league, and state bowling association tournaments. His wealth allowed for the sponsorship of numerous athletic clubs.[64]

Many other Polish politicians held park district positions or promoted sports in conjunction with their businesses. Among them, William Fuka, owner of a clothing store, sponsored an array of teams, including an interstate football champion, a baseball contingent, and basketball squads for both boys and girls. He also sponsored several bowling leagues, a softball team, and an athletic club that included a ladies' auxiliary. In return, he expected all team members to shop exclusively at his store.[65]

Harry Berkman, a former Turner instructor, physical director at the Hebrew Institute, chairman of the International Gymnastics Union, and a committee member of the Amateur Athletic Federation, was instrumental in bringing sport to the Jewish community. The Standard Club, composed of Chicago's wealthy Jewish businessmen, began playing baseball as early as 1891. By 1901 Jews had their own country club in Homewood. Like Berkman, most of these were northern European German-speaking Jews familiar with and accepting of the industrial process. They organized the Chicago Hebrew Institute to help assimilate their eastern European brethren, and sport played a pivotal role in that process. Historically, Jews fought discrimination, bias, and a negative stereotype. In the 1890s they were viewed as part of an international financial conspiracy. Their yearning for knowledge often presumed a neglect of the physical. Harry Berkman did much to overturn that presumption with a comprehensive athletic program that included baseball, football, basketball, wrestling, track, gymnastics, golf, and tennis.[66]

The organization's benefactors believed that life in the United States presented the most immediate answer to worldwide religious persecution. To attract the Jewish youth of the West Side, the institute offered dances, gifts, vocational courses, middle class entertainment, and, after 1914, a $100,000 gymnasium. The athletic program emphasized American sports intended to

> Improve physical bearing...and the loss of objectionable mannerisms peculiar to our people; and provide rapid assimilation through contact with other athletes. These results once accomplished much of the prejudice against our people will be removed, and the Jew will then possess those traits and characteristics held in common by the other peoples of the community, and still not lose his inborn Judaism, of which he is so justly proud.[67]

The organization's best athletes were sponsored and showcased at national meets as the Hebrew Institute sought to overcome native stereotypes. Like Catholics and other ethnics, the Jews sought acceptance without the loss of traditional values.

Under Berkman, sport served to bring greater contact between eastern European Jews and the mainstream culture in which the institute's officers operated. Much in the manner of a large settlement house, the institute offered help, education, and entertainment. Athletic spectacles provided much of the latter, including the city meets, the Sears and Western Electric Company tournaments, and indoor softball games that drew as many as 800 spectators. The Sears Athletic Meet of 1913 attracted more than 20,000 fans. Jewish businessmen donated the trophies, and politicians used such occasions as public forums.[68]

Harry Berz, an institute officer, presided over baseball leagues and the Mid-City Basketball League. He also served on the wrestling committee of the Amateur Athletic Federation, which numbered 200 groups, as the Hebrew Institute became a major player in the production of athletic events on the West Side. Not only Jews, but Italian, German, and Irish youths, as well as a Catholic high school team, used its facilities for practice. By 1914 the Chicago Hebrew Institute was fielding teams in a dozen different sports, and under careful tutelage, its athletes were overcoming the image of physical debility. Jimmy Lightbody, a three-time Olympian, was hired as the track coach in 1913, and Danny Goodman, a veteran of 225 professional fights, also joined the gym. Neighborhood boys, such as Jackie Fields and Barney Ross, later parlayed their skills into world championships. The exploits of such ethnic heroes fostered a perception of sport as a meritocracy, unlike the subjugation experienced in the factories and sweatshops. The institute programs thus introduced American sport forms to a largely orthodox group with little or no sporting culture. Despite parental misgivings, the opportunities available through sport attracted immigrant youth.[69]

Sport provided opportunities for independent Jewish promoters as well. Harry Cohen's Dodger Training Athletic Club and Nate Kaplan's Magnets team won acclaim, while Abe Saperstein's baseball and basketball ventures (one being the world-famous Harlem Globetrotters) eventually won him an international following. Such entrepreneurial ventures apparently made sport an attractive alternative, or at least a supplement to wage labor for small-time gamblers and neighborhood teams. The efforts of such promoters as well as the organized programs by the Jewish settlements helped forge a new Jewish-American culture that was no longer European, but not yet fully American.[70]

The Workplace and Popular Leisure

Chicago's employers, like the school and park administrators, saw benefit in sport and increased their efforts to organize teams and leagues. Following the lead of George Pullman, they expanded industrial recreation programs, often using the services of the YMCA, which formed its own industrial branch in 1902. By 1913 more than 60 percent of companies that responded to government surveys indicated that they sponsored teams or provided facilities for employee organized teams. In addition to providing English language and civics classes, employers sponsored baseball, bowling, and softball leagues. They also made an effort to include competition in football, track, basketball, and soccer and to cooperate with the park programs and settlement houses. A number of Chicago's major companies, including the railroads, meat packers, Sears-Roebuck, and Marshall Field, maintained close ties with the YMCA. The Field Company even offered to pay 50 percent of employees' membership fees in the association.[71]

Employers continued to be concerned about the leisure practices of their employees, particularly if they affected attendance and production. As early as the 1890s, the Chicago, Burlington and Quincy Railroad had fired employees who drank liquor, while the Chicago and Great Western Railroad dismissed workers who even boarded in houses adjacent to saloons. Many railroads worked with the YMCA to provide recreational facilities and organize athletic teams as alternatives to the saloon. In 1908 Aaron Montgomery Ward relocated his entire business to an isolated area along the north branch of the river, due to the noon-hour drinking habits of his employees. The city council obliged Ward by voting the territory within a half mile of his plant "dry." Ward had detectives conduct surveillance activities in saloons and photograph patrons. Employees so detected were fired. Some companies even made cash payments to discourage the use of saloon services, but the Chicago, Burlington and Quincy Railroad simply ordered workers to cash their checks with other merchants, checking the third-party signatures for evidence of liquor dealers. Such dictates soon led to heated debate over workers' use of their leisure hours.[72]

The temperance wars that were an aspect of this debate followed class and religious lines. Evangelical Protestants, the dominant powers in the Progressive Party, Swedish Lutherans, and the conservative Catholic Paulist order favored prohibition, citing alcohol as the root of disease, crime, vice, and poverty. The prohibitionists represented a distinct minority. Most Catholics, Lutherans, and Episcopalians, all of whom used wine in their religious rituals, and the overwhelming majority of laborers, to whom beer or the saloon were a way of life, violently opposed prohibition.[73]

Company reprisals and middle class crusades upset workers, who judged leisure time as their own. On May 26, 1906, a parade of 80,000 ethnics, consisting of Germans, Bohemians, Poles, Hungarians, Danes, and Norwegians, demonstrated against a prohibition law. In that same year 1,087 ethnic organizations allied in the United Societies for Local Self-Government under the leadership of Anton Cermak to oppose the Anti-Saloon League. In 1910, Cermak, as alderman, studied alternative means of income for the city and concluded that without the revenue derived from taxes on liquor sales, Chicago would go bankrupt.[74]

The economics of the situation probably meant little to the masses, who continued to pursue their traditional leisure pastimes as well as the newer commercialized entertainments. Chicago had one saloon for every 335 residents and an unknown number of unlicensed "blind pigs." The United Breweries of Chicago allied with ethnic groups to present a formidable lobby against the evangelical crusade. The United Societies required aldermen to sign an antiprohibition pledge in order to gain the support of ethnic voting blocs. Consequently, in 1914 a coalition of the Anti-Saloon League, the Law and Order League, and churches failed to win their prohibition campaign, garnering only 90,000 of the required 171,000 signatures. By 1916 the few Catholic temperance societies reported "greatly diminished numbers," and temperance speakers were no longer welcome in Catholic churches, although they continued their Sunday harangues from Protestant pulpits.[75]

Despite the inability of the various groups to stem the flow of alcohol, Catholics and other conservative ethnic groups agreed with the need to reduce vice and gambling, and such support may have encouraged other actions by the reformers. Middle class social agencies, such as the Juvenile Protective League, founded by the Chicago Women's Club in 1906, and the Immigrant Protective League, established by Hull House workers in 1908, united in their opposition to commercial dance halls and cabarets. They believed not only that the dancing was lewd but that such places served as haunts for white slave traders, who sold unknowing or drunken girls into lives of prostitution. In 1909 evangelist Gypsy Smith led an unsuccessful raid against the South Side vice district known as the Levee. After Virginia Brooks marched with 5,000 supporters against the district in 1912, Mayor Harrison closed the area, which cost him the renomination of the Democrats in the subsequent election. With the closing of the Levee, vice became a decentralized operation, with gangs vying for control of the lucrative business.[76]

Commercialized leisure afforded new and exciting experiences for the ethnic youths and young adults mired in the drudgery of industrial work. Dancing in particular apparently held great fascination for many young people. Although reformers judged the new dances to be "more athletic and sexually suggestive," they gained great popularity among youths. Surveys conducted between 1910 and 1917 found that 75 percent of young women attended the dances, with 86,000 dancers counted on some evenings.[77] For immigrants, such practices served as a break from the traditional courtship rituals of Europe. A young Italian claimed that "he could date a Polish girl and have a 'red hot' time, but if he saw an Italian girl it would be assumed that he intended to marry her."[78] The participation of ethnic youth in such activities (conducted by private clubs, saloons, or so-called taxi dance halls) signaled a transition from private or communal forms of leisure, practiced in the home or neighborhood, to a more public sphere.[79]

Once again, various groups tried to restrict, or restrain, the most offensive forms. In Cicero the town council prohibited the tango and other "disorderly" dances, and no dances were allowed without a police permit. Some churches did hold dances as fundraisers, but there too, proper decorum reigned. The Rev. Kruszas of St. George Lithuanian Church received

the following letter from the office of the archdiocese after it
had received a complaint:

> Word has reached us that in the Parish Hall, there is (sic)
> conducted dances which are absolutely contrary to the rules
> of the Diocese. All face to face dances, shimmy dances, and
> such dances that are forbidden in any decent hall, cannot be
> tolerated in your parish. We trust that you will see to this
> and forbid at once any dances that are forbidden.[80]

Such "public dancing" was banned in 1913, until challenged
by wealthy dancers who enjoyed their rhythmic pastimes at
the posh Drake Hotel. The Supreme Court ruled the ban
unconstitutional in 1916.[81]

Unable to control private leisure practices, reformers instituted alternate leisure forms, such as supervised dancing in
the parks, concerts, and lectures to "elevate standards and
direct social desires in high and worthy channels." [82] Consistent with the attempt to inculcate high culture, also, all park
statuary was subjected to the approval of the Municipal Art
League as part of an ongoing progressive effort to address
aesthetic concerns.[83]

All of these efforts were in keeping with a fairly comprehensive design for orderly and efficient growth: the Burnham
Plan of 1909. A product of the Commercial Club and Daniel
Burnham, the chief architect of the 1893 World's Fair, it
presented the view that "Chicago was a city in the making,
and was considered a logical place in which to experiment with
municipal and regional planning."[84] The scheme called for
increasing parks, playgrounds, and boulevards in relation to
population density. The lakefront was to be secured from
private gain and saved as parkland, and a system of forest
preserves developed. Forest preserves were seen as an escape
by the middle class visionaries. "Natural scenery furnishes
the contrasting element to the artificiality of the city...where
mind and body are restored...."[85]

Reformers rationalized the plan as a necessity due to the
"influx of people without a common tradition and the rising
crime rate which posed a threat to order and civic unity
essential to material advancement."[86] The Chicago board of
education thought so highly of the plan that it distributed

15,000 abridged versions to be used as civics texts. Reformers, commercial interests, and city planners considered the Burnham plan an exciting opportunity, not only to bring orderly and aesthetic growth but to socially engineer wholesome morality and greater profit.[87]

The voters, however, thought otherwise. Forest preserves, accessible only by car in the early years of the century, were denounced by labor leaders as "picnic grounds for the rich" and "pandering to the taste of the idle and nonproductive classes."[88] Teachers, already allied with labor, suspected an increase in the bureaucracy and a further drain on the tax base that supported the school system. Ethnics feared the loss of political power in the parks if the system became centralized. Despite the lobbying efforts of the board of education and business groups, the forest preserve plan, first proposed in 1893, was defeated in a referendum in 1905 and not achieved until 1916. The reformers' failure to fully structure the physical and aesthetic environment of the city allowed ethnic and working class traditions to persist in the neighborhoods and public spaces.[89]

Middle class crusades for prohibition and the elimination of vice, gambling, and juvenile delinquency had limited success. Reformers achieved greater control over the informal and unregulated play of the street culture by incorporating the athletic interests of youths and various ethnic groups within organized structures supported by commercial interests and administered by persons bent on the amelioration of cultural differences. In the schools, parks, playgrounds, and workplaces, coaches and trained instructors intended to build character by the inculcation of a particular value system that stressed competition, the work ethic, and a distinct middle class vision of morality.[90]

The progressives established no timetable for their reform movement, but, frustrated by their inability to fully achieve their goals, the movement lost some of its benevolent characteristics as America pondered entry into World War I. Jane Addams lost respect and leadership within the movement to nativist factions as she crusaded for world peace. The nativists resorted to harsh legislation to effect their objectives, using the same strategy of government intervention that crippled the radical movement of the late nineteenth century. The eighteenth amendment prohibited the manufacture, sale, or transport of alcohol; while the Red Scare, following World War I, brought further intervention against trade unions and ethnic organizations, culminating in restrictive immigration laws.[91]

Subordinate groups accepted, or were forced to accept, such an hierarchical relationship—but often on their terms. They blatantly circumvented prohibition and often limited their participation in the Americanization programs. Sport, however, had become firmly established across all ethnic, class, racial, and religious lines. Sport, based on the physical prowess so esteemed by the working class, provided opportunities for psychic rewards and immediate gratification not available in the drudgery of work. For some, sport provided material gain and at least the perception of a meritocracy. However, different class and ethnic values continued to pose problems for the assimilationists. While administrators tried to channel ethnic nationalism into more acceptable athletic competitions, such events often exacerbated rivalries and created heroes that reinforced ethnic pride. Boxing, in particular, produced a bevy of champions in a sport most reviled by reformers and outlawed in Illinois. In the years following World War I, sporting practices played a significant role in the evolution of a mass popular culture amenable to such pluralistic values.

Notes

1. Rosenzweig, *Eight Hours for What We Will,* 146, 249; Richard Butsch, "Introduction: Leisure and Hegemony in America," in Butsch, ed., *For Fun and Profit,* 3-27. See Stephen Hardy and Alan Ingham, "Games, Structure, and Agency: Historians on the American Play Movement," *Journal of Social History,* 17 (Winter 1983): 285-301, for valuable insights.

2. Cavallo, *Muscles and Morals,* 88-106; T. R. Young, "The Sociology of Sport: Structural Marxist and Cultural Marxist Approaches," *Sociological Perspectives,* 29 (1986): 3-28; Donald J. Mrozek, *Sport and American Mentality, 1880-1910* (Knoxville: University of Tennessee Press, 1983).

3. Bernheimer, *The Russian Jew,* 212, states that only 3 percent of the students completed eighth grade in 1905. John Bodnar, "Immigration and Modernization: The Case of Slavic Peasants in Industrial America," in Milton Cantor, ed., *American Working Class Culture* (Westport, CT: Greenwood Press, 1979), 333-360, asserts that only 4 percent of Poles and Slavs attended school beyond grade six. Five percent of blacks, 16 Polish Jews, 3 percent of Italians, and 2 percent of Poles went to high school in 1910.
See Ronald A. Smith, *Sports and Freedom: The Rise of Big-Time College Athletics* (New York: Oxford University Press, 1988) for early, student-controlled organizations; and Hardy, *How Boston Played,* 111-22, for similar concerns and patterns of development in the East. *The High School Journal,* 10:3 (Nov. 1890): 43-4; 10:6 (Feb. 1890): 87; 10:7 (Mar. 1891): 105; *Englewood High School Journal,* 1:1 (Feb. 1893): 9; *The High School Weekly,* 1:1 (June 12, 1893): 19, 20-1; *Chicago Tribune,* Mar. 30, 1890, 14; July 3, 1890, 6; July 4, 1890, 2; July 6, 1890, 5; Oct. 6, 1890, 3; Archie Oboler, ed., *The Oski-Wow-Wow,* 5, 17-8, 21.

4. Everett, ed., *High School Journal,* 10:3 (November 1890): 37-44; 10:5 (Jan. 1891): 75; 10:8 (Apr. 1891): 120; *Chicago Tribune,* November 14, 1890, 6. The *Tribune,* November 20, 1890, 6; November 21, 1890, 6.
Hardy, *How Boston Played,* 113-15, found a similar school spirit and bonding among Boston interscholastic teams.

5. Everett, ed., *High School Journal,* 10:8 (April 1891): 120; 10:7 (March 1891): 102, 105-6; Oboler, ed., *The Oski-Wow-Wow,* 2; Rader, *American Sports,* 161; Hardy, *How Boston Played,* 116-19; and Mirel, "From Student Control to Institutional Control," detailed similar abuses in Boston and Michigan cities.

6. B. "Yank" Adams, ed., *The Sporting and Theatrical Journal,* 11:7 (December 24, 1887): 8-9; Pesavento, "A Historical Study of the Development of Physical Education in the Chicago Public Schools," 56, 64, 105; Guy Lewis, "Adoption of the Sports Program, 1906-39," *Quest,* 12 (May 1969): 34-46; Ronald A. Smith, "The Historic Amateur — Professional Dilemma in American College Sport," *British Journal of Sports History,* 2:3 (Dec. 1985): 221-31; Rader, *American Sports,* 55-61.

7. See Bob Braunwart and Bob Carroll, *The Alphabet Wars: The Birth of Professional Football, 1890-1892* (Professional Football Researchers Association, 1981), 42; and J. Thomas Jable, "The Birth of Professional Football: Pittsburgh Athletic Clubs Ring in Professionals in 1892," *The Western Pennsylvania Historical Magazine,* 62:2

(April 1979): 136-47, on Heffelfinger as the first professional football player. Although the nature of his "expenses" is not clear, it is likely that he was first paid by the Chicago team.

See Robin Lester, *Stagg's University: The Rise, Decline, and Fall of Big-Time Football at Chicago* (Urbana, IL: University of Illinois, 1995), on the commercialization of intercollegiate athletics, and Amos Alonzo Stagg Papers; Boxes 12-13 on recruitment, at the University of Chicago, Special Collections.

Bonnie S. Rockne, ed., *The Autobiography of Knute K. Rockne* (Indianapolis, IN: Bobbs-Merrill, 1930), 63-4, on the emulation of athletes.

8. *The High School Weekly,* 1:1 (June 12, 1893): 3-4, 18-21; *Englewood High School Journal,* 1:1 (Feb. 1893): 9, in the Neighborhood History Collection, Chicago Cultural Center, NHRC 57, EHS, file 1/1.

9. Minutes of Cook County Indoor Baseball League, 1895-1899, at Chicago Historical Society; Oboler, ed., *The Oski-Wow-Wow,* 5; Medill High School *Echo,* 2:2 (Oct. 1897): 15-16; Chicago *Tribune,* Jan. 6, 1900, 7. See *Tribune,* Feb. 25, 1900, 18; Mar. 25, 1900, 18; Jan. 25, 1903, 11; and *Chicago American,* Oct. 18, 1902, 20, on the growth of girls' sports. For issues engendered by such activities and the transition from feminine ideals of the past, see *New York Times,* Nov. 29, 1903, 8; Deborah Gorham, *The Victorian Girl and the Feminine Ideal* (Bloomington: Indiana University Press, 1982); Bruce Haley, *The Healthy Body and Victorian Culture* (Cambridge, MA: Harvard University Press, 1978); Mrozek, *Sport and American Mentality,* 136-60; Allen Guttmann, *Women's Sports: A History* (New York: Columbia University Press, 1991), 85-134; Seymour, *Baseball: The People's Game,* 443-527; Mary Lou Squires, "Sport and the Cult of True Womanhood: A Paradox at the Turn of the Century," in Reet Howell, ed., *Her Story in Sport* (New York: Leisure Press, 1982), 101-06; Goodman, *Choosing Sides,* 119-29; Ronald A. Smith, "The Rise of Basketball for Women in Colleges," and Dudley Sargent, "Are Athletics Making Girls Masculine? A Practical Answer to a Question Every Girl Asks," in Steven Riess, ed., *The American Sporting Experience* (New York: Leisure Press, 1984), 239-54; and 255-63, respectively. Joanna Davenport, "The Eastern Legacy: The Early History of Physical Education for Women, *Quest,* 32:2 (1980): 226-36; Mangan and Park, eds., *From Fair Sex to Feminism.*

10. Minutes of Cook County Indoor Baseball League, Jan. 2, 1896; Dec. 18, 1896; Dec. 3, 1897; Dec. 7, 13, 19, 1898. Spalding started courting the students as early as 1886; see ads in *The High School,* 1:1 (May 1886): 1.

11. Minutes of Cook County Indoor Baseball League, Dec. 19, 1898, Jan. 5, 1899; Medill *Echo,* 2:6 (Feb. 1898), 14-15; 2:7 (March 1898), 15-16; *Chicago Tribune,* Mar. 13, 1904, 6.

12. *The Medill Light,* 4:1 (Sept. 1902), 13; Medill *Echo,* 2:10 (June 1898), 23; *Chicago Tribune,* January 25, 1903, 11.

13. Frank Palmer, ed., *The Review,* 7:6 (March 1900), 7.

14. Walter E. Cuneo, ed., ibid., 10:1 (September 1902), 2.

15. City of Chicago, *Proceedings of the Board of Education, July 6, 1904 - June 21, 1905* (Chicago: Barnard and Miller, 1905), 254; and City of Chicago, *Board of Education Proceedings, 1904-1905,* 324, established new rules for afternoon basketball and softball use, to be held under the supervision of school principals, and eliminating admission fees.

16. Helen Lefkowitz Horowitz, *Campus Life: Underground Cultures from the End of the Eighteenth Century to the Present* (New York: Alfred A. Knopf, 1987); William Graebner, "Outlawing Teenage Populism: The Campaigns against Secret Societies in the American High Schools," *Journal of American History,* 74:2 (September 1987): 411-35; Hardy, *How Boston Played,* 114-23.

17. Hyde Park High School, *Libethrian* (Chicago: The Windermere Press, 1904), n.p.

18. *Chicago Tribune,* May 16, 1902, 6; James A. Peterson, *Eckersall of Chicago* (Chicago: Hinckley & Schmitt, 1957), n.p. Walter Eckersall of Hyde Park, the Illinois state sprint champion, had already been declared a professional for playing baseball with the Spalding team. Oboler, *Oski-Wow-Wow,* 15-17.

19. John R. Kelly, *Leisure Identities and Interactions* (London: George Allen & Unwin, 1983), 102-03; *Chicago Tribune,* March 13, 1904, 6; *Libethrian,* n.p.
On similar moves aimed at control of interscholastic athletics in New York, see Goodman, *Choosing Sides,* 51-5; Rader, *American Sports,* 157-64; and J. Thomas Jable, "The Public Schools Athletic League of New York City: Organized Athletics for City School Children, 1903-1914," in *Sport and American Education: History and Perspective* (Washington, DC: American Alliance for Health, Physical Education, Recreation, and Dance, 1979), Chapter 1.

20. *New York Times,* Dec. 7, 1902, 17, details the Hyde Park victory over Brooklyn Poly. Ibid., Nov. 21, 1903, 7; Nov. 29, 1903, 16, provide accounts of North Division's win over Brooklyn Boys' High School, who were routed despite inducing a Hyde Park coach to defect after

124   The Interplay of Commercialism and Popular Culture

the 1902 season. The latter game concluded early due to darkness. The onslaught had already reached 60-0 at the half. *Chicago Daily News,* Nov. 6, 1902, 2; Nov. 16, 1903, 4; Nov. 21, 1903, 1; Nov. 23, 1903, 4; *Chicago Tribune,* May 16, 1902, 6.

21. *Chicago Tribune,* May 16, 1902, 6.

22. Ibid., Jan. 27, 1898, 4; Amos Alonzo Stagg and Wesley W. Stout, *Touchdown* (New York: Longmans, Green & Co., 1927), 165, 189, 240. See Lefty Farnsworth, "Shanghaid Maroon?" *College Football Historical Society,* 3:2 (Feb. 1990): 5, on the alleged kidnapping of Walter Steffen, who actually defected temporarily over internecine squabbles with Eckersall at Chicago. See Amos Alonzo Stagg Papers, University of Chicago Regenstein Library, Special Collections, on his guarded correspondence with athletes.

23. *Chicago Tribune,* Jan. 25, 1903, 11; Mar. 13, 1904, 6; *New York Times,* Nov. 28, 1903, 14; Peterson, *Eckersall of Chicago.* The Hyde Park teams of 1901-03 featured a number of outstanding athletes who earned All-American status in college or turned professional, and included Sammy Ransom, one of the first great African-American stars in Chicago.

24. *Chicago Daily News,* Nov. 7, 1903, 2; Nov. 12, 1902, 6; Nov. 19, 1903, 6; Nov. 21, 1903, 1; *Libethrian,* 1904; *Chicago Tribune,* May 16, 1902, 6; Amos Alonzo Stagg Papers, University of Chicago, correspondence with athletes, Box 13, Folder 19.

Axel Bundgaard, "World's Greatest Interscholastic," unpublished manuscript; Seymour, *Baseball: The People's Game,* 168-87, on international competition with Japanese schools; and Hal Lawson and Alan Ingham, "Conflicting Ideologies Concerning the University and Inter-Collegiate Athletics: Harper and Hutchins at Chicago, 1892-1940," *Journal of Sport History,* 7 (Winter 1980): 37-63 on the demise of such events.

25. *Chicago Tribune,* Jan. 16, 1908, 6; Jan. 17, 1908, 10; May 18, 1911, 11; Dec. 31, 1911, Sec. 3:2; *Chicago Daily News,* Nov. 20, 1902, 6; Nov. 9, 1903, 4; Nov. 21, 1903, 1; *Chicago American,* Nov. 21, 1902, 13; Nov. 22, 1902, n.p.; Chicago Public Schools Archives, Interscholastic Athletic Championships file.

On the New York Interscholastic League, see Jable, "Public Schools Athletic League of New York"; Rader, *American Sports,* 152-60; Goodman, *Choosing Sides,* 51-5; Riess, *City Games,* 160-4. See Hardy, *How Boston Played,* 107-23, on the evolution of adult control in Boston. Joel Spring, "Mass Culture and School Sports," *History of Education Quarterly,* 14 (Winter 1974): 483-500; and Timothy P. O'Hanlon, "Interscholastic Athletics, 1900-1940," *Educa-*

tion Theory, 30 (Spring 1980): 89-103, offer alternative interpretations.

26. John Hargreaves, "Sport, Culture, and Ideology," 30-61; Chicago Cultural Center, "A Breath of Fresh Air: Chicago's Neighborhood Parks of the Progressive Era, 1900-1925," July 22, 1989 - Nov. 11, 1989, and CHS, "Prairie in the City." Both exhibited original drafts of park plans depicting the transition from classical, aesthetic, and passive intentions to more functional, active usage. See Rader, *American Sports,* 157-60; Rosenzweig, *Eight Hours for What We Will,* 143-56; Cavallo, *Muscles and Morals,* 23-48; Goodman, *Choosing Sides,* 74-80, 108-12; Hardy, *How Boston Played,* 85-106; Riess, *City Games,* 132-40; and Boyer, *Urban Masses and Moral Order,* 242-51, on playgrounds and social reform in eastern cities.

27. Perkins, *Report of the Special Parks Commission* (Chicago: W. J. Hartman, 1904), 10, 27-8, 31, 140. In 1901 the South Parks Commission issued bonds for $1.5 million, and the West Parks Commission issued another $1 million. Lincoln Park issued $500,000 in park bonds that year, but another $1 million was issued in 1903 for a reclamation project that added 215 acres to the park.
Special Parks Commission, *A Plea for Playgrounds,* 1905, 17, stated playground attendance as 1,015,000 for 1904.
Goodman, *Choosing Sides,* 79; Cavallo, *Muscles and Morals,* 45; Riess, *City Games,* 167, identified 504 cities that had supervised recreation programs based on the Chicago model by 1917.

28. Special Parks Commission, *A Plea for Playgrounds,* 17; Todd, *Chicago Recreation Survey,* 1 (1937): 4; Cavallo, *Muscles and Morals,* 40-5.

29. Todd, *Chicago Recreation Survey,* 1 (1937): 22; Richard S. Gruneau, "Modernization or Hegemony: Two Views on Sport and Social Development," in Jean Harvey and Hart Cantelon, eds., *Not Just a Game* (Ottawa: University of Ottawa Press, 1988), 9-32.

30. Special Parks Commission, *Annual Reports, 1904,* 10-14; *1907,* 4-10; *1910,* 3, 6-7, 24; Goodman, *Choosing Sides,* 61-80.
Jane Addams, "Public Recreation and Social Morality," in Edward T. Devine, ed., *Charities and the Commons,* 18:18 (August 3, 1907): 492-94. The issue focuses on the playground movement in Chicago with other articles by Mary McDowell, "The Fieldhouses of Chicago and Their Possibilities," 535-38; Dwight H. Perkins, "Union of Playgrounds and Public Schools," 538-41; and Charles Zeublin, "Playgrounds and the Board of Education," 543-45.

31. Hogan, *Class and Reform,* 70.

32. Graham H. Taylor, "How They Played in Chicago," *Charities and the Commons,* 18:18 (August 3, 1907): 471-80; quote is from page 474.

33. Playground Association of Chicago, pamphlet, 1907, 7.

34. Halsey, *The Development of Public Recreation,* 32; Cavallo, *Muscles and Morals,* 97, 102. Goodman, *Choosing Sides,* 67-8, 102-08; 137-51, indicates similar values were taught in the New York playgrounds.

35. Halsey, *The Development of Public Recreation,* 34; Goodman, *Choosing Sides,* 71, 151-9, for a discussion of the faulty conclusions of the Burns study. Rosenzweig, *Eight Hours for What We Will,* 150, found that the playgrounds had no effect on delinquency in Worcester.

36. *Annual Report, Special Parks Commission, 1904,* 7. Independent teams that avoided the administrative control of park directors became known as prairie league teams. A rough style and gambling often characterized their play. Surreptitious tactics included punching and spitting or throwing dirt in the eyes of opposing linemen.

37. John J. Bradley, chairman, *Report of the Special Parks Commission,* in the *29th Annual Report, Department of Public Works, 1904,* 527-8, 534. The Merchants Club had been making an annual donation since 1901. Special Parks Commission, *Annual Report, 1907* (Chicago: 1908), 4, 10.

38. Robert E. Park, Ernest W. Burgess, and Roderick D. McKenzie, *The City* (Chicago: University of Chicago Press, 1925), 112; Thrasher, *The Gang,* 197, 275, 316, 328, relates another story where gang members affronted a park instructor and then took over the facilities. They were arrested, but released due to their political connections. See Boyer, *Urban Masses and Moral Order,* 246, for an apparently successful case.

39. Steven A. Riess, "Sport, Race and Ethnicity," 5, manuscript in author's possession, gives details on the founding of Ragen's Colts in 1908. Lindberg, *Chicago Ragtime,* 205-6, 248, on the Colts and the newspaper wars. Between 1910-1913 twenty-seven vendors were killed. The Annenbergs eventually bought the wire service of gambling kingpin Mont Tennes, the son of German immigrants, who made much of his illegal money from sporting ventures.

Thrasher, *The Gang,* 52, 316, states that more than 300 gangs, or social-athletic clubs, were organized by politicians. More than one notable politician got his early political and athletic experience in such clubs. Edward J. Kelly, a fifth grade dropout, rose from the ranks of the Brighton A.C. to become mayor, as did Richard J. Daley, president of the Bridgeport Hamburgs. See Roger Biles, *Big City Boss in Depression and War: Mayor Edward J. Kelly of Chicago* (De Kalb: Northern Illinois University Press, 1984), 6-7,10; Katz, ed., *The Negro in Chicago,* 14-15; Mary McDowell Papers, Box 2, Folder 10, at the Chicago Historical Society.

40. See Thrasher, *The Gang,* Chapter 12; 45-8; 150, for quote; P. E. Burkholder, "The Gang Leader," n.p., Ernest W. Burgess Papers, University of Chicago, Special Collections, Box 128, Folder 1. Reiss, "A Fighting Chance: The Jewish-American Boxing Experience, 1890-1940," *American Jewish History,* 74:3 (March 1985): 223-54, especially 244, on the Miller brothers gang.

41. Katz, ed., *The Negro in Chicago,* 272, 274, 282-3, 287-8, 290-1, 295; Special Parks Commission, *Annual Report, 1907* (Chicago: 1908), 6, 19, 20, 22, 24.

42. Thrasher, *The Gang,* 24, 30, 37-8, 74, 126, 134-5, 138, 247; *Chicago Herald,* April 16, 1917, 15.

43. The Eclipse story is derived from materials in the NHC, Chicago Cultural Center, Box CRCC, file 4/4, including clippings from the *South End Reporter,* April 23, 1925; April 16, 1931; and from an anonymous manuscript, pages 4, 7 in file 4/31.

Lincoln Park Souvenir (Chicago: Illinois Engraving Co., 1896), 13, states that Lincoln Park rules forbid professional games at the main North Side park. The restriction proved a boon to sporting entrepreneurs. Billy Niesen's Gunthers team, which started as a semipro unit in 1906, eventually built a park with a seating capacity of 4,000-5,000 for its games on the North Side. The location is the current site of Chase Park, in NHC, Sulzer Library Special Collections, Box RLVCC, file 12/14.

44. John D. Shoop, *Report of Social Centers in the City of Chicago, 1912* (Chicago: Board of Education, 1912), 8, 9, 13.

45. *Report of the South Parks Commissioners, 1908-1909,* 110-1, 115-6. Cavallo, *Muscles and Morals,* 24, 29.

46. Shoop, *Report of Social Centers,* 19-20, 22, 33-6, 40-1. *Chicago Schools Journal,* 1:1 (Sept. 1918): 21. Jane Addams, *Twenty Years at Hull House,* 105, 442, expressed similar concerns regarding boys' activities at her settlement.

47. City of Chicago, *Annual Report of the Committee on Parks, Playgrounds and Beaches, 1916,* 34. The athletic proficiency tests were given to girls starting in 1912 and buttons were awarded for

128   The Interplay of Commercialism and Popular Culture

attendance. From Special Parks Commission, *Annual Report, 1913*, 35, 39. Cavallo, *Muscles and Morals*, 43.

48. Special Parks Commission, *Annual Report, 1912*, 39; 34 on suspensions. See Goodman, *Choosing Sides*, 3-19, 44-5, 55, 83-5, 93, on New York street life and the use of police. Rosenzweig, *Eight Hours for What We Will*, 149, states that children in Worcester, Massachusetts, also reshaped playgrounds to meet their own needs and values.

49. Special Parks Commission, *Annual Report, 1912*, 44.

50. Ibid., *1913*, 39, shows a reduction in suspensions by 244, but an increase is noted again in ibid.,*1914*, 40 and *1915*, 39.

51. City of Chicago, *Annual Report of the Committee on Parks, Playgrounds and Beaches, 1916* (Chicago: Bernard and Miller), 5, 7, 10.

52. Ibid., 37, 39. Special Parks Commission, *Annual Report, 1909*, 31. Sexes had been segregated on public beaches until 1913, a move admittedly unpopular with the bathers. Goodman, *Choosing Sides*, 125.

See Special Parks Commission,*Annual Report, 1912*, 42. The park district authorities recognized the cumbersome nature of traditional swimming attire after the tragic *Eastland* disaster in 1915 in which so many drowned. Swimming, life saving, and artificial respiration classes, along with new rules for swimsuits, were initiated thereafter. See ibid., *1915*, 43. In 1925 a fine of $5-$200 was imposed for indecent exposure at the beaches. From *Municipal Code of the South Park Commissioners* (Chicago: 1925), 46.

53. Special Parks Commission, *Annual Report, 1912*, 30.

54. City of Chicago, *Annual Report of the Committee on Parks, Playgrounds and Beaches, 1916*, 34. Ted Vincent, *Mudville's Revenge: The Rise and Fall of American Sport* (New York: Seaview Books, 1981), 226; *Annual Report, 1909*, 21-2, *Annual Report, 1914*, 33, lists prizes as bats, balls, pocket knives, etc., for boys; and bracelets, brooches, dolls, and handbags for girls.

55. Program, July 4, 1911, Festival of the Playground Association of America; Eric J. Hobsbawm, *The Age of Empire, 1875-1914* (New York: Pantheon Books, 1987), 105-07; Michael R. Olneck, "Americanization and the Education of Immigrants, 1900-1925: An Analysis of Symbolic Action," *American Journal of Education*, 97:4 (August 1989): 399-423; Rosenzweig, *Eight Hours for What We Will*, 65-90; Cavallo, *Muscles and Morals*, 43-5.

Paul Connerton, *How Societies Remember* (Cambridge: Cambridge University Press, 1991); Mary Jo Deegan, *American Ritual*

Dramas: Social Rules and Cultural Meanings (Westport, CT: Greenwood Press, 1989).

56. Special Parks Commission, *Annual Report, 1912,* 32. The athletic meet was extended to include grammar schools in 1913. Ibid., *1913,* 34. In 1914 a grammar school championship in playground ball was introduced; ibid., *1914,* 33. In 1915 awards for swimming and diving were offered by businessmen and the 6th Ward Republican Club; ibid., *1915,* 45.

57. *Denni Hlasatel,* Sept. 9, 1918; quote is from ibid., July 20, 1917. Also see ibid., Oct. 11, 1911; Sept. 6, 1914; June 20, 1915; Sept. 15, 1915; Oct. 13, 1915; Apr. 16, 1917; May 3, 1917; Oct. 20, 1918; July 29, 1922; Aug. 26, 1922; Sept. 20, 1922 for Czech soccer activities (FLPS).

58. Ibid., Mar. 6, 1918 (FLPS). Laura Bergquist, et al., *History of Englewood High School,* 118; *Lane Tech Yearbook, 1914,* 205; Peter J. Peel, a Scottish physician, was the driving force behind soccer organizations in the city. He donated trophies symbolic of the city championship for high school and adult teams. By 1910 the Chicago League, the Association League of Chicago, and the Gaelic Football League showcased numerous ethnic teams from around the city. See *Chicago Tribune,* Apr. 4, 1910, 10; Apr. 11, 1910, 12; July 4, 1910, 11; Nov. 14, 1910, 13. Special Parks Commission, *Annual Report, 1915,* 34, cites the adoption of rugby and soccer competition in the playground system in that year.

Parker High School, *The Green and White,* 1:18 (Nov. 19, 1919), 1, on the decline of soccer; Adeline Loughlin, "A Community Study of South Lawndale," 21 in Box LCCC, file 4/4 of NIIC, Chicago Cultural Center.

59. *Denni Hlasatel,* June 20, 1915 (FLPS).

60. *Svornost,* Apr. 8, 1890, indicated that there were already several teams by that date; June 2, 1890 reported a game between the Pilsen Sokol and Klatovsky Sokol. On baseball among the Bohemians, see ibid., Mar. 31, 1901; July 2, 1901; and Apr. 2, 1910 (FLPS); *Rozhledy,* 1905-06.

The quote is from *Denni Hlasatel,* Sept. 16, 1911 (FLPS).

Bohemians had their own cycling club by 1891, in *Svornost,* May 20, 1891 (FLPS), and the Poles soon followed.

61. *Denni Hlasatel,* Jan. 11, 1914 (FLPS); Amateur Athletic Federation, *1914 Rule and Year Book,* 6, 17, 19, 53-4, 128; *Amateur Athletic Federation Handbook, 1929-30,* 7, 9.

See *Pamatnica* (Passaic, NJ: Slovak Catholic Sokol, 1965), 61-2, for similar developments in the East.

62. On Cermak, see *Denni Hlasatel*, Oct. 11, 1911; Apr. 30, 1922; Aug. 26, 1922 (FLPS); Duis, *The Saloon*, 261. Alex Gottfried, *Boss Cermak of Chicago* (Seattle: University of Washington Press, 1962), 45, 127; Vlasta Vraz, ed., *Panorama: Historical Review of Czechs and Slovaks in the United States* (Cicero, IL: Czechoslovak National Council, 1970), 312; American Sokol Organization, *Centennial*, n.p., and *Chicago American*, Nov. 20, 1936, 29, on Smidl, whose Lindblom gymnastics team won thirteen consecutive public league championships. Joseph Cermak served Medill High as Director of Physical Education for 38 years, while Jaroslav Zmrhal provided 22 years as superintendent of schools. Along with immigrants Jarka Kosar and Jarka Jelinek, they provided publications and translations that fostered common ideology or unity.

63. On Kowalski, see Duis, *The Saloon*, 137-8; Krzywonos, ed., *The Poles in Chicago*, 5, 145-7.
The Polish teams played top flight competition. According to Casimir Wronski, "Early Days of Sport Among Polish-Americans in Chicago," in Krzywonos, ed., *The Poles in Chicago*, 145-8, the football team defeated the University of Chicago team under Amos Alonzo Stagg; and the Royal (a.k.a. Kosciusko) Colts, whose roster included Poles, Irish, Germans, and Swedes, beat the black American Giants of Rube Foster in 1908.
Dziennik Chicagoski, June 27, 1915 (FLPS).
In the East, the church fostered Catholic athletic groups to oppose the radical clubs. See *Pamatnica*, 52, 58.

64. Krzywonos, ed., *The Poles in Chicago*, 147, 256; Riess, *City Games*, 76-8; Paul W. Kearney, "Ten Million Keglers Can't Be Wrong," in Herb Graffis, ed., *Esquire's First Sports Reader* (New York: A. S. Barnes, 1945), 226-38.

65. Krzywonos, ed., *The Poles in Chicago*, 189-256, gives biographical sketches of prominent Poles and their athletic activities. On Fuka, see Slayton, *Back of the Yards*, 59.

66. *The Reform Advocate*, 42 (Jan. 13, 1912): 817; Edward Mazur, "Jewish Chicago," in Holli and Jones, eds., *The Ethnic Frontier*, 272; *Chicago Hebrew Institute Observer*, 1:1 (Nov. 1912), 7-9, 17; 1:2 (Dec. 1912), 5; 1:9 (Aug. 1913), 12; 1:10 (Sept. 1913), 9; 2:12 (Nov. 1914), 9; *Daily Jewish Courier*, Apr. 26, 1914 (FLPS); ibid., Nov. 29, 1909; *Chicago Tribune*, Sept. 6, 1910, 14. See Gerald R. Gems, "Sport and the Forging of a Jewish-American Culture: The Chicago Hebrew

Institute," *Journal of American Jewish History,* 83:1 (March 1995): 15-26, for detailed coverage.

John Higham, *Send These to Me: Immigrants in Urban America* (Baltimore, MD: Johns Hopkins University Press, 1984), 126, attests to the success and rapid rise in socioeconomic status among early Jewish immigrants. An 1890 survey showed that 7,000 of 10,000 had house servants. The institute's officers were among the city's wealthiest businessmen: Jacob Loeb, Julius Rosenwald, president of Sears, and Charles Shaffner; *The Observer,* 1:4 (March 1913).

67. *Observer,* 1:1 (Nov. 1912), 9; 1:3 (Feb. 1913), 4-6. Objectives are stated in ibid., 1:3 (Feb. 1913), 5-6; 1:5 (Apr. 1913), 9.

68. Ibid., 1:10 (Sept. 1913), 9-11; 1:11 (Oct. 1913), 11-2; 1:12 (Nov. 1913), 9-12; 2:1 (Dec. 1913), 11. Berkman, who served many years as an intercollegiate gymnastics judge, was an active promoter of track activities, sponsoring the Post Office Meet at Dexter Pavilion and inaugurating the annual Women's Olympic Track Meet in coordination with the *Daily News.* From the *Reform Advocate,* 71 (Mar. 20, 1926), 207.

69. *Observer,* 2:1 (Dec. 1913), 12; 2:2 (Jan. 1914), 11; 1:6 (May 1913), 10; 1:7 (June 1913), 27; 3:12 (Nov. 1915), 12; 3:7-8 (June-July, 1915), 20, for figures on prizes won. The institute also provided athletic competition for girls, but its monthly magazine focused almost entirely on male efforts in its sports coverage.

Ira Berkow, *Maxwell Street,* 141-7, 182-6, 336-46; Barney Ross and Martin Abramson, *No Man Stands Alone* (New York: J. B. Lippincott, 1957). For complete coverage, see Ken Blady, *The Jewish Boxers' Hall of Fame* (New York: Shapolsky Books, 1988); and Steven Riess, "A Fighting Chance."

Despite the efforts to assimilate, Jews continued to face anti-Semitism. The *Daily Jewish Forward,* July 16, 1923, reported the resignation of Jewish golf clubs from the Western Golf Association in 1921 and its ban on Jewish women. Farlin B. Hall, president of the golf association, had no rationale for the discriminatory decision, simply stating that "applicants must please the executive committee."

70. Ruck, *Sandlot Seasons,* 120; Bruno, *Italians in Chicago,* 46; Jones and Holli, eds., *Ethnic Chicago,* 56, 68, 202. In addition to the Hebrew Institute, the recreation center at Sinai Temple, founded in 1912, conducted a comprehensive athletic program for boys and girls that produced numerous champions. See *Tribune,* Dec. 19, 1920, Pt. 2:2; Riess, *City Games,* 100-01, 104-05.

71.   Elizabeth Lewis Otey, U.S. Bureau of Labor Statistics, *Bulletin No. 123,* "Employers Welfare Work," May 15, 1913, 52; U.S. Bureau of Labor Statistics, *Bulletin No. 250,* February 1919, 74; and *Bulletin No. 458,* February 1928, 33, 37; along with the *American Physical Education Review,* 27 (March 1922): 223, and the *Chicago Recreation Survey,* 2 (1937): 73-4; Johnson, *History of YMCA,* 123, 231; all attest to the ongoing involvement of the YMCA in such matters.

Leonard J. Diehl and Floyd R. Eastwood, *Industrial Recreation: Its Development and Present Status* (Lafayette, IN: Purdue University Press, 1940), 8-9, cite early studies of the industrial recreation movement (1913-1919) that were designed to better relations between labor and management and increase loyalty to the company.

See Seymour, *Baseball: The People's Game,* 213-57, for a complete history of industrial baseball teams; Riess, *City Games,* 82-6; John R. Schleppi, "It Pays: John N. Patterson and Industrial Recreation at the National Cash Register Company," *Journal of Sport History,* 6 (Winter 1979): 20-8. Company sponsorship of baseball started in the 1860s, while bowling and softball teams appeared in Chicago by the 1890s.

72.   Melendy, "The Saloon in Chicago," 298; Duis, *The Saloon,* 182-3, on company reprisals. Ironically, Ward sold liquor through the company's catalog sales division.

73.   Rosenzweig, *Eight Hours for What We Will,* 93-112, 124-5, 183-90; James H. Timberlake, *Prohibition and the Progressive Movement, 1900-1920* (Cambridge, MA: Harvard University Press, 1963), 2, 5-6, 40.

74.   See "Guardianship Not Necessary," *Chicago Arbeiter Zeitung,* Mar. 23, 1910, in Keil and Jentz, eds., *German Workers in Chicago,* 354-7; *The Social Evil in Chicago* (Chicago: Vice Commission, 1911), 116-40. Klaus Ensslen and Heinz Ickstadt, "German Working Class Culture in Chicago: Continuity and Change in the Decade from 1900-1910," in Keil and Jentz, eds., *German Workers in Industrial Chicago,* 236-52; Hogan, *Class and Reform,* 76-7; *Denni Hlasatel,* Feb. 28, 1910 (FLPS); Duis, *The Saloon,* 115-6, 258, states only 319 ethnic organizations in the United Societies, but a membership of 100,000.

75.   Vice Commission, *The Social Evil,* 120-2; Kingsdale, "The Poor Man's Club," 473; Rosenzweig, *Eight Hours for What We Will,* 53-64; Timberlake, *Prohibition and the Progressive Movement,* 102-4, 138, 150. By 1907 prohibitionists succeeded in declaring Hyde Park, a bastion of the middle class, a dry district, and 160 other Chicago

precincts refused to grant licenses, causing the closure of 199 saloons. Duis, *The Saloon,* 288, on the 1914 petition. Rev. Thomas L. Harmon, *Church of the Annunciation, A Parish History, 1866-1916* (Chicago: D. B. Hansen & Sons, 1916), 25, on the "greatly diminished numbers."

76. "Protection of Immigrant Girls on Arrival at Interior Points," from *First Annual Report of the Immigrants' Protective League of Chicago,* 13-18, in Stanley Feldstein and Lawrence Costello, eds., *The Ordeal of Assimilation: A Documentary History of the White Working Class, 1830-1970s* (Garden City, NY: Anchor Books, 1974), 86-91; Department of Public Works, *Social Service Directory* (City of Chicago, 1915), 14-15; Vice Commission, *The Social Evil in Chicago.*

Joanne J. Meyerowitz, *Women Adrift: Independent Wage Earners in Chicago, 1880-1930* (Chicago: University of Chicago Press, 1988); Mark Norman, *Mayors, Madams and Madmen* (Chicago: Chicago Review Press, 1979), 15-17; Duis, *The Saloon,* 264, 268, 278, 282; Hogan, *Class and Reform,* 78-9. Hogan cites Eric Anderson's study of the so-called committee of Fifteen, although fifty-five members served between 1913-1916. Most were Protestant Republican businessmen or Progressive Party members. None were Democrats. Twenty-six of the fifty-six directors during the period belonged to the Union League Club.

Max Kaplan, *Leisure in America* (New York: John Wiley, 1960), 131, estimates the Chicago vice trade at $10 million annually, based on the 5,000 prostitutes in the 400 brothels during the 1930s. There were 3,500 brothels in 1913. The 1911 Vice Commission Report, 32, stated that profits from prostitution exceeded $15 million a year. Boyer, *Urban Masses and Moral Order,* 191-219, covers anti-vice crusades in Chicago and elsewhere.

77. Mina Carson, *Settlement Folk,* 172; Perry R. Duis, "Yesterday's City: Tripping the Light Fantastic," *Chicago History,* 18:4 (Winter 1989-1990): 82-94. The 1913 survey is cited in Robert A. Slayton, *Back of the Yards,* 61-2.

Kathy Piess, *Cheap Amusements,* presents a significant study of gender, industrialization, and commercialized leisure. Lewis A. Erenberg, *Steppin' Out: New York Nightlife and the Transformation of American Culture, 1890-1930* (Chicago: University of Chicago Press, 1984) analyzes elements of class, ethnicity, and gender in the development of commercialized popular leisure.

78. Paul F. Cressey, "The Succession of Cultural Groups," Ph.D. Dissertation, University of Chicago, 279-280; Maria Interlandi, born in Sicily in 1918, testified that she was not allowed to go to the

dances, in Interlandi interview, 28, Italians in Chicago, 1860-1965 (Oral History Project of the University of Illinois at Chicago). Valentino Lazzaretti, as a boy, was permitted to go to the dances and dated girls from other ethnic groups. Lazzaretti came from a northern Italian family, traditionally more liberal; from the Lazzaretti interview, 40, 43.

79. Paul G. Cressey, *The Taxi Dance Hall* (Chicago: University of Chicago Press, 1932), xix, 58, 63-6, 75-8, 111-14, 177-95, 252-3, 286.

80. On Cicero dances, see *Denni Hlasatel,* Dec. 7, 1913 (FLPS). The letter to Rev. Kruszas, dated Jan. 28, 1921, is at the archives of the Archdiocese of Chicago. See Cressey, *Taxi Dance Hall,* 190-3, on the shimmy and other dances considered to be too sensual and indecent.

81. Vice Commission, *The Social Evil in Chicago,* 31, acknowledged and criticized the double standard applied between the rich and poor dancers.

82. *Forty-Third Annual Report of the West Chicago Parks Commissioners, 1911,* 14.

83. Ibid., 16.

84. Todd, *Chicago Recreation Survey,* 1 (1937): 5, 7, 23.

85. Ibid., 16.

86. Cited in Hogan, *Class and Reform,* 72. Paul Boyer, *Urban Masses and Moral Order in America,* 272-6, characterizes the Burnham Plan as an attempt to impose physical order on the city that a particular moral order might also be achieved.

87. Burgess, "Idealism and Arrogance"; see Don S. Kirschner, "The Perils of Pleasure: Commercial Recreation, Social Disorder, and Moral Reform in the Progressive Era," *American Studies,* 21 (Fall 1980): 27-42; Harry Jebsen, "The Public Acceptance of Sports in Dallas, 1880-1930," *Journal of Sport History,* 6 (Winter 1979): 5-19; Alan Havig, "Mass Commercial Amusements in Kansas City before World War I," *Missouri Historical Review,* 75 (April 1981): 316-45, for developments elsewhere.

88. *Chicago Tribune,* November 6, 1905, 4, cited in McCarthy, "Politics and the Parks," 171; Todd, *Chicago Recreation Survey,* 1 (1937): 22-3.

89. Alfred A. Baker & Co., *The Forest Preserve Proposition,* November 3, 1905; Henry G. Foreman, Outer Belt Commission Report, *Country Playfields for the People of Chicago and Cook County* (Chicago: October 30, 1905); Riess, *City Games,* 140.

90. Whitson, "Sport and Hegemony;" Hargreaves, *Sport, Power and Culture,* 38-42.

91. Dawley, *Struggles for Justice,* 196-259, 277-82.

The 1893 Lake View High School football team practices in a public park. Note the heavy sweaters and canvas or mole-skin pants and jackets that served as protection. (*Courtesy Sulzer Regional Library, The Chicago Public Library*)

Tennis court in a middle-class neighborhood, 1890-1891. (*Courtesy Sulzer Regional Library, The Chicago Public Library*)

Members of the Illinois Cycling Club exhibit their vehicles in 1890. These bicycles show the advent of the transition from the dangerous high wheel to the more practical "safety" bicycle. (*Courtesy Sulzer Regional Library, The Chicago Public Library*)

Arthur Bennett in cycling tights, c 1890s. Bennett was the son of R. J. Bennett, builder of the Wilson Avenue YMCA, the first YMCA in the Lake View neighborhood. (*Courtesy Sulzer Regional Library, The Chicago Public Library*)

The 1904 Lake View High School girls' basketball team.
(*Courtesy Sulzer Regional Library, The Chicago Public Library*)

The Woodlawn (*aka* Midway) Thistles in 1903 practicing in an enclosed stadium, signaling the transition to semipro play before paying spectators. On the ground can be seen several pieces of the primitive headgear being worn at that time. (*Courtesy Sulzer Regional Library, The Chicago Public Library*)

A game of "playground ball" at the Marshal Swenie playground, which served the "Little Italy" neighborhood. (*Courtesy Harold Washington Library, Municipal Reference Collection*)

Girls in a rope-climbing contest at the Max Beutner play-ground. (*Courtesy Harold Washington Library, Municipal Reference Collection*)

A Knights of Columbus baseball team in 1908. Sport proved to be a primary means of inclusion in the mainstream culture for Catholics. (*Courtesy Sulzer Regional Library, The Chicago Public Library*)

The Parker High School football team, c 1917, practicing in a public park as the coach looks on. (*Courtesy Sulzer Regional Library, The Chicago Public Library*)

The Roseland Eclipse baseball team in 1911. The team had become semipro and was playing before paying spectators. (*Courtesy Sulzer Regional Library, The Chicago Public Library*)

CHAPTER 5

The Emergence of a Mass Culture

Throughout the early twentieth century, labor relations, nativism, war hysteria, and mounting racial tensions fragmented and alienated segments of American society. The onset of armed conflict, however, produced a critical historical moment, since World War I forced ethnics to examine and identify their primary loyalties as the United States entered the European hostilities. Following the armistice, many ethnics returned to newly independent homelands, while those that remained were drawn closer to the mainstream as the Americanization of Catholicism, immigration quota laws, and public education contributed to the ongoing dismantling of traditional ethnic cultures.[1]

The process of cultural evolution was an uneasy one, producing tensions within ethnic communities and across generations. Rather than the homogenized culture envisioned by the progressives, the synthesis of diverse values produced a more popular, mass culture, influenced from the bottom upward. New forms of art and leisure, such as jazz and dance styles, emerged, to be condemned as decadent by the social elites. Other forms of commercialized leisure took on added importance as ethnics selectively participated in entertainment such as movies, radio, and the record industry that produced both English and foreign language materials. As ethnic groups, particularly the American-born children of immigrants, adopted American sport forms, the working class also found reasons for accommodation in the free expression and exultation of physical prowess. Commercialized leisure activities allowed for the adaptation of working class values that had previously threatened the interests of the middle and upper classes. By the 1920s American athletic heroes such as Babe Ruth, Jack Dempsey, and Red Grange personified the physicality inherent in the working class identity and nurtured dreams of opportunity. This popular sporting culture moved toward a greater degree of stability, as it amalgamated class, ethnic, and religious interests throughout the years following the "great war."[2]

World War I and Americanization

Nativism and the international nature of the First World War altered the relations between nativist and ethnic Chicagoans, especially the Germans. Previously among the most stable and entrenched of Chicago's ethnic groups, the Germans had solidified a political power base and enjoyed widespread influence throughout the city. The enigmatic populist mayor, "Big Bill" Thompson, whose pro-German, anti-British stance had gained German support through the war, allowed German groups to retain a measure of political weight. However, as many other Chicagoans began to shift their loyalties to the Allied powers during the war, the German-Americans' base of support crumbled. Authorities revoked the charters of fraternal organizations, moved to ban the Teutonic language from the schools, and suppressed German-language papers. In July 1918, the police, assisted by 10,000 members of the American Protective League, apprehended 100,000 Chicagoans and accused them of un-American activities. In effect, ethnics came under intense pressure to prove themselves as loyal Americans.[3]

Unlike the Germans, some ethnic groups were able to adopt the Allied cause as congruent with their own independence movements. Poles, in particular, became strident in their pro-Allies stance. The Polish Falcons issued a call to arms, and 215,000 answered. Other groups sent $200 million for the Polish cause in support of a national army, while individual Poles bought $67 million in Liberty Bonds.

For nativists, the war provided an excuse to counteract ethnic influences. An indication of things to come occurred early in 1917, when Congress required immigrants to pass a literacy test. Four years later, Congress imposed a limit on the number of emigres, eventually restricting immigration to a maximum of 150,000 per year. The policy particularly discriminated against southern and eastern Europeans. Poles, for example, first permitted to immigrate at a rate of 30,977 per year, were limited to only 5,982 by 1924. The consequences of such restricted immigration for ethnic cultures in Chicago would eventually be dire ones.[4]

Nativist opposition to ethnic culture and influence extended well beyond the matter of demography. Reductions in the numbers of immigrants had their parallel in the educational system, where earlier ethnic curricular themes were displaced. In the case of physical education, a curriculum that had emphasized German gymnastics and American games began to stress military preparation after 1915. By 1917 an investigation of the German system, which had dominated the physical education curriculum since 1885, went so far as to condemn its use. A 1920 report stated that "the peculiar needs of the American child require teachers who possess and understand the American spirit...."[5] Nobody could miss the emphasis on "American." As American sports and games had already comprised part of the curriculum for nearly two decades, the intent to remove all ethnic influences became explicit.

Administrative "reforms" carried over to the extracurricular program. When the Public Schools Athletic League became subsumed by the Bureau of Physical Education in 1920, it made its intentions clear: "The purposes and aims of the league are to promote and provide for American sports and games among the students of the Chicago public schools... and to make a wider use of the splendid park and playground system of the city of Chicago."[6] The program, run in conjunction with the parks, was extensive, with as many as 200 schools in competitions for both boys and girls.[7]

While the reformers curtailed the flow of European immigrants and reduced their influence in the schools, businessmen worked to impart "loyalty." In the wake of the patriotic fervor and the Red Scare that followed the war, Rotary clubs organized loyalty days to coincide with traditional working-class celebrations during May. The commercial interests coordinated with the board of education, the playgrounds, and the administrators of the Jewish Peoples' Institute to turn May Day into a youth loyalty demonstration to "train and shape the coming generation."[8]

Newly constructed public facilities, such as Soldier Field, memorialized veterans and tied patriotism to sport as Chicago hosted numerous national athletic spectacles at the site in the ensuing years, including ethnic sport festivals. The merger of American patriotism and ethnic nationalism proved less subtle in other matters. This was particularly true of the Catholic Church, where Old World pastors enjoyed a good deal of autonomy in operating ethnic parishes within their neighborhood enclaves. They not only supported but often directed programs with nationalistic aims and a very extensive educational system that reinforced ethnic cultures and retarded the assimilation process. The accession of George Mundelein to the archbishopric in 1916, however, marked the real beginning of an "American" Catholicism. Chicago served as a stage for this process, and Mundelein became a prime mover and a national figure.[9]

An American-born, Roman-trained prelate, Mundelein became the youngest archbishop in the United States in 1915. With his appointment to Chicago, he determined to seek greater control over the archdiocese and bring greater efficiency to its operations. A financial wizard, he provided the economic bureaucracy, standardization, and order found in business corporations. New parishes were denied the autonomy formerly enjoyed by the nationalistic parishes. Furthermore, Mundelein declared a building moratorium on national parishes and increased control by strategic appointments, if not diplomacy. By handpicking the school board, Mundelein standardized schools in his first year at the helm—only reading and religion continued to be taught in native tongues. The action, to be sure, was not well received in the ethnic parishes. Poles, in particular, fought it bitterly. However, with centralization of the administrative bureaucracy, the nationalistic parishes lost their political clout within the Catholic power structure.[10]

The clergyman also had close ties to the Democratic Party, counting local politicians and, in later years, Franklin D. Roosevelt, among his friends. Mundelein, a German speaker, used the World War I mobilization efforts to win greater acceptance for Catholicism and foster his own program of assimilation. In a show of patriotism, the archbishop personally bought $10,000 worth of Liberty Bonds, ordered the purchase of at least $100 in bonds from each parish, and had the bonds sold in church vestibules. The *New World,* a Catholic paper, urged parishioners to enlist in the military service. During the Red Scare following the war, Mundelein forestalled the rising class consciousness by opposing the radicals, and his program of church reform pushed the ethnics closer to Americanization.[11]

The encroachment of the Americanization process on ethnic leisure practices, did, of course, have its limits. When reform touched upon religious issues, such as the proposed ban on alcohol, even the Catholic hierarchy resisted, for wine was central to its rituals. Nevertheless, wartime rationing and hygiene laws had allowed middle class crusaders to have free lunches banned from the saloons. Anti-German sentiment closed many German establishments during the war, and class, ethnic, and religious lines were clearly drawn for the showdown vote in 1919. Chicagoans opposed prohibition by a three-to-one margin, with more than 90 percent of the ethnics voting against the measure; yet the state passed the regulation. Chicagoans, particularly Catholics, who were supported by the clergy, refused to observe the law. Police estimated there were two to three stills per block in the city, and only 12 percent of the bars actually closed. The rest converted to soft drink parlors that continued to sell alcohol clandestinely. Bootleggers became local heroes, voters continually rejected "dry" politicians, and elements of the ethnic and working-class cultures continued to flourish in the saloons.[12]

Previously bastions of the radical labor movement, saloons moved into the mainstream as their owners succumbed to exorbitant license fees and dependence upon politicians and breweries even before prohibition. Still a haven for masculinity and sporting interests, tavern-sponsored bowling and softball teams found park leagues convenient structures in which to exercise neighborhood rivalries.[13]

Ethnics also adopted and practiced the American sport forms within the extensive fraternal or church organizations.

Catholic parishes had formed an athletic league early in the century, and such practices became more common and centrally controlled under Archbishop Mundelein.

During the war, Mundelein had each parish create a Holy Name Society to coordinate religious functions, social programs, and athletic activities. Membership languished, however, until the organization assumed the latter role. The *New World,* official organ of the archdiocese, stated that "the injection of athletics into our church societies has added interest far beyond all expectations."[14] Some of the teams developed into semipro units, and the program took on greater organization when Father Bernard J. Sheil, Cook County Jail chaplain in 1919, inherited the task. As Catholics played intra- and inter-parish matches, they "drew tremendous crowds of several thousand excited fans."[15] Social relationships began to expand as urban developments replaced the sandlots and the athletic club fields. Both church and community teams were forced to use public facilities and abide by the stated rules. The cooperation and coordination of the Catholic authorities and the fraternal organizations with the park administrators facilitated greater accommodation between the private clubs and the public administrators.[16]

Not only ethnic but traditional class differences, such as gambling, also found resolution as laborers found the means to practice such actions within the mainstream leisure structures. Like the bootleggers, gambling racketeers and bookmakers earned prestige and status in working class communities for their ability to earn a living, often a handsome one, as they challenged middle class precepts of morality. But even such illegal activities, often operated by ethnics, forced greater accommodation with the dominant culture as racketeers networked with police and politicians to circumvent constraints on their activities.[17]

Sport and gambling had long enjoyed a close relationship. Even young boys' teams had openly challenged rivals in newspaper ads of the 1880s and 1890s for large sums of money. Among the adults, the Chicago Bowling Association found it necessary to limit players to three leagues in order to restrict the use of "ringers." The *Western Bowlers' Journal* distinguished between gambling and nongambling leagues, with the latter clearly a minority. Bowling tournaments offered money prizes that not only enticed entrants but encouraged widespread gambling in side bets among participants and their supporters, similar to the traditional practices in boxing and billiards. With the expansion of industrial recreation programs, the ethnic working class readily adopted bowling, with its opportunities for financial gain. Substantial winnings allowed some to purchase saloons or bowling establishments on the road to entrepreneurship.[18]

The working class faced a double standard relevant to sport and gambling. Gambling among gentlemen at the horse track or country club seemed more acceptable than that which occurred in saloons or billiard parlors. The *Sporting News* noted the distinction in its issue of June 10, 1920, in a poem entitled "The Gamboleers."

> Gaze on the wicked gamboleer
> He is a thing of shame
> He bets a dollar and a half
> Upon a baseball game;
> They sting him with a fine and heap
> Disgrace upon his name.
> Gaze on the noble financier
> Who proudly walks the street;
> A pillar of the church is he
> Whom one is proud to meet;
> He does not bet on baseball games
> He bets on corn and wheat.[19]

Laborers and ethnic youth quickly learned to adapt their gambling practices to the athletic programs in the city spaces, despite the supervision.

By 1920 the public parks had enacted regulations against gambling and initiated a point system to stress the middle class values of discipline, teamwork, and sportsmanship; but the endemic nature of gambling encouraged the use of "professional" players, who derived income from their physical abilities and won wagers for their neighborhood supporters. Widespread professionalism forced the park directors to make concessions. The *Annual Report of 1921-22* stated that the

generally acceptable amateur rules are intolerable...many
of the pro baseball players can't be in the park programs.
This inequity has moved several of these men to gather their
friends and admirers into athletic clubs, resentful of the
parks...without leadership they fast degenerated into de-
moralizing neighborhood influence, of great weight among
the younger generation.[20]

Supervisors agreed to let the professional players compete
on teams in sports other than those in which they made a
living, in order to avoid the "evasion and deception" of ali-
ases.[21]

By the end of World War I, a transition in the sporting
culture had become more evident. The separate, private,
nationalistic, and sometimes antagonistic sporting practices
of the early immigrants subsided, replaced by the "Americanized," public, and commercialized ventures of their offspring.
The Turners, Sokols, and Falcons no longer threatened the
establishment—they became part of it. Laborers who may
have become disgruntled with the effects of the industrial
economy also found ways to make the capitalist system more
agreeable in commercialized leisure practices. For the children of southern or eastern European peasants, who had little
or no sporting culture, the American games enabled more
widespread participation and profitable opportunities for the
underclass through the regularly scheduled programs of the
public agencies.

The exclusive athletic clubs induced some of the best ethnic
and working class athletes to compete for them with offers of
membership, sponsorship in international events, use of their
outstanding facilities, and tutelage under professional
coaches. The Illinois Athletic Club enrolled Johnny Weissmuller, a local Catholic swimming champion, in 1922. He soon
achieved fame as an Olympic hero in 1924 and as a Hollywood
movie star thereafter. Both men and women benefited from
such sponsorship.[22]

As professional female physical educators deemphasized
competitive sports for girls in the schools, the parks, playgrounds, and private clubs expanded opportunities for
women. Bertha Severin founded the Illinois Women's Athletic
Club in 1918. The venture proved remarkably successful, with

a $100,000 site and $60,000 in memberships subscribed in the first year. While Mrs. Severin opposed prohibition and supported the legalization of boxing and horseracing in Illinois, she remained more conservative in promoting sports for women. Working class girls, recruited to "bring fame and enhance the name of the club," might train for free, so long as they adhered to amateurism and modest dress.[23]

Those who did so earned fame, if not money. Sybil Bauer, a protege of the Illinois Athletic Club, held nine swimming records by 1922, even surpassing the men's mark in the backstroke. The *New York Times* speculated that "the discussion prior to the 1924 Olympics was whether Bauer would swim against women or men."[24] The club produced several individual and team champions at both local and national levels in swimming, basketball, and track as the IWAC became a major power in women's sports by 1930.[25]

Promising athletes were conscripted as early as their high school years. Annette Rogers, who ran for the Illinois Catholic Women's Club track team as a fourteen-year-old, won a gold medal at the 1932 Olympics. Such ethnic and working class athletes helped the elite clubs achieve their goals as they vied with intracity rivals for athletic and social status. Recruitment of working class athletes produced athletic heroes that bridged ethnic and class divisions and also enhanced the perception of sport as a meritocracy.[26]

Schools

Recruitment of athletes had been an established practice for more than fifty years. It was not limited to the aspiring clubs; colleges and even high schools practiced it. Within the interscholastic programs, the working class value of physical prowess converged with the middle class perception of sport as character building, but commercialization and professionalization undermined the concept of amateurism. Success provided recognition and even greater opportunities as sponsors, promoters, and managers courted talent for industrial, semipro, and professional teams.[27]

Even among the "amateur" players of the college ranks, alumni provided substantial sums for spending money and charge accounts at local stores. Many college stars earned additional money as boxers, pool players, and hirelings on the burgeoning pro football circuit. Such practices proved particularly helpful to Notre Dame players, who often traveled by train to Chicago and other midwestern locations on Sundays to avail themselves of the opportunities. George Gipp seemed particularly peripatetic, and it was not unusual for him to carry $600 in his pocket as a result of gambling ventures. Like Gipp, many others supplemented their incomes with billiard cues and bowling balls, or simply sold their services to the highest bidder. Some, like George Halas, Paddy Driscoll, and "Hippo" Vaughn, became full-fledged professionals. Such athletes were recruited and rewarded by middle class promoters specifically for the physical skills so admired by the working class. Social mobility gained through such means made capitalism not only tolerable but agreeable to the favored children of immigrants.[28]

Despite the amateur ideals and regulations designed to counteract abuses, the street culture of the working class persisted in high school athletics. In 1923 Lindblom High School protested its loss to the New York City champs in the intercity baseball series because the New Yorkers had used a twenty-one-year-old catcher. In the quest for profit and victories, struggling promoters even conscripted from the high school ranks. Ambrose McGuirk, a Chicagoan who owned the Milwaukee Badgers franchise in the fledgling National Football League, hired four Englewood High School players for an impromptu game with Chris O'Brien's Chicago Cardinals in 1925. The practice of high school athletes competing with and against adults was common, and both the city council and the board of education addressed the issue and the violation of the amateur ideology. The city council urged leniency for the suspended high schoolers, citing ignorance on the part of the young players and the ambiguous nature of "pro" football; but the board suggested that the process of recruitment was already a systematic one, as professional agents had infiltrated high school sports. Its report recommended that all teachers and coaches affiliated with professional teams should be prohibited from such activities during the season in which they coached interscholastic teams.[29]

Semipro teams and even professional players practiced alongside high schoolers in the parks, and star players were well aware of the weekly opportunities to capitalize on their abilities. In addition to neighborhood affairs, hundreds of games between rivals willing to pay for an edge occurred within a train ride of Chicago. The Aurora Yellow Jackets, a professional football team, hired Ted Londros, a high school star, for a game against the Chicago Cardinals. The Cubs also offered Londros a baseball contract before his graduation. Several years later, Londros was allegedly still playing for an eastern college. Such tramp athletes continued to change teams or schools by the season.[30]

The Public Schools Athletic League struggled with rule changes throughout the 1920s and 1930s in an attempt to address the ongoing abuses associated with professionalism and the persistent elements of the street culture that affected good sportsmanship and playing conditions. The administrators struggled in vain. In 1919, the aldermen of the city council, perhaps courting favor with their working class clientele, passed a resolution that guaranteed sports fans "the inalienable right to freely express themselves," including the right to throw bottles at game officials.[31]

By 1926 the football season featured "riotous conditions," eligibility violations, disputes over game receipts, teams practicing and playing with colleges, and multiple games in one day in order to increase revenue. School administrators emphasized the commercial aspects of the athletic programs as they rationalized their educational value. In 1928 the league executives curtailed the intercity matches when opponents offered to pay only expenses rather than share the profits. The administrators soon found a solution to the problem by inviting the Catholic schools to compete, thereby drawing upon the natural ethnic and religious rivalries within the city. The "championship" game brought widespread media coverage, including a radio broadcast and game films. By 1931 such games were being played throughout the season, more fully incorporating alternative groups into the mainstream.[32]

The ability of divergent groups to earn profits within the commercialized sport structure promoted the perception of greater inclusion in American society, but it did not produce wholesale acceptance of the reformers' value system. Championships were contested in two weight divisions, with the intention of equalizing play according to size and providing greater opportunity for all, but the widespread use of ineligible players negated the aims of the authorities. The 1927 lightweight basketball championship game between Englewood and Roosevelt high schools proved disastrous. Street youths commandeered the floor during halftime, and the rowdyism and property damage that ensued after the game caused the league to threaten to withhold the championship shield. One of the teams had employed an ineligible (overaged) player during the semifinal round as well. Lindblom High, which stood to gain a tie for the divisional championship if the league enforced the forfeiture, graciously declined to contest the matter, provided it received a share of the game profits. It had become readily apparent that commercialized sport and the quest for profit had undermined the best intentions of the progressive reformers by the 1920s.[33]

Such activities were not limited to the men and boys. Whereas middle class women had brought a sense of moral balance to the reform movements, working class women actively participated in the transition to commercialized leisure and sporting practices. As women entered the work force in ever-increasing numbers, employers began to organize women's teams in bowling and track after 1900. A dislike for the formal gymnastic routines of scholastic physical training programs led women to seek more competitive games and athletic pastimes. Physical educators, who denounced the competitive male model as inappropriate for women, introduced the concept of play-days to girls' interscholastic programs in the 1920s. But industrial teams continued to provide an alternative by expanding competition in basketball, softball, tennis, and volleyball.[34]

The Western Electric Company provided perhaps the world's largest industrial recreation program, with 28,000 members by 1923. It offered opportunities for women in several sports, including an eight-team women's baseball league. The annual track meet drew more than 10,000 spectators on its twentieth anniversary in 1930. The year before, the company entered twenty-six women's bowling teams in the national tournament held in Chicago. Fifty-two thousand Chicagoans showed up to watch.[35]

That women had such competitive inclinations so decried by the physical educators and medical professionals is evident by the widespread activity and success of Chicago's women's teams. High school girls engaged in interscholastic competition well before the war, having started basketball play as early as 1895. The Chicago Stars, a women's professional baseball team, barnstormed the country in 1902. Chicagoans were prominent in the founding of the Woman's International Bowling Congress in 1916, although women's tournaments had been conducted since 1907. By 1920 they were offering more than $2,000 in prize money at the national tournament. During the 1920s, Chicago women won numerous national championships in bowling, basketball, swimming, and track and field. When the *Chicago American* and the Park District hosted a track meet for girls and women, more than 1,400 entered the competition. At least 900 women's teams played in a local softball tournament, while 1,200 teams vied for the basketball championship. Such widespread enthusiasm soon produced a variety of world records and women's Olympic team members.[36]

It was evident that schoolgirls unable to find competitive opportunities in the schools could still be accommodated on industrial teams, ethnic and private athletic clubs, and in the Chicago parks. Despite the misgivings of physical educators, corporate promoters, newspapers, and the public agencies thus inducted women into the male-dominated sport structures. For working class women, like their male counterparts, sport provided opportunities for some material gain in the form of cash or prizes, greater freedom of expression, and otherwise unavailable occasions for travel .

Semipro Teams

Commercialized sport afforded opportunites to both athletes and their backers that work did not. Youngsters gambled in the playground leagues, while school stars soon graduated to the neighborhood and industrial teams. Although many company teams maintained membership in the Amateur Athletic Union, they were not always "amateur." The violation of some of the amateur principles by independent teams led to the murky designation of "semipro" clubs that played for money prizes or engaged in commercial contests at private grounds.[37]

The cloudy nature of the amateur-professional relationship is evident in the 1914 schedule of the semipro Roseland Eclipse baseball team. The Eclipse defeated the University of Chicago by a lopsided score and played against the professional Chicago Cubs as well. Such teams existed well before the turn of the century, and the ambiguity of their nature bridged not only the amateur-professional dichotomy, but alternative and sometimes oppositional value systems. Small towns, companies, neighborhoods within the city, or particular ethnic or racial groups formed their own teams that promoted communal pride and a sense of solidarity. The widespread opportunities for remuneration and the constant movement of players among teams fostered individualism. Middle class promoters eyed profits while they organized such teams within commercialized frameworks, yet players earned rewards based on the working class values of physical prowess. Even nonathletes shared in the vicissitudes of victory or defeat, often in the high stakes gambling that accompanied athletic contests.[38]

The company or craft-based teams even promoted the perception of democracy. Simon Mandel, owner of a large downtown department store, sponsored and played with his company team in a Sunday semipro league. Bosses at other industrial plants played ball with employees on noon hours, and steelworkers at the South Works plant reveled in their victories over administrators. Harry Blumberg, a semipro who starred for the workers and a city league team, provided particular delights when he struck out executives who proved inept as batsmen.[39]

For workers who felt stifled and oppressed by industrial labor, sport remained a relatively free market in which to test one's worth. When Jimmy Callahan, a White Sox player, sued Charles Comiskey for back pay in 1906, he was blacklisted. Undaunted, Callahan started his own semipro circuit of ten teams within the city and got his revenge when his Logan

Squares beat the Sox after their World Series victory. Others, like Art Rooney and Johnny Kling, quit their pro teams for greater profits and freedom among the semipros. For some, like Rube Foster and his American Giants, who were banned from organized baseball because of their race, the Chicago City League offered an opportunity and springboard to a better life.[40]

Semipro circuits became institutionalized structures in the city and proliferated throughout the country. Some teams openly recruited players through newspaper ads, while others, such as the Lutheran Baseball League, required church attendance and forbid remuneration, but allowed for admission charges. Other teams followed more clearly professional practices, paying local stars on a per game basis for their services.[41]

Competition among the independent semipro and community athletic clubs involved both prestige and money. Promoters and team managers also vied with employers for the best players, regardless of ethnic or religious affiliation. The *New World,* a Catholic weekly, even listed the numerous papists on city league teams. Many industrial teams played in the city's semipro circuits, and rampant gambling led to the recruitment of nonemployees, including professional players and college stars for high stakes games. In addition to the industrial players who were nonemployees, others became full-time athletes on company time, as employers sought publicity through sport.[42]

Rampant professionalism marked city league baseball play by World War I. Henry Penn, a former pitcher for the University of Illinois and a star of the semipro Eclipse team, indicated that he had turned down professional contracts with four different teams. He did so because the amounts offered simply could not compare to his salary as an engineer and his "semipro" earnings. The semipro players actually enjoyed the enviable position of the earliest professionals—a free market in which to sell their services. Unlike the professional teams, players were not bound by a reserve clause, and they had the luxury of entertaining multiple offers. As early as the 1890s, neighborhood teams had sought out and recruited youngsters in a similar manner, thus reinforcing the notion that the physical skills so esteemed by the working class could provide one with a measure of success within the commercial system.[43]

Itinerant ball players could earn $100 a game or more if willing to travel. Street-smart players gained even more by hustling less sophisticated opponents. Arthur Hardy, a member of a black barnstorming baseball team, stated that they played ineptly, just well enough to win, in order to gain a rematch. It was in the carnival which followed the game that he and his teammates "got all the money."[44] Rematches increased the stakes and led to bidding wars for the talent that would give one team the edge.

Three separate semipro baseball leagues, with at least forty-six teams, operated in the city by 1918. Players in the Chicago Industrial League were paid $10-$20 for their participation in Sunday games. Wagering might augment that sum considerably, particularly in local leagues, where neighborhood or trade pride was at stake. Such loose associations, often organized by local promoters, proved a boon to players, and even professionals from the Cubs and Sox joined the "semipros" on their off days. In 1920 employers reacted by uniting with Bill Veeck, Cubs president, to organize their own league with fifty-four company teams. The league was to serve as a major league farm system, rally workers to the company, and thwart Communism in the ranks of labor. When league commissioners, including Avery Brundage, tried to enforce amateur status, participation dwindled to fourteen teams. The following year the Midwest League organized as an independent association. By 1924 it held sway as the largest in the country and included Paddy Driscoll, who would gain more lasting fame as a professional football star. The best players clearly sought the autonomy and remunerative opportunities of such alternative leagues.[45]

Among the independent teams, competition proved plentiful, and the stakes were high. Mario Bruno, an Italian immigrant who acted as player-manager for the Chicago Heights Athletic Association of the Manufacturers' League, stated that "you couldn't afford to come out and throw your money away, so you went out and got a good team together."[46] The addition of top athletes to one or both rosters sent wagering even higher. Winning players and their supporters often topped their weekly salaries in weekend games, while losers upped the ante for rematches. Even small towns raised $10,000 for football rivalries and offered $500 of it to a player who could insure a win, although the procurement of several players at much lower sums was most common. Commercialized sport thus provided ample opportunities for many to become small-time capitalists.[47]

As companies vied for athletic prestige and publicity, they provided team members with time to practice and play. Lew Menchetti stated that he was employed by International Harvester for forty years, but during his tenure on the company baseball team he practiced mornings and played games in the afternoon. In addition to the release time allowed for sports contests, consistent winners enjoyed lucrative remuneration. The extensive support network of team sponsors, managers, local backers, gamblers, and neighborhood followers minimized the financial risks of such endeavors for individual players.[48]

Chicago's largest employers indulged their employees with extensive recreation programs. Workers found in sport a means to rationalize competition in a manner consistent with their own values. Strikes and government intervention during the war insured at least a subsistence wage for most, but sporting activities provided added psychological and financial benefits for winners. Athletic contests allowed workers to test their rivals and social superiors in the physical arena, where athletic prowess reinforced the physical skills necessary for work and admired by peers. At the South Works steel mills, workers collected money to uniform their team. Forty cars and a truckload of fans, including a band, soon followed the squad. Many more turned out to witness the workers humiliate bosses in the intracompany league.[49]

Competition was a daily reality for workers, whose wages often fell short of their basic needs, and the success of individuals in competitive athletics continued to foster the American dream. Abe Saperstein started as a booking agent for local teams, but his barnstorming tours with the black "Savoy 5" basketball team eventually gained him wealth and an international reputation as owner of the Harlem Globetrotters.

Others, such as Mario Bruno, a colleague of Saperstein's on the Chicago semipro circuit, asserted that his sporting activities expanded his social network and led to other opportunities, including local political offices. John Kikulski, a former president of the Polish Falcons, became the president of a labor union and a candidate for city office until he was assassinated in a labor dispute.[50]

For the most fortunate or highly skilled, sport served as the entré to the middle class. Although denied the extensive remunerative opportunities for men, women also enjoyed limited benefits. The Chicago Bloomer Girls and other women's softball teams drew thousands of fans. Eva Skrzydlewski, a three-sport star for the Western Electric Company, was rewarded with an administrative post after her athletic career. Most, however, found their greatest measure of self-esteem in these leisure activities that provided high visibility, psychic rewards, and peer acknowledgment, if only at the neighborhood level. Such leisure roles, often enhanced by the thrill of gambling, certainly superceded the mundane existence of the working world for the common laborer. Alan Metcalfe, in his study of Canadian and English miners, found gambling and money to be central to working class sporting ventures. For them, money was not to be saved, but spent for immediate fulfillment. Within such a context, the thrill of gambling proved more important than the prize itself.[51]

The Pros

Players on the industrial teams combined their labor and leisure lives, a combination that allowed at least one immigrant's son to learn well the lessons of capitalism. George Halas's parents had migrated to Chicago from Bohemia in the 1860s. His early life revolved around the Pilsen Sokol, but his athletic successes in the parks and at Crane Tech led him into the native sport structure. By sixteen, he had already gleaned the financial benefits of semipro athletic competition. He spent following summers playing for two industrial teams and the semipro Logan Squares. His athletic prowess at the University of Illinois earned him a job offer from the Staley Starch Company in Decatur after a brief stint in professional baseball with the Yankees and another with the Hammond Pros football team. The responsibilities of Halas's new position included performance on the company baseball and football teams. The removal of the Bears to Chicago in 1921 and Halas's consequent rise to millionaire status present a detailed picture of semipro operations and ethnic American hopes.[52]

The Staley team, playing against small-town rivals and in the large Chicago market, turned a profit in 1920. Each player got $1,900 besides his weekly paycheck. When a business recession curtailed the Staley athletic program in 1921, the employer agreed to keep the players on the payroll but allowed Halas to pursue profits in Chicago, where the company would be publicized at Halas's expense. The team was required to retain the Staley name for one year, with a $5,000 advance to Halas. In addition to the advertising, Halas acted as trainer, manager, coach, player, and ticket seller at Cubs Park, then run by Bill Veeck, Sr. With Veeck getting at least 15 percent of the gate and the rights to all concessions, Halas and his partner, Edward "Dutch" Sternaman, were left with the proceeds from program sales and a large debt to Staley. Players received $75-$100 per game, and the team showed a $71.63 loss that year.[53]

The Chicago Bears Football Club incorporated in 1922 with Halas, Sternaman, and Paddy Driscoll as shareholders. The choice of the word "club" was significant, for teams were not yet considered full-time businesses. Players held a primary job and played football on weekends. The Bears practiced in a vacant lot and vied with at least twenty other semipro games each Sunday for patronage, but they showed a profit of $1,476.92 in their second year. By 1924 the team earned $20,000 in profit, and the addition of "Red" Grange the following year assured the success of professional football. Promoters with small-time roots, such as Halas, who managed to succeed against the odds, sustained the perception of sport as the one true meritocracy for the working class. For most, however, the realities of free market opportunities brought only temporary gains or dismal disappointments.[54]

The roots of the pro game in Chicago lay in the working class. The original Bear fight song was composed in 1922, and the lyrics, with their improper English, suggest that it could have been created by any laborer in any bar on any Saturday night.

From the East and from the West,
They send their very best
To play against the pride of old Chicago.
There is none of them compare with our Chicago Bears.
Through the line they go,
Hold them down Chicago, Hold (sic) them down,
Is the cry of everybody in our town.
Just watch the way they meet and tumble their foe,
Out to win Chicago Bears, they will always go.
Cross that line Chicago, cross that line,
That's the way to play, you're doing fine,
And when the season's o'er and you have to play no more,
Chicago Bears will stand out fore.[55]

Fight songs proclaiming the team's prowess were commonplace among the social-athletic clubs or gangs of the era.

The Wizard Arrows, a North Side prairie league team, also declared their stature and territoriality in verse.

We are the Wizard Arrows and we come from Agassiz
(public school playground).
We play the best of teams that come around.
Pride of the prairie, the Wizard Arrow team,
We are the best team, the best you'll ever see.
Once we get started we will never stop.
Pride of the prairie, the Wizard Arrow team.[56]

To nearby competitors, the claim of a particular territory, such as the playground, evinced communal pride, served as a challenge, and informed other clubs where games or bets might be made. The support systems of the neighborhood teams often included the ward alderman—who secured clubhouses, fields, permits, jobs, and prestige in exchange for political favors at election time—and local businessmen—who might enjoy the patronage of players and their supporters or, at any rate, did not wish to offend the group of young men.

Teams raised additional funds through regular social affairs, such as dances or raffles, similar to the radical labor groups of the past. The majority of such clubs lacked private grounds for contests and simply "passed the hat" among spectators that lined the perimeter of the public fields. The Wizards purposely scheduled teams in affluent areas and used child mascots who worked the crowd with well-rehearsed appeals to increase donations. Lacking the capital resources of Halas and the Bears, who played nearby, the Wizard Arrows enjoyed a long history but never evolved into a professional club.[57]

Chicago's other professional football team, the Cardinals, started in a similar manner. Organized in 1899 by Chris O'Brien, a South Side painting contractor, they earned their name by the color of the hand-me-down jerseys received from the University of Chicago. With a clubhouse on South Racine Avenue, they became known as the Racine Cardinals, or the Morgan Athletic Club. They were only one of many clubs that evolved from semipro units, and won the territorial and franchise rights in the new professional league in a showdown match with the Chicago Tigers, 6-3, on a Paddy Driscoll score. New ownership provided sound financial backing by the late 1920s.[58]

Other local teams were not as well organized or as well endowed with players or financial support. The number of local teams—all of which vied for patrons, gate receipts, and winning wagers—made Chicago a player's marketplace. The city offered sixty baseball leagues, more than forty semipro football teams, with over twenty fully professional football clubs in the Midwest, and a large number of boxing clubs, where fighters could earn money on a nightly basis. The best athletes earned handsome sums by playing baseball in the summer, football in the fall, and indoor baseball in the winter. With the inception of pro basketball in Chicago in the 1920s and additional wrestling, bowling, and billiards matches, sport provided year-round opportunities for profit through one's physical abilities, an alternative to the middle class emphasis on education.[59]

Though George Halas personified the prototypical success story, every ethnic group could point to similar, if less lofty, attainments. *Who's Who in Major League Baseball, 1933* listed at least twenty-seven active Chicagoans. A later source listed 154 major leaguers from the Windy City. Many others played for minor or semipro league teams, with Chicago's own City League as the most visible example. Professional scouts roamed the ball fields looking for talent. Fred Lindstrom, a standout on park and parochial school teams, signed his first of many pro contracts with the Giants in 1921 at the tender age of sixteen. The recruitment of such players, and the allegiance of their followers, brought about a gradual transition in shared loyalty and identity—from that of a particular ethnic or religious group to a larger geographical area, such as a park district, city league, or national professional team. In the process, participants, spectators, and followers moved beyond the restricted boundaries of ethnic neighborhoods to the larger public sphere.[60]

The Resurgence of Boxing

As pro scouts recruited youthful players for the burgeoning semipro and professional circuits in baseball and football, boxing agents and promoters found a wealth of ready volunteers who offered their services in the numerous gyms throughout the city. Although Chicago contributed a fair share of its residents to the ranks of professional boxing in the nineteenth century, the city had never been a mecca of pugilism. As early as 1884 the *Sporting and Theatrical Journal* declared Chicago "the deadest town in the Union for fistic sport."[61] Progressive reformers managed to enact legislation that banned the sport altogether, but athletic clubs managed to circumvent such prohibitions by staging "exhibitions" for "members" who paid their dues at the door. That flimsy subterfuge proved unnecessary as World War I rationalized the need for self-defense training, and the military camps around Chicago became centers of boxing action.[62]

By 1924 even the *Chicago Tribune* openly challenged the boxing ban by staging tournaments, and lawmakers relented by repealing the law in 1926. The widespread interest was apparent a year later when more than 100,000 flocked to Soldier Field to witness the Jack Dempsey-Gene Tunney heavyweight championship bout.[63]

The resurgence of boxing set the stage for greater inclusion of blacks and working class ethnic groups within the sporting mainstream. As baseball and football strove for middle class standards of propriety and recruited their talent more heavily from college ranks, boxing remained the sport of the downtrodden with no pretensions of respectability. Gangsters had already encroached upon the administration of the fight game by the 1920s, thus insuring an illegitimate character. In conjunction with such illicit enterprises, even the more pristine promotions—the *Tribune*-sponsored Golden Gloves, the Knights of Columbus, and Catholic Youth Organization tournaments—relied on and showcased ethnic boxers from the city's blighted areas. Rooted in urban ghettoes, boxing allowed working class youths to reinforce their own valued toughness and gain a measure of esteem, or at least spending money, in the established system of commercialized sport.[64]

Ethnic and working class athletes thus found in sport the means to accommodate with the commercialized leisure forms. Such athletes, however, chose only those sport forms, such as combative or team sports, that agreed with preexisting cultural values. Inner city youth did not adopt middle class individual sports such as tennis or golf. The few that did were characterized as effeminate or snobbish. Even George Lott, who gained international stature as a tennis star, lost the favor of his boyhood peers. Despite the intentions of middle class administrators to enforce amateurism, the sporting practices of the working class enabled them to maintain and reinforce their traditional values. Year-round competition in team sports at the scholastic, semipro, and professional levels bolstered communal solidarity even as it drew segregated groups into the growing athletic network. Both team sports and boxing promoted ethnic pride and offered regular opportunities for gambling. The widespread opportunities for profit available to athletes and their neighborhood supporters throughout periods of financial hardship and the boom times of the 1920s gave youth little cause to question the capitalist system, as their parents had. Whereas the Turners and Sokols led the radical opposition in the nineteenth century, interscholastic athletics, parks, and industrial recreation programs brought the leisure practices of succeeding generations ever

closer to the mainstream. While the working class still har-
bored no love for the rich, they tended to blame problems on
individual employers or politicians, as their sporting experiences maintained hopes in the rhetoric of democracy, equality,
and opportunity.[65]
Racial, ethnic, class, and religious lines remained clearly
visible in Chicago and America following World War I, but the
perceived promise of sport provided hope for many. Labor
disputes continued, but the radical threat paled in comparison
to the armed conflict of Haymarket and Pullman. As alternative groups expanded their sporting practices and immigrant
children adopted American sport forms, they increasingly
accepted native and middle class organizations and their
regulatory agencies, but they did not desert cultural, class, or
religious values in the transition. The process of accommodation moved all participants toward a mass culture that encom-
passed pluralistic meanings and values.[66]

Notes

1. Dawley, *Struggles for Justice,* 172-7, 184-9, 254-68; Hoare and
Smith, *Selections from the Prison Notebooks,* 210, 265, 327; Kammen,
Mystic Chords of Memory, 230-1; Greene, *For God and Country,* 18,
21; Frank Renkiewicz, ed., *Poles in America* (Dobbs Ferry, NY:
Oceana Pub., 1973), 21; Joseph Szeplacki, *Hungarians in America*
(Dobbs Ferry, NY: Oceana Pub., 1975), 27; Steven Bela Vardy, *The
Hungarian-Americans* (Boston: Twayne Pub., 1985), 25-6, 91; Hum-
bert S. Nelli, *From Immigrant to Ethnic: The Italian Americans* (New
York: Oxford University Press, 1983), 46, 124.
Charles Shanabruch, "The Catholic Church's Role in the Ameri-
canization of Chicago's Immigrants, 1833-1928," Ph.D. Dissertation,
University of Chicago, 1975, 505.

2. Hobsbawm, *The Age of Empire,* 220-4, 236-7; Catherine Sardo
Weidner, "Building a Better Life," *Chicago History,* 18:4 (Winter
1989-90): 4-25; Lizabeth Cohen, "Encountering Mass Culture at the
Grassroots: The Experience of Chicago Workers in the 1920s," *Ameri-
can Quarterly,* 41:1 (March 1989): 6-33; Lizabeth Cohen, *Making a
New Deal: Industrial Workers in Chicago, 1919-1939* (New York:
Cambridge University Press, 1990), 104-06, 123-5, 146-7; Rosen-
zweig, *Eight Hours for What We Will,* 191-215; Victor Greene, "Old

Time Folk Dancing and Music among the Second Generation, 1920-1950," in Kivisto and Blank, eds., *American Immigrants,* 142-63. See Benjamin G. Rader, "Compensatory Sport Heroes: Ruth, Grange, and Dempsey," *Journal of Popular Culture,* 16:4 (Spring 1983): 11-22. For examples of biographies that treat ethnic and racial sports heroes, see Isenberg, *John L. Sullivan;* Roberts, *Papa Jack;* and John M. Carroll, *Fritz Pollard: Pioneer in Racial Advancement.*

3. Allswang, *A House for All Peoples,* 23, 33; *Chicago Tribune,* July 5-31, 1918; *Chicago Evening American,* July 9, 1918, 2; *Chicago American,* July 12, 1918, 1; July 13, 1918, 1; July 15, 1918, 3.

On the colorful but corrupt Thompson, see Thomas M. Coffey, *The Long Thirst: Prohibition in America, 1920-1933* (New York: W. W. Norton, 1975), 6, 33, 50-1, 87, 149, 203, 285.

On anti-German nativism, see Howard B. Furer, *The Germans in America, 1607-1970* (Dobbs Ferry, NY: Oceana Pub., 1973), 133; and Roderick Nash, *The Nervous Generation: American Thought, 1917-1930* (Chicago: Rand McNally, 1970), 142, who asserts that 20,000 of the arrested were detained. *Chicago American,* July 15, 1918, 3, estimated 150,000 apprehensions. Anti-German sentiment was prevalent among other ethnic groups as well. See *Denni Hlasatel,* June 24, 1915; June 21, 1915; Mar. 2, 1917; Apr. 20, 1918 (Works Progress Administration, Foreign Language Press Survey, 1942, hereafter abbreviated as FLPS); *Diamond Jubilee Book of St. Aloysius, 1884-1959* (Chicago: 1959), 41, on the transition to English language usage during World War I.

4. Davis, *Spearheads for Reform,* 221; Dawley, *Struggles for Justice,* 277-82.

John Higham, *Send These to Me,* 52; Rev. Anthony F. Lo Gatto, *The Italians in America, 1492-1972* (Dobbs Ferry, NY: Oceana Pub., 1972), 14-15; Renkiewicz, *The Poles in America,* 22; *Chicago Tribune,* July 29, 1918, 7.

5. Wilma J. Pesavento, "The Historical Study of the Development of Physical Education in the Chicago Public Schools"; Marie Broderick, "The Chicago Public Schools and World War I," M.Ed. Thesis, Chicago Teachers College, 1956, 20-2, 32-40, 129-30.

City of Chicago, *Proceedings of the Board of Education, May 27, 1919 - July 2, 1920* (Chicago: Board of Education, 1920), 769, 774, 1051, 1673, 1775.

6. E. C. Delaporte, "Administration and Control of Athletics in Public Schools," *American Physical Education Review* (March 1922), 100-02.

7. Chicago Public School Athletic League files, 1920; *Chicago Tribune,* July 22, 1920, 10; Sept. 5, 1920, part 2: 2.

8. Rotary International, International Boys Week program, 1923, 43; Chicago Board of Education Archives, Boys' Week file, 1923-1931; *Chicago American,* Sept. 22, 1925, 11.

9. *Chicago Tribune,* July 5, 1918, 4; July 31, 1918, 3; "The Use of Polish in the Church," *Zgoda,* Dec. 20, 1900, in Feldstein and Costello, eds., *The Ordeal of Assimilation,* 136-8; Slayton, *Back of the Yards,* 22-3, 50-1, 126, 131-3; Hogan, *Class and Reform,* 125-7; Carbaugh, ed., *Human Welfare Work in Chicago,* 181. The public school system enrolled 45,440 students in its 24 high schools, and 406,440 in the 268 elementary schools in 1920.

10. Edward R. Kantowicz, "Cardinal Mundelein of Chicago and the Shaping of Twentieth Century American Catholicism," *The Journal of American History,* 68:1 (June 1981): 52-68; Slayton, *Back of the Yards,* 135-6, 138. Father Louis Grudzinski, a member of Mundelein's board of consultants, led a protest of sixty-eight clerics unhappy with the changes. Grudzinski, replaced in 1921, was awarded a Polish Commander's Cross by the Polish government, which was delivered by world-renowned pianist Ignace Paderewski.

11. Kantowicz, 64; Shanabruch, "The Catholic Church's Role," 500; *Chicago Tribune,* July 8, 1918, 7.

12. Duis, *The Saloon,* 296-9. Of the 14,000 bartenders in the city, 5,000 lacked American citizenship, raising questions of loyalty. Timberlake, *Prohibition and the Progressive Movement,* 179.

Thomas M. Coffey, *The Long Thirst: Prohibition in America, 1920-1933* (New York: W. W. Norton, 1975), 52; Allswang, *A House for All Peoples,* 119-20, 129; Hogan, *Class and Reform,* 76-7.

13. Duis, *The Saloon,* 25, 72, 76, 118, 297-8.

14. *New World,* Apr. 6, 1920, 6.

15. Ibid., May 20, 1921, 10; Feb. 16, 1923, 5; *Chicago American,* Sept. 10, 1925, 22.

16. *Chicago American,* Sept. 11, 1925, 23; Sept. 19, 1925, 21; Slayton, *Back of the Yards,* 98; *Diamond Jubilee Book of St. Aloysius,* 99, 101; *CYO* (Chicago: Catholic Youth Organization, n.d.), 5; A. F. Hammesfahr, "Cook County Amateur Athletic Federation Championships," in *Spalding's Official Basketball Guide, 1922-23,* 191-6, lists more than 100 church teams.

Rev. Florian Girometta, *St. Anthony of Padua Italian National Parish Diamond Jubilee Book, 1903-1978* (Chicago: 1978), 16-17,

states that Holy Name Society meetings continued to be conducted in Italian until 1935.
On the history and decline of a Turner group, see "The Aurora Turnverein," *Der Westen: Frauen-Zeitung,* Nov. 15, Nov. 22, 1896, in Keil and Jentz, *German Workers in Chicago,* 160-69. See Robert J. Previts and John Grabowski, "Sandlot Baseball in Cleveland, Ohio, 1919-1929," presented at Baseball in American Culture Conference, Cooperstown, NY, June 6-8, 1990, on inclusion of Catholic teams in that city.

17. See Commission on the Review of the National Policy toward Gambling, Appendix I, 34-5, 44-5, 102-43, 373; and Mark Haller, "Organized Crime in Urban Society: Chicago in the Twentieth Century," *Journal of Social History,* 5 (Winter 1971-72): 210-34, for ethnic control and networking in Chicago; and Ruck, *Sandlot Seasons,* on black racketeers and sport in Pittsburgh.

18. American Bowling Congress, *The First Fifty Years,* 112; Hemmer and Kenna, eds., *Western Bowlers' Journal,* 76. Examples of baseball betting, already endemic, can be found in *Chicago Tribune,* July 4, 1890, 2; and Sept. 1, 1890, 3, 6.

19. Cited in Richard Crepeau, *Baseball: America's Diamond Mind* (Orlando: University Presses of Florida, 1980), 7-8. See *Boston American,* Oct. 4, 1919, 1; and *Chicago Tribune,* Sept. 24, 1920, 1, on baseball betting among the wealthy.

20. *Annual Report of the South Park Commissioners, 1921-1922* (Chicago, n.p., 1922), 74.

21. Ibid., 74-5.

22. The exclusivity of the elite athletic clubs can be ascertained by club publications. William A. Cameron, president of the Chicago Athletic Association, maintained in the *Annual Report, 1908,* 6, that the club already had a waiting list of 517 at that time. His successor, Everett C. Brown, stated in the *1910 Report,* 7, that the waiting list had reached 1,200 and urged fearlessness in rejecting undesirable applicants. By 1922 the club had decided that the judges of the U.S. District Court in northern Illinois were among the desirables and awarded them honorary memberships; from the *1922 Annual Report,* 15.
The Midwest Review (July 1924), 16, the official publication of the Midwest Athletic Club, stated in its bylaws that all athletic memberships were recruited.
New World, Feb. 16, 1923, 5.

23. Bertha Severin Papers, CHS, letter of Aug. 2, 1923; Illinois Women's Athletic Club, *Woman Athletic,* 12:3 (March 1927), 28 (quote); 4:15 (Apr. 1930), 10. Scott Johnson, "Not Altogether Lady-like: The Premature Demise of Girls' Interscholastic Basketball in Illinois," presented at North American Society for Sport History Convention, Chicago, May 26, 1991.

24. *New York Times,* Mar. 9, 1924, Sec. 9: 2, cited in Evans, "Status of American Women in Sport," 151.

25. *Chicago American,* Sept. 10, 1925, 25; Mar. 1, 1929, 53; Mar. 2, 1929, 1, 13-16; Mar. 4, 1929, 15; Mar. 5, 1929, 21; June 28, 1930, 17; July 8, 1931, 18-19; July 10, 1931, 36; July 18, 1931, 5; *Chicago Tribune,* July 4, 1930, 15; July 5, 1930, 15.

26. On Rogers, see Paula Welch, "'32 Track and Field's Annette Rogers," *The Olympian,* 10 (February 1984): 12-14; and *Chicago American,* June 26, 1930, 18; *Chicago Evening American,* July 3, 1930, 10; July 5, 1930, 13-14, states that five of the nine members of the Illinois Women's A.C. National Championship team were still students.

27. *Chicago Tribune,* May 18, 1911, 11; Don Dawson, "Social Class in Leisure: Reproduction and Resistance," *Journal of Leisure Science,* 10:3 (1988): 193-202. On the history of commercialization and professionalism in interscholastic athletics, see Smith, "The Historic Amateur-Professional Dilemma," David L. Westby and Alan Sack, "The Commercialization and Functional Rationalization of College Football," *Journal of Higher Education,* 47 (Nov.-Dec. 1976): 625-47; Roberta Park, "From Football to Rugby—and Back, 1906-1919," *Journal of Sport History,* 11 (Winter 1984): 5-40; Mirel, "From Student Control to Institutional Control of High School Athletics"; J. Hammond Moore, "Football's Ugly Decades, 1893-1913," *Smithsonian Journal of History,* 11 (Fall 1967): 49-68; Hal Lawson and Alan Ingham, "Conflicting Ideologies Concerning the University and Intercollegiate Athletics," *Journal of Sport History,* 7 (Winter 1980): 29-40.

28. *Chicago Tribune,* May 18, 1911, 11; Dec. 17, 1930, 23; *Chicago American,* Nov. 9, 1935, 17; Nov. 12, 1936, 23-4. Chet Grant, *Before Rockne at Notre Dame* (Notre Dame, IN: Dujarie Press, 1968), 38; Patrick Chelland, *One for the Gipper,* 45, 104, 106, 125-6, 142-3, 163, 166. Emil Klosinski, "When Notre Dame Won the Rockford City Championship," *Coffin Corner,* 11-12 (Nov.-Dec., 1985): 3-5, states that Gipp and five other Notre Dame players earned $400 each for one game in 1919. Curly Lambeau founded the Packers after he and

George Trafton were expelled from school for such practices. Numerous accounts indict Rockne as a co-participant in the pro games. David L. Porter, *Biographical Dictionary of American Sports: Football* (Westport, CT: Greenwood Press, 1987), 13-14, 152, 211-12, 504-07, 601-02; ibid., *Biographical Dictionary of American Sports: Baseball* (Westport, CT: Greenwood Press, 1987), 109, 310-11, 570-1; Ruck, *Sandlot Seasons,* 27, 29-30, 39, 41, 118; Hemmer and Kenna, *Western Bowlers' Journal.*

29. Letter of Harry Keeler, Lindblom High School principal, to E. C. Delaporte, Nov. 29, 1923; Al F. Gorman, city clerk, Resolution of the City Council, Jan. 16, 1926; Report of the Committee on Relation of Professional Athletics as it Concerns High School Athletics, Coaches, and Officials, Jan. 20, 1926 in the football file, 1924-1930 of the PSAL Archives; Bob Carroll, "Bulldogs on Sunday," *Coffin Corner,* 11:1 (Winter 1989): 56-7. Paddy Driscoll, star of the Chicago Cardinals, was among the professionals who taught, coached, and refereed at the high schools.

30. *Chicago American,* Nov. 9, 1935, 17. *Chicago Tribune,* July 30, 1918, 11, lists at least forty-six semipro baseball teams in the city. Emil Klosinski, *Pro Football in the Days of Rockne* (New York: Carlton Press, 1970), 49, 56, 64, 73, 76, 91, 111, mentions more than fifty Chicago area semipro teams in the World War I era. The National Football League also fielded more than twenty teams in its early years, eighteen of them from the Midwest; in Carroll, *Bulldogs on Sunday,* 46, 64-5.

31. PSAL Archives, *Chicago Tribune,* July 3, 1918, 11; *Chicago American,* Nov. 17, 1936, 23; Nov. 18, 1936, 29.

32. *Chicago Tribune,* Sept. 5, 1920, part 2, 4; H. R. Crook, Report of 1926 Football Season, Dec. 8, 1926; Chicago PSAL Football, Suggested Schedule Plan, May 11, 1928, 1; 3rd Meeting of Executive Committee, City Championship Football Game, Nov. 22, 1928; PSAL 1931 Football Schedule.

33. Report of the Basketball Committee to the Board of Control; Chicago PSAL Basketball Regulations, VII. 9:4.

34. Schaper, "Industrial Recreation for Women," 103-13. Women's earlier sporting movements often emanated from the ethnic fraternal orders or feminist issues. Catholic priests incorporated such efforts within parish organizations to reasssert their patriarchy and redirect the women's efforts toward religious perspectives. See Gerald R. Gems, "Sport and the Americanization of Ethnic Women," in George Eisen and David Wiggins, eds., *Ethnicity and Sport in North*

American History and Culture (Westport, CT: Praeger, 1995), 177-200, for a fuller treatment of the subject.

A survey of Chicago high school yearbooks during the interwar years suggests that the play-day concept had only limited success, as not all schools adhered to the remonstrations of the physical educators.

35. *Hawthorne Microphone,* Dec. 31, 1928, 3; *Chicago American,* Mar. 4, 1929, 17; Mar. 17, 1931, 23; July 6, 1931, 12; *Chicago Tribune,* Sept. 14, 1930, part 2: 4; July 5, 1931, part 2: 4.

36. *Chicago Tribune,* Mar. 25, 1900, 20, on girls' high school basketball. Seymour, *Baseball, The People's Game,* 479, 496-8. Women's International Bowling Congress, *WIBC History: A Story of 50 Years of Progress, 1916-17 - 1966-67* (WIBC: 1967), 4, 9, 11-12; Bernice Amanda Miller,"Growing Need for Physical Recreation Among Employed Women," *Journal of Health and Physical Education,* 1:10 (December 1930): 3-8, 43-5. Chicago Tribune, *Sports Almanac,* 225; Evans, "The Status of American Women in Sport, 1912-1932," 118-19; *Chicago American,* Mar. 1, 1929, 49; Mar. 2, 1929, 1, 13, 16; Mar. 5, 1929, 20-1; June 28, 1930, 17; July 30, 1931, 11; Apr. 4, 1932, 47; *Chicago Tribune,* July 4, 1930, 15; July 5, 1930, 15; Sept. 3, 1930, 17; Sept. 14, 1930, part 2, 4, on track.

37. A census analysis of early industrial team rosters (1890, 1900) confirmed the implications of the secondary sources that teams used nonemployees in important games. For city leagues, see *Chicago Tribune,* July 9, 1900, 8; Aug. 9, 1900, 8; Apr. 2, 1910, 11; Apr. 4, 1910, 10; July 3, 1910, part 3, 4; Sept. 4, 1910, part 3, 2; July 4, 1920, part 2, 2; Sept. 5, 1920, part 2, 2; July 4, 1930, 16; July 13, 1930, part 2, 6.

38. CNHC, Box CRCC, file 4/14. See Seymour, *Baseball: The People's Game,* 258-75, on the development of semipro baseball teams; and Robert W. Peterson, *Cages to Jump Shots: Pro Basketball's Early Years* (New York: Oxford University Press, 1990), 6-11, 32-9, 45-7, 64-8, on basketball. See *Chicago Tribune,* July 6, 1918, 9, for a brief team history, starting in 1887. Previts and Grabowsky, "Sandlot Baseball in Cleveland," 1, state that the 1915 championship game drew 100,000 fans.

39. Seymour, *Baseball: The People's Game,* 222, 240, 496-7; *Chicago Tribune,* Sept. 9, 1900, 19; *South Works Review,* May-June, 1919, 18-19; Jan. 1921, 28.

40. Seymour, *Baseball: The People's Game,* 267-70; Donald Gropman, *Say It Ain't So, Joe!* (New York: Lynx Books, 1988), 11-32,

214-16; John Holway, *Blackball Stars* (Westport, CT: Meckler Books, 1988), 8-33; Ruck, *Sandlot Seasons*, 41, 118. Herbert N. Ribalow, *The Jew in American Sports* (New York: Bloch Pub., 1948), 17; *Chicago Defender,* Jan. 22, 1910, 1; Feb. 5, 1910, 1; Mar. 12, 1910, 1.

41. The *Chicago Tribune,* Sept. 9, 1900, 19; Oct. 14, 1918; Ribalow, *The Jew in American Sports*, 13, 17; Emil Klosinski, *Pro Football in the Days of Rockne,* 11, 23; Schaper, "Industrial Recreation for Women," 107, alludes to a gambling problem.
Lutheran Baseball League of Cook County, 1917, in Box RLVCC, file 11/7, NHC, in the Sulzer Library, Special Collections.

42. *New World,* Apr. 16, 1920, 6, lists forty Catholic stars on at least ten teams. Seymour, *Baseball: The People's Game,* 179, 213-57; Gropman, *Say It Ain't So, Joe!,* 19, 24, 27; Ruck, *Sandlot Seasons,* 29-30. *Chicago Commerce,* Feb. 7, 1920, 59, acknowledges the "well-known fact" of using athletes in such a manner.

43. Penn manuscript, CNHC, CCC, Box CRCC, file 4/31; and *South End Reporter,* April 23, 1915; April 16, 1931 (clippings); *The Calumet Index,* April 16, 1956; *South End Reporter,* April 23, 1925, 3; *Chicago Tribune,* July 29, 1918, 13.

44. Donn Rogosin, *Invisible Men: Life in Baseball's Negro Leagues* (New York: Atheneum, 1983), 119, 122; John Holway, *Blackball Stars,* 26, 36, 57, 262; Seymour, *Baseball: The People's Game,* 270; Peterson, *Cages to Jump Shots,* 54-5, 64-8, 75-6. See Richard Pagano, "Robert 'Tiny' Maxwell," *College Football Historical Society,* 1:4 (May 1988): 1-3, for the itinerant career of one Chicago athlete leading to pro football.

45. Bureau of Labor Statistics, *Bulletin No. 458,* "Health and Recreational Activities in Industrial Establishments, 1926" (February 1928), 46. Seymour, *Baseball: The People's Game,* 225, claims that sixty leagues operated in Chicago. See *Chicago Sun-Times,* May 14, 1989, 14, on the banning of Dickie Kerr.
On industrial league teams, see CNHC, CCC, Box ACC, file 3/13; Box CRCC; *Chicago Herald,* Apr. 16, 1917, 15; *Chicago Commerce,* Jan. 31, 1920, 9; Feb. 7, 1920, 32; May 8, 1920, 11; May 3, 1924, 22; *South Works Review,* May-June 1919, 19; Jan. 1921, 28; *Chicago Tribune,* July 30, 1918, 11; Apr. 25, 1920, part 2, 3; July 4, 1920, part 2, 2; Sept. 5, 1920, part 2, 2; Sept. 15, 1920, 19; July 4, 1930, 16; July 13, 1930, 2, 6; Sept. 1, 1930, 20; Box WGP, file 5/13; the *Midwest Review* (July, 1924), 6, on the Midwest League and Driscoll.
See Robert J. Previts and John Grabowski, "Sandlot Baseball in Cleveland," on similar developments, including a national industrial team tournament.

46. Bruno Interview, Italians in Chicago, CHS, Box 3: 47.

47. Ibid.; Carroll, *Fritz Pollard,* 132, 143; Emil Klosinski, "When Notre Dame Won the Rockford City Championship," *Coffin Corner,* 11-12 (Nov.-Dec. 1985): 3-5.

48. *Chicago Sun Times,* Sept. 14, 1988, 15; Seymour, *Baseball: The People's Game,* 218, 223-4, 228-9, 242-6, 252; Rob Ruck, *Sandlot Seasons* for similar developments in Pittsburgh.

49. *South Works Review,* July, 1916, 12; August 1916, 10; May-June 1919, 18-19.

50. Bruno Interview, Italians in Chicago, 44-5, 50, 55; Barrett, *Work and Community,* 196, 229; Kaplan, *Leisure in America,* 108; Peterson, *Cages to Jump Shots,* 105-07; Pacyga, *Polish Immigrants and Industrial Chicago,* 184-5, 188, 218, 240-7.

51. Herb Graffis, "Belles of the Ball," in Graffis, ed., *Esquire's First Sports Reader,* 160-67; *The Hawthorne Microphone,* Dec. 31, 1928, 3; *Chicago Tribune,* Sept. 14, 1930, 2, 4; July 5, 1931, 2, 4. See Gems, "Working Class Women and Sport: An Untold Story," on opportunities for women.

Alan Metcalfe, "Leisure, Sport and Working Class Culture: Some Insights from Montreal and the Northeast Coalfields of England," in Hart Cantelon and Robert Hollands, eds., *Leisure, Sport and Working Class Cultures: Theory and History* (Toronto: Garamond Press, 1988), 65-76. Di Liberto interview, Italians in Chicago, 26, 40, indicates similar conditions in Chicago, including more than $1,000 wagered in a single dice game.

52. George Halas, with Gwen Morgan and Arthur Veysey, *Halas by Halas* (New York: McGraw-Hill, 1970), 25; Richard Whittingham, *The Chicago Bears* (New York: Simon and Schuster, 1986), 16.

John Carroll, *Fritz Pollard* (Urbana, IL: University of Illinois, 1992) presents a portrait of another athlete who used sport as a springboard to achieve success despite social discrimination.

53. Whittingham, *The Chicago Bears,* 19, 21-3; Bob Carroll, ed., "Bulldogs on Sunday," in *Coffin Corner,* 9:1 (Sept. 1987): 25-8.

54. For less successful ventures, see Carroll, *Fritz Pollard,* 132-67; Lance Trusty, "From Prairie Football to the NFL: The Hammond, Indiana Pros, 1917-1926," presentation delivered at North American Society for Sport History Convention, Clemson, SC, May 28, 1989; Bob Braunwart and Bob Carroll, "Ollie's All-Stars," *Coffin Corner,* 6:7 (July 1983): 7-8.

55. Whittingham, *The Chicago Bears,* 12, 27-8, 30-1, 36; *Coffin Corner* (July 1983): 7-8, and (January 1984): 4, detail the origins of pro football in St. Louis and Green Bay, respectively, under similar circumstances.

56. Lyrics supplied by Francis Patrick "Lefty" Dorgan, Gerald J. Gems, and Frank Di Benedetto, former club members.

57. Wizard Arrows information is gleaned from the personal papers of Frank Di Benedetto, club officer, conversations with members, club records, team programs, dance programs, and newspaper accounts. Gerald R. Gems, "The Neighborhood Athletic Club: An Ethnographic Study of a Working-Class Athletic Fraternity in Chicago, 1917-1984," *Colby Quarterly,* 32:1 (Mar. 1996): 36-44, includes the team history.

The Vernon Park Club made $4,000 on a dance that featured a brief appearance by Sophie Tucker; from Di Liberto interview, Italians in Chicago. Thrasher, *The Gang,* 45-8, 316; *Chicago American,* Oct. 9, 1935, 35; Oct. 10, 1935, 20; Nov. 14, 1936, 16; Nov. 23, 1936, 23.

58. Whittingham, *Chicago Bears,* 18-19, 62, 89; Bob Carroll, ed., *Bulldogs on Sunday 1920* (Pro Football Researchers Assn., 1991), 23-4. *The Coffin Corner,* official publication of the Professional Football Researchers Association, provides serial coverage of early games, including the recruitment of Halas, Driscoll, Knute Rockne, and other college stars by semipro teams for important games. The Bears continued to play semipro contingents during the Depression. The 1933 season included a 60-0 rout of the Cicero Boosters and a 55-0 win over the Arizona All-Stars.

Like the neighborhood clubs who solidified their political support within the local arena, the Bears issued season's passes for the 1926 season to William Wrigley and Bill Veeck, Sr., their landlords, A. E. Staley, their original benefactor, the chief of police, the local politician, a traffic cop, and Grover Cleveland Alexander, the colorful star pitcher whose attendance would probably generate newspaper publicity.

59. *Chicago Daily Journal,* Jan. 10, 1925, 14; *Chicago Evening Post,* Jan. 14, 1925, 10; Porter, *Biographical Dictionary: Football,* 424, indicates that Ernie Nevers earned $60,000 in 1926 playing baseball, basketball, and football; while Peterson, *Cages to Jump Shots,* 54-5, states that Joe Lapchick got $7,500 during the 1919 basketball season. Seymour, *Baseball: The People's Game,* 225; Klosinski, *Pro Football in the Days of Rockne;* Carroll, *Bulldogs on Sunday,* 46, 64-5; Interviews with club fighters, Judge Abraham

Lincoln Marovitz, Dec. 10, 1990; Gerald J. Gems, and Frank Di Benedetto; Ross and Abramson, *No Man Stands Alone,* 71-9.

60. Riess, *City Games,* 88, lists Chicago as a major source for professional baseball players up to 1905. Old Timers' Baseball Association of Chicago, dinner program, Feb. 1, 1945 (from the scrapbook of William C. "Billy" Niesen) in the Special Collections of the Sulzer Library, listed 154 Chicagoans as major league players. The *27th Annual Reunion and Dinner Program, 1946,* in Box RLVCC, file 12/14 of the Sulzer Collection, claimed that baseball "is the avenue of escape for thousands of boys born to poverty," and that it "provided common ground for bartenders, bishops, clergy, bosses, bankers, and laborers in a democracy that works." See *Chicago Herald,* Apr. 16, 1917, 15, on the geographical scope of the city league that not only covered the city but reached into Indiana and Wisconsin.

Porter, ed., *Biographical Dictionary of American Sports: Baseball* presents biographical information on numerous Chicago-area players, many of whose athletic careers started on park or industrial semipro teams. See pages 332-3 for the Lindstrom story. Chicago Park District, *Third Annual Report, 1938,* 146, states that nineteen players in that season alone earned professional tryouts.

John R. Kelly, *Leisure Identities and Interactions* (London: George Allen & Unwin, 1983), 109-10. See Reiff, "Manufacturing a Community," on sense of community and empowerment in Pullman; and Joseph R. Healey, "An Exploration of the Relationship between Memory and Sport," *Sociology of Sport Journal,* 8:3 (September 1991): 213-27.

61. *Sporting and Theatrical Journal,* Apr. 26, 1884, 388.

62. *Chicago Record-Herald,* May 22, 1907, 6; *Chicago Tribune,* July 5, 1918, 5, 8; July 25, 1918, 8; Aug. 1, 1918, 12; Aug. 2, 1918, 3,8; Riess, *City Games,* 172-7.

63. Thomas Littlewood, *Arch, a Promoter, Not a Poet: The Story of Arch Ward* (Ames: Iowa State University Press, 1990), 37-9, 43-4; Raymond O'Keefe, Sec. of United Sportsmen's League, to George Getz, local promoter for Tex Rickard, July 28, 1927, at CHS, indicated that 100,000 had petitioned to bring the bout to Chicago.

64. Riess, *City Games,* 109-13, 177-81; ibid., "A Fighting Chance"; ibid., "Professional Sports as an Avenue of Social Mobility in America," in Kyle and Stark, eds., *Essays on Sport History and Sport Mythology,* 83-117; Berkow, *Maxwell Street,* 141-7, 182-6, 336-46; Mark Haller, "Organized Crime in Urban Society"; S. Kirson Weinburg and Henry Arond, "The Occupational Culture of the Boxer," in

Riess, ed., *The American Sporting Experience* (New York: Leisure Press, 1984), 334-47.

Malcolm X, who engaged in a short-lived amateur career during the 1930s, declared that the boxing ring was the only place a black could beat a white without being lynched; from *The Autobiography of Malcolm X* (New York: Ballantine Books, 1992 ed.), 29.

65. Jones, *Sport, Politics, and the Working Class,* 61, 66; James T. Farrell, *My Baseball Diary* (New York: A. S. Barnes, 1957), 16; George Lott, "A Living from Tennis," in Graffis, ed., *Esquire's First Sports Reader,* 71-5; Bob Neville, *Who's Who in Sports* (New York: Modern Sports Pub. Co., 1931), 45.

Frank Stricker, "Affluence for Whom? Another Look at Prosperity and the Working Class in the 1920s," *Labor History,* 24:1 (Winter 1983): 5-33, challenges the period as a boom time for workers.

66. Andrew W. Miracle, "Functions of School Athletics: Boundary Maintenance and System Integration," in Salter, ed., *Play: Anthropological Perspectives,* 176-84, asserts that athletics can be both inclusive and exclusive of participants, giving mixed messages. Steven J. Jackson, "Sport Spectatorship, Meaning, and Identity," presented at the North American Society for the Sociology of Sport Convention, Nov. 9-12, 1988, at Cincinnati, stated that sport is created both for us and by us, with the form and meaning being dependent upon needs and desires, even though others may act as producers.

CHAPTER 6

The Consolidation of the Sporting Culture

Class consciousness seemed less overt in second generation ethnic youth. The earliest immigrants, particularly the Irish and northern Europeans, had integrated more readily with the native-born Americans, and World War I forced further Americanization upon more recalcitrant groups. Southern and eastern Europeans, who followed northern emigres by a generation or more, found a different America. The radical culture had been largely subdued, and capitalism remained firmly entrenched. While the older generation clung to traditional ethnic values and lifestyles, ethnic youth wrestled with the differences in their private and public lives. Public education and commercialized leisure practices allowed for greater inclusion in mainstream society, and the children of immigrants increasingly assumed a hyphenated ethnic-American identity throughout the first three decades of the twentieth century. The process of transition from separate, alternative, and at times antagonistic ethnic cultures to a more homogeneous, stable, and pluralistic American one became quite evident in the sporting practices of the populace. Neighborhoods remained pockets of ethnicity, religious differences persisted, and the working class maintained alternative perspectives, but all became increasingly engaged in a common sporting culture that fostered some common interests and alliances.

Lizabeth Cohen has documented the adherence to ethnicity and labor militancy during the interwar period in Chicago. Her analysis indicates a resistance to cultural homogeneity but fails to account for the role of sport in sustaining working class consciousness during the transition to a more acceptable form of capitalism, particularly among the ethnic offspring. In their domestic lives, ethnic youths continued to speak in European tongues, listen to ethnic music, eat ethnic foods, and participate in ethnic festivals and dances, whether voluntarily or involuntarily, as the autocratic familial structure dictated. Most ethnic youths enjoyed a much wider social sphere as well. The schools insured that they spoke English, and they attended English-language films and popular dance halls where English served as the medium of communication among diverse nationalities. Just as they patronized small neighborhood stores and theaters, they also frequented parks, playgrounds, and ballrooms that presented conflicting values.[1]

These experiences, different from those of their parents, presented the second generation with a muddled perception of ethnicity and class. The armed conflict of the nineteenth century, emanating from clearly defined hostile camps, became a rarity by the 1930s. Arbitration and negotiation replaced gunfire as the labor movement became part of the system rather than opposed to it. Particularly during the Depression, workers "could feel; but they no longer understood" such oppression as clearly as their immigrant forefathers. Class consciousness, grounded in the Marxist doctrines of European ethnics, became diluted by the experience of second generation Americans. Throughout the 1930s and thereafter, increasing unionization continued to threaten management, but no longer threatened the capitalist system.[2]

Sporting practices played an instrumental role in the process, reinforcing both the dominant system and working class culture. Athletic programs and facilities were among the earliest of workers' demands. Employers even initiated such programs with their own intentions of channeling workers' aggressiveness, instilling productive values, and promoting loyalty to the company. As such programs brought workers closer to, and under greater regulation by, the dominant culture; they also allowed the working class to retain a sense of self-esteem, prowess, and identity. Sport extolled physicality, afforded regular opportunities for gambling, and provided an acceptable means of socioeconomic gain for the working class. By the 1920s the ideology of sport as the one true meritocracy in American society permeated the working class perspective. Even Communist organizers for the Congress of Industrial Organizations (CIO) initiated their recruitment efforts with sports talk. When Babe Ruth responded to a query about making more money than the President of the United States, he rationalized that he had a better year. He undoubtedly satisfied both employers, who measured his productivity, and workers, who admired his brawn.[3]

Commercialized sport depended upon mass patronage and the satisfaction of diverse groups. Profit required compromise, and natives soon accepted some ethnic sports, while reformers acquiesced in their failure to eradicate baser activities such as boxing. Working class groups both adopted and adapted the previously middle class pastimes of bowling and softball to meet their own needs. Each of these gained inclusion in the sporting culture, albeit under the regulation of, or even aided by, the dominant group for its own benefit. The Brunswick Sporting Goods Company sponsored a Polish music show on radio, perhaps to attract the large number of Polish bowlers but also because it produced demands for its fledgling records division. More often, ethnic clubs, faced with the loss of youthful members to the athletic programs of the schools, parks, and playgrounds, turned to the wholesale adoption of American sport forms. Religious groups, too, formalized their sporting activities in the Catholic Youth Organization (CYO) and the B'nai B'rith Youth Organization (BBYO) to attract and retain youth while averting the proselytizing influences of the Protestant YMCA. The maintenance of religious separation precluded full cultural unification, but it also reinforced the common bonds of sport. The process of amalgamation resulted in parallel sporting cultures that shared the same forms but held different values and meanings by race, ethnicity, class, gender, and even religion.[4]

The American Media and a Popular Culture

As the ethnic sporting practices waned, the Chicago media played a prominent role in fostering a more homogeneous

"American" sporting culture. By the 1920s both ethnic and native media catered to constitutents' pastimes and promoted sporting interests, especially as a self-serving means to greater financial profit.

Radio proved a wondrous technology that brought entertainment to the home and privatized leisure, while it presented a homogenized culture. Aided by the Federal Radio Act of 1927, native commercial interests quickly incorporated the multitude of early broadcasters into consolidated networks, enhancing power in the hands of a few. While programming catered to a large variety of popular tastes in music and drama, sports broadcasts focused on American games. As immigrant children learned to speak English in the schools and were attracted to competitive athletics in the parks and playgrounds, a more uniform sporting culture and language began to take shape. Despite the reality of unsavory practices, the media extolled the virtues, character-building qualities, and rags-to-riches opportunities available through sport. Middle class listeners requested "educational and uplifting programs," particularly "baseball stories that taught children to play right."[5]

Media coverage played on, and perhaps helped to increase, the appeal of sport. Native sportswriters and broadcasters sensationalized and dramatized events, and sport provided the opportunity for journalists to indulge themselves. The first national broadcast of a football game featured the University of Chicago in a 21-18 loss to Princeton in 1922. Soon, the Notre Dame backfield became the "Four Horsemen" (of the Apocalypse), to be followed by Red Grange as the "Galloping Ghost." Even the Fordham linemen were no longer mere mortals; they became the "Seven Blocks of Granite." Interviews with prominent sport personalities created an even more intimate relationship between fans and their heroes. There was money to be made by marketing sports, and both broadcasters and their commercial sponsors quickly grasped the opportunities for promoting their products and American patriotism. The Cubs began playing "The Star Spangled Banner" at the 1918 World Series, thirteen years before its adoption as the national anthem. The 1921 Dempsey-Carpentier fight featured nationalistic overtones, while the World Series,

Indy 500, Kentucky Derby, and Rose Bowl soon linked listeners to American sporting traditions. Seven different radio stations broadcast Cub games simultaneously in the 1920s, and attendance still increased by 119 percent.[6] As Cohen notes, many ethnics preferred traditional programs, but their children often turned to the mainstream. In the case of sports programming, neither had much choice as baseball, football, and boxing filled the airwaves. Ethnic papers, being commercial enterprises, took note. The *Bohemian Review* and the Italian *Vita Nuova* began publication in English, and the Polish press reported sports coverage in English "in deference to youth."[7] By 1926 the Polish paper *Dziennik Zjednoczenia* included a sports page, followed by a German and English version of *Arbieter-Sport in America*. Polish boys and girls formed an athletic association at Holy Trinity High School to play American sports. By the end of the decade an Italian team had won the Boys' Club baseball championship, and Poles created a Commission of Sports and Youth to finance athletic teams. Despite such accommodations, the use of English and the esoteric language and lure of sport further separated ethnic youth from their parents.[8]

In the 1920s media exposure created instant national and local heroes, as the names of Ruth, Grange, and Dempsey joined the American hagiography alongside those of Washington and Lincoln. By the 1930s even previously excluded blacks enjoyed the inclusion of Jesse Owens and Joe Louis in the cast. Despite Ruth's working class roots and a background fixed firmly in the street culture, the middle class media lionized his prodigious physical feats rather than his gluttonous appetite, womanizing, and boorish manners. The children of the immigrants readily identified with these new heroes, as a survey of Polish youth discovered. More than 80 percent could identify Ruth, while only 53 percent knew Joseph Pilsudski, the Polish president. Jewish youth, too, idolized athletes, much to the consternation of their parents, who considered a ballplayer to be "king of the loafers."[9] By 1925 the *Jewish Daily Bulletin* even proclaimed lightweight champ Benny Leonard greater than Einstein, for although millions knew both, only a few could understand the latter.[10]

Newspapers also created an interest in sport by playing upon ethnic and religious loyalties. For the 1930 fight between Primo Carnera and Jack Gross, the *Tribune* overstated the case, advising that "Every man, woman, or child with a drop of Italian blood in their veins should see the Greatest Italian Fighter of all times....Jack Gross is the best Jewish fighter in the world...."[11] Chicagoans had an abundance of local ethnic talent as well. Such stars as Johnny Weismuller, Knute Rockne, and Phil Cavaretta earned a national reputation, but almost every neighborhood and ethnic group claimed its share of professional athletes and a newfound stake in American culture.[12]

Both boys and girls attributed their popularity and acceptance in the public schools to their athletic abilities. High school stars often received more media hype than the professional players. Austin's Bill De Correvont drew newspaper photographers, movie makers, and spectators to practice sessions as his name was splashed across the sports pages in the late 1930s. When Mt. Carmel, an Irish Catholic high school, faced Harrison Tech, with its multi-ethnic squad, for the 1931 city football championship, the *Tribune* touted the battle as the Irish against the world. For the American-born children of the immigrants, identification with ethnic athletic heroes or attainment of such status served an essential function. It allowed youth to retain a sense of ethnicity and permitted a level of aspiration within the American system acceptable to peers. Identification with heroes such as hard-drinking local favorites Grover Cleveland Alexander and Hack Wilson or Ruth, who adhered to the working class lifestyle despite a salary that surpassed that of the United States President, helped to minimize any sense of class consciousness. By 1936 Catholics joined with the public school bands, a thousand strong, to initiate the championship football game with "The Star Spangled Banner," and the professional Chicago Cardinals team supplied the halftime entertainment, as sport provided the venue for symbolic unity.[13]

Newspapers also sponsored, promoted, and created local sporting spectacles to attract readers. Despite objections from high school administrators, the *Chicago Tribune* continued to sponsor intercity athletic competition for high school athletes.

Within the city and outside the jurisdiction of school authorities, the newspapers also publicized their own competitions held in the city's parks.

Newspapers sponsored a wide variety of tournaments, drawing an international field to the competitions. The *Tribune*'s Silver Skates Derby, the *Daily News*'s Ice Skating Mardi Gras, and the Chicago *American*'s sponsorship of the Central AAU Track and Field Championships were only a few of the major events held in Chicago. Through the efforts of its sportswriter, Arch Ward, the *Chicago Tribune* initiated the baseball All-Star game at Comiskey Park in 1933 and the College All-Star Football Classic against the Bears in Soldier Field in 1934. The same site had been used to stage the 1927 Dempsey-Tunney fight, which drew 128,000 fans and $2.6 million for its promoters.[14]

While newspapers attracted followers with their own promotions, they also capitalized on interscholastic championships, which numbered fourteen by 1930. Throughout the year, the news media and the schools preached that athletics served to foster school spirit and communal pride. For second generation ethnics, who lacked the European backgrounds of their parents, such associational ties may have provided an identity that replaced an earlier sense of nationalism, and sport offered opportunities not otherwise available to them. Apart from the hero status that individual performances might bring, all team members shared in the glory of victory. Winning teams traveled to intercity matches, attracting large gates and reaping big profits for the hosts. Such promotions continued to perpetrate the perception of sport as a democratizing agent among the less fortunate.[15]

Publicity for intercity matches raised such sporting events to the level of the spectacular as high school teams received headlines and extensive coverage. It also sold newspapers at a time when they were desperately competing with radio stations and each other for advertising dollars. From the early 1920s onward, the daily papers sponsored numerous promotional events to attract readers by catering to particular ethnic and class interests. For example, the *Tribune* ranked only third among the eight daily Chicago papers in 1911. In the early 1920s the *Tribune* purchased radio time to broadcast sporting events, and soon bought its own station, WGN, along with several smaller ones. By 1925 it had a Sunday circulation of over 1 million, becoming the most profitable, and perhaps most powerful, paper in the country. Sports dominated the *Tribune*'s airwaves, and not even the Depression slowed the Golden Gloves or the All-Star extravaganzas. The *Tribune*'s sporting ventures proved so successful that it set up a charitable foundation with the profits in 1936.[16]

Sport promotions that proved a boon to the *Tribune* played havoc with the regulations of the Public Schools Athletic League. Spurred by civic boosters and powerful agencies like the media, school administrators felt somewhat helpless in their attempts to regulate, or at least profit from, such affairs. Despite the costs, schools felt compelled to meet the challenges of urban rivals and even small towns in pursuit of athletic glory. E. C. Delaporte, director of the program, resigned in 1929. August Pritzlaff replaced Delaporte, but the abuses continued. Athletes continued to play for outside teams, and the quest for profits led teams to schedule an excessive number of games. During the 1930-31 basketball season, Harrison High played thirty-nine games, while five other schools exceeded thirty contests, and another thirteen teams played more than twenty games. Pritzlaff imposed a twenty-game limit for the next season.[17]

Pritzlaff faced similar problems in baseball. Teams played three games per week, left school early for extra batting practice, and used nonuniformed players in games. Each team continued to use its star pitcher in each game, despite the arm injuries incurred, and Edward Ruzicka, chairman of the baseball committee, finally urged a limit on games or innings pitched.[18]

In football, the street culture persisted in game conduct. A 1934 game between Calumet and Hyde Park high schools resulted in a fight. Neighborhood toughs swarmed the field at the half and then besieged the Hyde Parkers in their dressing room. The police finally arrived to extract the beleaguered team.[19]

Amid such conditions and practices, the league administrators encouraged soccer as a substitute for football. The sport was still popular among ethnic adults, but their offspring

favored American football. By 1936 only two city schools
fielded soccer teams, and principals favored the retention of
football because it generated much more revenue.[20]

More than a dozen intercity football games marked the
1931 and 1932 interscholastic schedules, and eight schools
requested permission to play out-of-town games on Thanks-
giving Day of 1932. In 1940, Fenger High School, the city
champ, played thirteen football games (five more than the
colleges of the Big Ten), including three in a ten-day span.[21]

In the quest for glory and profit, both administrators and
opponents accused coaches of cheating to insure victories. At
Lane Tech, the coach rigged a phone to the school's rooftop in
order to spy on his opponents during contests. Civic pride, too,
took precedence over academics. In 1938 Mayor Ed Kelly
intervened to allow the Fenger team and its coaches to miss
school without penalty for a road trip. By 1940 even the
newspapers that had contributed to the commercialism of
high school sports railed against its abuses.[22]

If the newspaper publishers had their own way with the
schools, they courted others more assiduously. In a largely
Catholic city, papers needed to cultivate and hold the allegiance of the predominant religious group. The *Tribune* did so
in the person of its Irish-Catholic sportswriter, Arch Ward,
who got his start as Rockne's press agent at Notre Dame. As
boxing promoters, both Ward and the *Tribune* successfully
challenged the state ban on boxing in 1924. By 1928 the
Chicago Tribune initiated the Golden Gloves boxing tournaments that met with widespread success. Ward became sports
editor in 1930, and his contacts with the Catholic hierarchy
engendered cooperative efforts and a steady supply of fighters
from the Catholic parishes. National broadcasts and international boxing ventures even brought stardom to unknown
street kids and school dropouts. The *Chicago Recreation Survey* noted in 1937 that "due to such promotional activities, the
number of boys who had taken up boxing has shown a tremendous increase in the last decade."[23]

The success of such cooperative sporting ventures proved
critical to the accommodation of Catholics within the mainstream culture. Ethnic Catholics adopted purely American
sport forms, such as softball, as early as the 1890s, but often

practiced such pastimes within their own circles. The Americanization programs of Cardinal Mundelein met with disdain in the nationalistic parishes, but sports provided such groups an entré into American society on their own terms. The alliance of the *Tribune* and the Catholic Youth Organization brought previously divergent groups together in a common cause, created favorable publicity for both, and fostered greater acceptance of each other. Sporting relationships created strange bedfellows as the liberal Catholic hierarchy under Mundelein combined with archconservatives at the *Tribune* to lead an ethnic, working class constituency closer to the dominant culture.[24]

Given a free rein by Mundelein, Bishop Bernard J. Sheil centralized the bureaucracy of the CYO but allowed autonomy in program selection at the parish level. An avid sportsman and a major league prospect as a pitcher with the Logan Squares early in the century, Sheil, like the progressives, saw in sport the answer to social problems. He stated his intentions as such:

> We'll knock the hoodlum off his pedestal and we'll put another neighborhood boy in his place. He'll be dressed in C.Y.O. boxing shorts and a pair of leather mitts, and he'll make a new hero. Those kids love to fight. We'll let them fight. We'll find champions right in the neighborhood.[25]

Sheil organized the city amateur boxing tournament in 1931 and soon instituted a comprehensive athletic program for both sexes that surpassed that of the public schools in size and scope. The basketball tournament of 1931 had 415 teams, and the winner, St. Joseph, was sent off to play the New York champion, St. Nicholas of Tolentine. The swim meet for that year was held at the Lake Shore Athletic Club, and the boxing tournament, held at the Chicago Stadium, involved every parish in Cook County as well as the five surrounding counties. It drew 18,000 fans, and winners were guaranteed a trip to New York. The boxing program, in particular, appealed to working class youths. Sheil accepted all races and creeds on the condition that they swore allegiance to God and country. Thousands responded to the provision of free medical care and the chance to win a full suit of clothes, national team trips with all expenses paid, college scholarships, and management of professional boxing careers. Within a few years the boxing program reached international proportions with trips to Panama, Hawaii, and Europe. Three CYO fighters made the 1936 Olympic team, while others went on to pro careers.[26]

By recruiting boxing instructors such as Benny Leonard and featuring Barney Ross, both Jewish lightweight champions, the CYO programs also forged bonds between the Christian and Jewish communities. Under the guidance of Sheil, competitive ventures between CYO and B'nai B'rith teams endured a long and harmonioius relationship.[27]

Through Sheil's efforts and the attraction of sport, Chicago's athletes won local and national acclaim. Catholic organizations sponsored events such as the National Catholic Interscholastic Basketball Tournament held at Loyola University after 1923. It served as a parallel to Amos Alonzo Stagg's national tournament, held at the University of Chicago since 1918. Soon the CYO offered the largest baskeball program in the entire country. As with the newspapers, profits from such athletic promotions provided substantial remuneration for the church during the Depression. More importantly, the CYO encouraged the transition from private to public sporting practices, which would bring the ethnics closer to the mainstream. Mundelein brought a halt to nationalism in the parishes, and Sheil used religion to transfer ethnic rivalries into more acceptable leisure practices through athletic competition.[28]

Sheil, a controversial figure like his mentor, was closer to the people. The incorporation of the Catholic Youth Organization in 1932 and funding from the Chicago Tribune Charities, the Knights of Columbus, and other groups brought even greater expansion to its programs as it solidified middle class leadership. Vacation schools operated in conjunction with the park district, using the public facilities for parochial programs. The agency provided extensive social services as well as athletic programs in seventeen sports. By the end of the decade, the CYO numbered almost 84,000 participants at the local level and 150,000 nationally. All programs and policies came under the auspices of Bishop Sheil, who mixed social and religious motives, eventually extending CYO services to the Indian, Hispanic, Asian, and African-American communities in the city.[29]

Sheil also became a prominent social activist, opposing anti-Semitism and discrimination against blacks. In 1939, as a labor mediator, he settled a planned strike against the meat packers of the stockyards. The governor and the mayor cochaired a testimonial dinner for Sheil in 1941, and Marshall Field III served on the executive committee. The affair served as a testimonial to one of the American-born prelates who led a conglomeration of ethnic groups closer to the American mainstream. Sheil's influence extended all the way to the White House, and the image of the bishop as the champion of labor and the poor forestalled any resurgent class consciousness for most Catholics during the Depression and buttressed the church's opposition to Communism. Under such leadership, ethnic Chicagoans would no longer instill the fears of the Haymarket radicals.[30]

The emergence of Catholic champions, both secular and athletic, coincided with the transition to, and inclusion in, the commercialized leisure structures. Ethnics who had previously opposed each other united under the banner of religion to face secular foes. The 1930 football game between two undefeated teams, Notre Dame and Army, got headline coverage and 110,000 fans to see a 7-6 Catholic win in the rain at Soldier Field. The *New World* lauded Catholic athletes who succeeded in the secular world and celebrated Catholic pride in triumphs over Protestant institutions. Victories, such as those against the symbols of nativist power, assuaged years of bitter acrimony and provided at least a temporary sense of power. Promoters, both civic and religious, capitalized on such rivalries to realize financial as well as psychological profits.[31]

The city high school championship football game between the Catholic and public school teams brought the parallel educational systems together in athletic competition from the 1920s onward. In 1937 a charity football game between two Catholic high schools gathered 20,000 spectators, the public high school championship game drew 25,000 fans, and its Catholic counterpart only 12,000. When the two champions met the following week for the city championship, however,

120,000 showed up to cheer their favorites, and promoters realized more than $100,000. Clearly the combination of religious rivalries and American sport forms brought large numbers of Chicagoans together in what was becoming a public, mass culture, and sporting practices, particularly those of the CYO, helped foster the transition of identification from a single ethnic group to a larger Catholic and, eventually, an American one.[32]

Postwar Ethnic Clubs

The American sports and games of the schools, parks, and playgrounds proved attractive to ethnic youth. Park records indicated a continually rising rate of attendance and participation, and neighborhood groups clamored for more recreational facilities than the city could possibly provide.

As youth adopted the American practices, the ethnic clubs, who were denied the steady flow of European recruits by the restrictive immigration laws of the 1920s, found it difficult to sustain traditional practices. They competed with both the park district and church teams for athletes and took measures to forestall the Americanization process.

This was especially true of the Chicago Sokols, who traveled to national meets, or *slets,* and international competitions in the homeland. Since its inception in 1890, the Slovak Gymnastic Union had sent delegations to the competitions held in Prague, Czechoslovakia. Slets, similar to Olympic festivals, were held every four years in Chicago, and world *slets* were held in Prague every six years. Teams from Prague, the Ukraine, and Yugoslavia, as well as the president of Czechoslovakia and the president of the Czech national association, attended the first mass meeting of the American Sokol Union in 1921.[33]

Despite such ties to homeland and culture, evidence of fragmentation among the Sokols appeared. With limited resources for such excursions, competitions were mainly of a local nature, and increased contact with other ethnics and native governing bodies necessitated the use of English and cross-class alliances in order to form leagues for ethnic sports such as soccer. Organizers printed *slet* programs in Czech until 1937, and teams from Czechoslovakia continued to compete in the gymnastic festivals, but the Americanization of the event was evident by 1941. The Chicago *slet* drew 4,000 participants and 60,000 spectators, but included competition in volleyball, basketball, and tennis in addition to the customary gymnastics.[34]

The dilution of ethnicity became noticeable in other ways among the Czech and other groups, as well. The Polish Roman Catholic Union began using English in its journal "to attract youth" in 1929.[35] The Sokol journal lamented the loss of nationalism among its younger members who had lost the original ideals. Older members blamed the American schools, not only for requiring the use of English, but for the inculcation of games that emphasized individualism and materialism that undermined the communal experience of the fraternal clubs.[36]

A preference for American sports, especially among young ethnic-Americans, rose sharply during the 1920s. Ethnic athletic clubs compromised or withered away. Despite an incompatibility with their aims, the German Turners formed a basketball league to appease younger Americanized members. A sokol team won the small parks basketball championship as early as 1921. Even the more strident nationalists, such as the Poles, Slovaks, and Lithuanians, initiated their own baseball, bowling, and basketball leagues. Both the ethnic and native papers extolled successes, and groups who previously felt excluded basked in athletic glory. Italian boys won a city baseball championship in 1927, and a Slovak captured the city golf title three years later. In 1928, Morton High School, with a team of southern and eastern European ethnics, claimed the national basketball laurels.[37] Ethnic sport forms, especially gymnastics, were central to the maintenance of ethnic culture; but despite the importation of European instructors, Sokol leaders were "unable to change American-born interests."[38] Facing the loss of half their membership, the Sokols fielded football, volleyball, and baseball teams. By 1934 a Chicago team had won a national Sokol basketball championship.[39]

Even traditional ethnic pastimes fell prey to native regulators. The Amateur Athletic Union held jurisdiction over the American athletic competitions in which the Turners, Sokols and Falcons engaged. Middle class white, native, Protestant athletic clubs composed the charter membership of the Midwest branch of the AAU, and ethnic groups who aspired to compete at the highest levels were enticed to accept the native leadership. By the 1930s the AAU controlled amateur competition in track, basketball, boxing, gymnastics, handball, swimming, wrestling, weight lifting, volleyball, softball, and ice hockey. Participation in the best and biggest events required AAU affiliation, and the major ethnic clubs had all become members before World War II.[40]

In return, the AAU acknowledged the significance of the ethnic organizations by adopting the Turner gymnastics program of individual and apparatus events. Such accommodations provided opportunities to showcase ethnic pride, as Turners, Falcons, or Sokols often swept the gymnastic honors.[41]

Among the eastern Europeans, soccer still drew several thousand spectators. The Czech Sparta team even claimed the national championship in 1938, but homogeneous ethnic teams became a rarity as immigration laws severly limited recruits and American football increasingly won the hearts of ethnic youth. As recruitment became more difficult, ethnic teams contrived to import European players by giving them jobs or to field consolidated teams of mixed ethnic groups. By 1937 Chicago still had sixty-one soccer clubs playing in the various leagues, but they were more ethnically heterogeneous than before. Most ethnic clubs lacked the human and financial resources to conduct effective recruiting campaigns in competition with the public and private agencies. Consequently, the Turners, previously among the most formidable of the ethnic fraternal groups, dwindled from sixteen in 1926 to six by 1938.[42]

The economic woes of the Depression made it increasingly difficult for the purely ethnic social-athletic clubs to continue their activities. Some ethnic clubs and most of the athletic gangs lacked their own fields and facilities. Open land and vacant lots fell prey to the urban development of the 1920s, so practice required the use of public facilities. Such use required independent groups to accept greater regulation from the civil governing bodies, who tried to instill particular values with rules about eligibility, sportsmanship, and time discipline via permits and scheduling. The West Parks alone claimed to have "registered" 30,000 boys and girls. That did not mean that alternative groups accepted the middle class ideology, however. The recreation commission of 1937 commented that "we are concerned with the widespread public participation in gambling."[43] More than four decades of progressive reform efforts had failed to curtail such working class habits; but a second generation of "Americanized" ethnic youth transformed the private, communal leisure practices of their parents into public, commercialized competitions that drew from elements of the divergent cultures in the process. Only vestiges of the European leisure cultures that had been transplanted in the nineteenth century remained by 1940.

The Depression and the Last Gasp of the Radical Movement

Both religious and industrial recreational activities increased throughout the 1920s, as the larger companies added golf, tennis, riflery, and ice hockey teams to their programs. Some industrial organizers supported sport as a democratizing agent that would ameliorate class distinctions by associating shop men or women with middle class office personnel in a common purpose. Religious agencies, too, like the YMCA, the Jewish Peoples' Insitute, and later, the CYO, tied sport to religion and induced the ethnic working class to accept middle class governance. Alan Dawley charges that Catholicism, in particular, inculcated a corporate-feudal ideology in opposition to Socialist doctrine.[44]

Radicals denounced such programs as capitalist conspiracies and countered with movements of their own in an attempt to create class consciousness. Communists organized a sports program based on European models and designed to attract women and black workers. Unlike the radical groups of the nineteenth century, they included American sport forms, such as baseball, in addition to gymnastics and soccer. Chicago hosted the track and gymnastics competition of the Communist Labor Sports Union in 1927 and the International Workers' Olympics in 1931 and 1932, but drew less than 2,000 spectators to the latter. German athletic clubs published the *Arbeiter-Sport in Amerika* (Proletarian Sports in America) from 1927-1932, and an association of fifteen workers' clubs formed the Arbeiterkultur-und Sportkartel in Chicago in 1931. Still, the attempt to resurrect the radical culture of the nineteenth century proved fruitless. One young convert, an aspiring lawyer, tempered his radical activities when such actions jeopardized his admittance to the bar. Ward politicans supplied immediate economic needs with patronage jobs, and the radical organizations enjoyed only a brief existence as the overwhelming number of laborers accepted the Democratic Party as the champion of labor and chose to work within the system.[45]

The unions vied with the Democractic political machine as a job provider. In so doing, the unions intended to strengthen their base and extend the scope of their organization by cultivating a labor tradition and a labor class consciousness. The Amalgamated and Clothing Textile Workers proclaimed that "its cultural program was centered on the objective of achieving the intellectual and emotional cohesion of the members...to unify the minds and hearts."[46] Sport was the most popular means of unification, with 5,000 members engaged in some form of activity. Such union programs served as a more moderate alternative to the radical movement; though they displayed a labor solidarity, they operated within the established economic structure.

Most workers supported the more moderate labor unions, who built expensive facilities and sponsored teams in competition with those of the corporate sponsors. The Chicago Association of Street, Electric Railway and Motor Coach Employees of America sponsored bowling teams and billiards at its $1 million facility. The Amalgamated Clothing Workers, with more than 16,000 members, had its own gym, handball courts, exercise room, wrestling and boxing facilities, bowling alleys, and billiard tables. The union sponsored both men's and women's teams in softball, bowling, basketball, and volleyball. For many, the union halls became the clubhouse and social center.[47]

The economic effects of the Depression had a direct impact on the industrial recreation programs, which were curtailed or eliminated altogether. In 1937, a city survey determined that 233 of 600 firms studied still maintained a recreation program for employees, but the unions and park district programs had become the primary providers of leisure pursuit for many workers. Within such programs, working class culture blossomed to meet the needs and values of the participants.[48]

During the enforced leisure of the Depression, both the formal and informal sport programs provided psychic and, more importantly, economic benefits. Softball, particularly the 16-inch version played in Chicago, allowed working class athletes to retain a measure of prowess and esteem well into middle age. The Windy City Softball League provided such opportunities from 1934 onward. Rocco "Lewa" Yacilla, a legendary player of Italian descent, pitched for more than fifty years. Nick Zaranti, another Italian, stated that every block had its athletic club during the 1920s and 1930s and that softball was played nightly. In addition, every precinct sponsored a softball team. Such neighborhood-based teams nourished community cohesiveness and identity. Women's teams proved of particular interest, outdrawing the White Sox during the summer. The *Evening American*'s city tournament drew over a million spectators to 4,800 games, 30,000 to the championship alone. The public schools reported that "if they didn't watch out softball will strangle them to death...and this is the most serious matter for high school baseball."[49] The grass roots development of softball paralleled that of the professional sports in their infancy, offering a free market for players and regular gambling opportunities for backers. In the tough times of the Depression, sport thus provided economic relief for some and psychic compensation for many.

Even with the advent of the Depression, the neighborhood teams continued to prosper, offering as much as $1,500 in prize money, the equivalant of the annual family income in 1933. Neighborhood leagues operated under the auspices of small-time gamblers and the local taverns, in effect operating an underground economy that kept money circulating within the community. Gangs played for money and pride, and even boys earned $10-20 each for winning efforts. Thousands of teams operated in the city, and cash proved more readily available through sporting ventures than through the established financial institutions, particularly during the Depression. Mario Bruno claimed that he garnered $1,650 on one game when the bank would not offer $100 for a paid-up home. Within such a context, even some religious teams turned semipro. For Bruno and others, ball teams continued to offer workers a measure of economic mobility or autonomy.[50]

Bowling surpassed even softball among industrial recreational offerings. After suffering a decline during World War I, the sport made a dramatic resurgence in the 1920s. Industrial teams continued to dominate the ABC and WIBC tournaments, where prize money provided additional incentive. The 1935 national women's tournament, held in Chicago, offered more than $15,000, and Marie Warmbier, a local favorite, garnered two titles. More than 15,000 Chicagoans held membership in the WIBC, accounting for the largest contingent in the organization. By 1938 there were 900 bowling leagues, 9,000 teams, and 500,000 bowlers in the city, including church leagues and major ethnic organizations. In 1939 the Public Schools Athletic League adopted bowling for interscholastic play, awarding diamond-studded medals to individual winners, further incorporating youth into the established sport structure.[51]

Boxing, supported by the newspapers, the CYO, and the park district, was also on the rise. After its legalization and regulation in 1926, clubs and gyms sponsored boxing events on a regular basis. Sanctioned amateur bouts offered medals that poor fighters pawned, while others fought for cash stakes in small neighborhood gyms. Barney Ross, who became a world champion, started fighting in such clubs in Chicago's Jewish ghetto at the age of fifteen. He fought almost every night, sometimes twice a night, except Sunday, and "didn't keep any of the medals or watches; but traded them all in for cash."[52] The Golden Gloves, a national boxing tournament sponsored locally by the *Tribune,* and the CYO fights produced ethnic heroes in each neighborhood. Such stars as Max Marek, who defeated Joe Louis as an amateur, and Leo Rodak even had their own booster clubs. Such opportunities allowed the working class to accommodate traditional values and practices as it integrated with the dominant culture.[53]

With such proliferation in sporting activity and the increased leisure time enforced by the Depression, the city admitted that it was unable to accommodate the overwhelming number of requests for baseball, basketball, and softball facilities. CYO programs filled the gaps as Bishop Sheil merged church facilities with public ones in a unified effort. Along with bowling and boxing, team sports formed the basis of working class and ethnic participation in the sporting culture. The alternative groups conducted that participation in accordance with their own values, focusing primarily on power sports that required a demonstration of physical prowess and activities that fostered communal solidarity and opportunities for gambling.[54]

Religious or ethnic-based sport programs proved more successful in amalgamating the diverse groups. As exercises in quelling labor discontent and improving social relations, industrial recreation programs produced only limited successes. Employers still perceived work and leisure as intertwined and attempted to inculcate work values into their employees' nonwork lives. The employers stated their perception of leisure in a 1940 study: "Recreation is a powerful force in preaching the gospel of clean living...employee energies find an outlet in games, and since there is little desire to violate laws or destroy property, he becomes a better citizen"[55] The assumption that laborers' leisure lives were immoral or needed direction points to the differences in employer-employee perspectives and suggests little change from those of the social reformers of a half-century before.

As workers adopted employers' offerings, they also adapted them to suit their own needs and values, just as their children did in the playgrounds and parks. Whereas the earlier immigrants divorced work and leisure and saw employers' incursions on their time as transgressions, second generation ethnic workers perceived some benefits, such as increased income or release time. As most companies funded recreational programs through employees' dues, "contributions" from the company store, or added expenses to production costs, workers still felt little sense of allegiance to their employer. The values of teamwork, discipline, and self-sacrifice that may have been learned through sport were not easily transferred to the workplace. Workers played hard to improve their own pecuniary or community status, but they were unlikely to do so to supplement company coffers in which they did not share. The participatory joys of some and the financial rewards inherent for others were likely to engender greater personal, rather than company, aggrandizement.[56]

Employers, too, reaped benefits from such programs. In addition to any good will that they generated, or the public relations value, newspaper coverage provided inestimable publicity for the company. Most importantly, both employers and employees had found in sport a means to achieve their own, sometimes conflicting, goals while they accommodated pluralistic values.

Accommodation Within the Dominant Culture

Americanization programs failed to produce a consensus culture. The anticipated melting pot still retained ethnic, racial, religious, gender, and class distinctions; but second generation ethnic-Americans had become active agents in producing a mass popular culture by the 1930s. Commercialized leisure activities allowed for greater inclusion in the American economic structure, and sporting practices permitted the retention of alternative and pluralistic values. Second generation ethnics forged a new identity and their own image of what it meant to be an American. As their unions, churches, and ethnic clubs moved closer to the mainstream, they sought greater empowerment within the established system. Sporting relationships brought the divergent groups together in the public parks, but such associations also germinated grassroots social movements that brought concessions from the dominant powers.

In a 1938 report, the Park District captured both the spirit and the import of this emergence. "Always our danger is that we...seek quick results by enforcements, instead of more enduring results by the slow evolving of a general determination to organize life...as...the people themselves desire...."[57] The new park programs emphasized the importance of individual communities, tacitly admitting that the progressive programs had failed to achieve a fully homogeneous society. Park officials no longer assumed that pliable immigrant groups were waiting to be molded into worthy Americans. Moreover, they recognized the significance of this one arena of mass culture. The parks "are our one secular social institute dedicated to neighborly friendliness, to the healing of those sharp differences of opinion which divide us into opposing factions."[58] The broader public, too, supported the parks, as votes revealed. Despite the protests of businessmen, who labeled the new park program an exercise in socialism and branded it too costly, voters approved more than eighty field-houses in referendums by 1934.[59]

The commercial interests that had directed the city's recreation programs lost much of their influence as the Depression gripped Chicago, but other groups assumed greater responsibility. New Deal programs such as the Works Progress Administration, the Civilian Conservation Corps, and the National Labor Relations Board brought even more ethnics and other working class groups into the middle class bureaucracy by providing jobs and some bargaining power within the established system. The Social Security Act promised a measure of protection for all. With the emergence of the Congress of Industrial Organizations in the 1930s, workers felt that solidarity provided even greater bargaining power and a better stake in American society.[60]

Whereas the West Side Advisory Council, composed of businessmen and professionals, gave direction to the West Parks Commission in the previous decade, a citizens' committee representing ethnics, labor, and women, as well as commerce, did so in the 1930s. They reported that

> it is difficult to advance any argument to support the policy of permitting private clubs, such as yacht clubs, boat clubs, gun clubs, lawn bowling clubs, or flycasting organizations, to continue the proprietary rights to some of the areas which they have acquired, to the exclusion of the general public.[61]

As ethnics and laborers gained greater control, middle class groups were being ejected from the very public spaces that they had used for assimilation purposes. Parks became havens for young adults, public lounges for dancing and drinking, as park commissioners faced concessions to the popular culture.[62]

The Back of the Yards Neighborhood Council, among the first of the grass-roots organizations, became a model for others and exemplified the emergent movement of empowerment. Covering an area from 39th to 55th Streets and Racine to Western Avenues west of the Union Stockyards, the council emerged as a self-governing body designed to bring cohesion and self-help to the area in 1939. The group had set a mean task, for the area's residents consisted of Poles, Slovaks, Lithuanians, Bohemians, and Mexicans whose antagonism toward each other was matched only by their hostility toward their common enemy, the meat packers that employed them.

The groundwork for unity had been built by Joseph Meegan, the director of Davis Square Park. Of working class origins, Meegan gained respect and achieved communal leadership through his efforts as park director. A free lunch program served as many as 1,500 kids each day. His park softball tournament brought local clubs together in an initial governing council in 1937, with Meegan serving as vice-president. With the inclusion of the Packingtown Youth Committee, an affiliate of the Congress of Industrial Organizations, to the council, the first resolutions were made: to increase jobs, and to increase recreational facilities.[63]

Meegan, whose brother was the secretary to Bishop Sheil of the CYO, enlisted the aid of Sheil in organizing alliances with the local churches. Sheil secured the aid of the young, native American assistant pastors who had been assigned to local parishes by Cardinal Mundelein in order to avoid ethnic rivalries. "Americanism" dinners were held to divert the traditional nationalism in the parishes, and Meegan offered $50 to local gangs for athletic uniforms and softball league play. Within a year he had induced thirty-six athletic clubs to join in the community projects.[64]

The neighborhood council achieved national distinction when the employees of the Armour Company, led by Bishop Sheil and Saul Alinsky, a CIO union organizer, threatened to strike in 1939. Acting as a mediator, Sheil won recognition for the union and a pay raise, although his labor activities won him the sobriquet of a Communist.[65]

Meegan, too, faced deprecation. When his community work began to replace the traditional political patronage system, officials transferred him to Ogden Park, but Meegan resigned. When the park district attempted to remove the council from Davis Square, it was thwarted by the overwhelming pressure of the clergy. The neighborhood union, fashioned from a softball association, led to a cohesive, class-conscious alliance that continued to oppose the meat packers and meet its own needs.[66] The successes of the community coalitions indicated that different perspectives and values continued to prevail, and programs failed to totally assimilate the alternative groups.

The "Americanization" programs of the companies, parks, playgrounds, and churches taught the English language to many immigrants and introduced them to American sport forms. In so doing, they brought ethnic groups closer to the mainstream culture, but different perceptions based on different ethnic, class, and historical experiences created a continual process of cultural transformation. Ethnic enclaves and vestiges of their alternative cultures remained but were no longer as isolated and autonomous from the mainstream culture. Immigrant offspring, who lacked their parents' European experiences and therefore failed to share their commitments, lived in two worlds. They upheld ethnic customs in their private lives, where parents ruled within the household. Their public lives, lived in the schools, parks, playgrounds, and streets, came increasingly under the influence of other adults or peers. Consequently, the workers of the 1930s had different perceptions of democracy than did those of the previous generation. The Depression brought recurring doubts about the economic system, and the working class was, to a degree, able to resurrect modified labor traditions and its sporting culture. But ethnic political power, relative economic mobility of the European immigrants in the past, an acceptance of the democratic values portrayed in sport and, above all, religious leadership made ethnic groups and laborers less reluctant to work within the system to meet their needs and values.[67]

Sport, as a common interest of the various ethnic, class, and religious factions, functioned as an important means of accommodation. Pluralistic values merged in a mass popular culture that featured common sport forms practiced within commercialized leisure structures and adhering to a democratic ideology that promised opportunity, if not full equality. The media fostered the perception of sport as a meritocracy, and religious leaders allied with commercial interests, social reformers, and the mainstream public agencies in promoting its benefits. Ethnic clubs, originally founded for alternative purposes, faced demise as they tried to retain Americanized youth who had been indoctrinated by the programs of the schools, parks, and playgrounds. Even after the oppressive realities of industrial capitalism became readily apparent to workers, sport, with its basis in the valued physical prowess of the working class, provided opportunities for the free expression of cultural values and continued to hold elements of the American dream for many youths.

Notes

1. Lizabeth Cohen, *Making a New Deal: Industrial Workers in Chicago, 1919-1939* (New York: Cambridge University Press, 1990). On the wider social sphere of ethnic youth, see Cressey, *Taxi Dance Hall;* Irene Smith Barlow, "Leisure Time Activities of Two Hundred High School Girls in Chicago," M.S. Thesis, University of Chicago, 1934; Joanna Meyerowitz, *Women Adrift: Independent Wage Earners in Chicago, 1880-1930;* Pacyga, *Polish Immigrants and Industrial Chicago,* 153-5; Italians in Chicago, and Chicago Polonia Oral History Projects, at the Chicago Historical Society; Burgess Papers at the University of Chicago, Box 130, Folder 2; Box 134, Folder 5; Box 135, Folder 4; Box 139, Folder 4; Box 142, Folder 3; Box 144, Folder 1; Frances Di Benedetto Gems, Oct. 26, 1991; and Victor Greene, "Old-Time Folk Dancing and Music among the Second Generation, 1920-1950," in Kivisto and Blanck, eds., *American Immigrants and Their Generations,* 142-63; Dominic Pacyga interview with August J. Ruf, Sr., *Daily Calumet,* Nov. 9, 1982, in Columbia College, Southeast Chicago Historical Project at CHS.

2. Hoare and Smith, *Selections from the Prison Notebooks of Antonio Gramsci,* 285-91, 418 (quote). Christopher Tomlins, *The State and the Unions* (New York: Cambridge University Press, 1985);

Dawley, *Struggles for Justice*, 151-5, 238,, 326-7, 359, 386-90; David Brody, *Workers in Industrial America* (New York: Oxford University Press, 1980); Nick Salvatore, "Response to Wilentz," *International Labor and Working Class History*, 27 (Spring 1985): 29; Nelson Lichtenstein, *Labor's War at Home: The CIO in World War II* (Cambridge: Cambridge University Press, 1982).

3. U.S. Bureau of Labor Statistics, *Bulletin No. 123*, May 15, 1913, *Bulletin No. 250*, Feb. 1919; *Bulletin No. 458*, Feb. 1928; Rader, "Compensatory Sport Heroes"; Cohen, *Making a New Deal*, 328, 498, n. 17.

4. Theodore C. Grame, *Ethnic Broadcasting in the United States* (Washington, DC: American Folklife Center, 1980), 49; Stephen Calt, "Paramount: Anatomy of a 'Race' Label," *78 Quarterly*, 1:4 (1989): 11, indicates that Brunswick was less supportive of black enterprises. Clarence G. Carleson, "How the YMCA Helps C.M.D. Industries," *Central Manufacturing District Magazine* (Jan. 1928): 101-04.

See Kammen, *Mystic Chords of Memory*, 407-20, 426-31, 434-43, 543, on the role of the media in the merger of populism with patriotism and the incorporation of folk culture with national culture during the interwar period.

See Terrence Cole, "The Great Indoors: The Story of Indoor Baseball," presented at the North American Society for Sport History Convention, Clemson, SC, May 28, 1989, on the transition from indoor baseball to softball and working class adoption in the playgrounds. Paul W. Kearney, "Ten Million Keglers Can't Be Wrong," in Graffis, ed., *Esquire's First Sports Reader,* 226-38, on pervasiveness of bowling among the working class.

5. Alice Goldfarb Marquis, *Hopes and Ashes: The Birth of Modern Times* (New York: Free Press, 1986); Harold L. Platt, "Samuel Insull and the Electric City," *Chicago History*, 15:1 (Spring 1986): 20-35. Lizabeth Cohen, "Encountering Mass Culture at the Grassroots: The Experience of Chicago Workers in the 1920s," *American Quarterly*, 41:1 (March 1989): 6-33, argues against the embourgeoisement thesis based on listening surveys that indicated allegiance to ethnic, religious, or class-based programs. Sport offerings provided less variety, however, and the appeal of sport crossed ethnic, class, racial, and religious boundaries. Bruce Linton, "A History of Chicago Radio Station Programming, 1921-1931," Ph.D. Dissertation, Northwestern University, 1953; Grame, *Ethnic Broadcasting;* J. Fred Macdonald, *Don't Touch That Dial: Radio Programming in American Life from 1920 to 1960* (Chicago: Nelson-Hall, 1979), 9, 42, 75; *Chicago*

Tribune Picture Book of Radio, 1928 (Chicago: Chicago Tribune, 1928), 13, 29, 39, 45, 57.

Steven A. Riess, "Professional Sports as an Avenue to Social Mobility in America: Some Myths and Realities," in Kyle and Stark, ed., *Essays on Sport History and Sport Mythology,* 83-117. Quote from Burgess Papers, University of Chicago, Special Collections, Box 93, Folder 7; Box 94, Folders 4-5.

6. Patrick Clark, *Sports Firsts* (New York: Facts on File, 1981), 42; Rader, *American Sports,* 196-200; Grantland Rice, *The Tumult and the Shouting* (New York: A.S. Barnes, 1954); Douglas A. Noverr and Lawrence E. Ziewacz, *The Games They Played* (Chicago: Nelson-Hall, 1983), 72; John Bowman and Joel Zoss, *Diamonds in the Rough* (New York: Macmillan, 1989), 96-7; Chicago Tribune, *Sports Almanac,* 1927, 367-369; John Fink, *WGN: A Pictorial History* (Chicago: WGN, 1961), 15, 18-19, 32-3; *Chicago Tribune Picture Book of Radio, 1928.*

7. Cohen, *Making a New Deal,* 105-06, 129-43; NBC, *This Fight Should Have Been Broadcast* (n.p., n.d.); *Denni Hlasatel,* Feb. 11, 1917; May 13, 1917; *Bulletin of the Italian American National Union* (April 1925); *Dziennik Zjednoczenia,* July 9, 1927 (Works Progress Administration, Foreign Language Press Survey, 1942, hereafter abbreviated as FLPS).

8. *Lietuva,* Nov. 7, 1913; *Dziennik Zjednoczenia,* July 7, 1926; July 9, 1927; Jan. 16, 1929; Apr. 27, 1929; Mar. 8, 1930 (FLPS); Pienkos, *PNA,* 230; Schiavo, *Italians in Chicago,* 60-1; Goodman, *Choosing Sides,* 89-90, on Yiddish press coverage of baseball.

Peter Burke and Roy Porter, eds., *The Social History of Language* (Cambridge: Cambridge University Press, 1987), 1-15; Walter L. Harrison, "Six Pointed Diamond: Baseball and American Jews," *Journal of Popular Culture,* 15:3 (Winter 1981): 112-18; and Leonard Covello, *The Social Background of the Italo-American School Child* (Totowa, NJ: Rowman and Littlefield, 1972), 300-26, on the alienation of elders. Hoerder and Harzig, eds., *The Immigrant Labor Press in North America,* 3:331, 389.

9. Harrison, "Six Pointed Diamond" 113; S. Kirson Weinberg, "Jewish Youth in the Lawndale Community," 227-8, in Ernest W. Burgess Papers, University of Chicago, Special Collections, Box 139, Folders 3-4. Randy Roberts, "Jack Dempsey: An American Hero in the 1920s," and Benjamin G. Rader, "Compensatory Sport Heroes: Ruth, Grange, and Dempsey"; quote from Eddie Cantor, *My Life in Your Hands,* 1928, cited in Harrison, "Six Pointed Diamond." Kantowicz, *Polish-American Politics,* 169-70.

10. *Jewish Daily Bulletin,* Mar. 25, 1925, cited in Ken Blady, *The Jewish Boxers' Hall of Fame* (New York: Shapolsky Pub., 1988), 125. Isadore Seligs, "A Study of the Basement Social Clubs of the Lawndale District, 1928," 11-15, in Burgess Papers, University of Chicago, Box 142, Folder 3, on hero worship, sports, and gambling among Jewish youth; and Silverman, *Jewish Athletes' Hall of Fame,* 91-2, on adulation shown Andy Cohen, Giants infielder, by Jewish fans during 1928 season.

See Peter Levine, *Ellis Island to Ebbets Field: Sport and the American Jewish Experience* (New York: Oxford University Press, 1992).

11. *Chicago Tribune,* Sept. 14, 1930, part 2: 5; Riess, "Sport and Ethnicity," undated manuscript, 25-6; Herbert N. Ribalow, *The Jew in American Sports,* 162. Harry Harris, a Chicagoan, was the first Jewish boxing champ. Barney Ross, another Chicagoan, who got his start in the Golden Gloves tournament, symbolically wore the Star of David on his trunks en route to becoming the lightweight and middleweight champion in 1932 and 1934, respectively.

Jeffrey T. Sammons, *Beyond the Ring: The Role of Boxing in American Society* (Urbana: University of Illinois Press, 1988), 86-91.

12. Steele, *Knute Rockne,* 7, 77; Rockne, *Autobiography,* 63-4; Chicago Park District, *Third Annual Report,* 1937, 145-6; Don W. Rizzs, *History of St. Donatus Parish* (n.p., 1980) lists a dozen pro athletes from a single neighborhood.

13. High school championship basketball broadcasts began as early as 1928; in Linton; "History of Chicago Radio Station Programming," 247. James T. Farrell, *My Baseball Diary,* passim, on aspiration among youth. A. William De Filippo, "Autobiography," 6; and autobiographies of Helen Razim, in Burgess Papers, Box 130, Folder 2, and Box 134, Folder 5, respectively. PSAL, 1937 Football File, on De Correvont. Hoare and Smith, eds., *Selections from the Prison Notebooks,* 210.

See *Chicago Tribune,* Oct. 17, 1937, part 2:8; Nov. 27, 1937, 17; Nov. 28, 1937, pt. 2:1,3 on De Correvont, who scored 57 points in one game and over 200 during the season. The city championship between Austin and the Catholic champ, Leo High School, drew 120,000 spectators. *Tribune,* Dec. 4, 1931, 27, lists at least seven ethnic groups represented on the Harrison team. *Chicago American,* Dec. 26, 1936, 16.

14. Bureau of Recreation of the Board of Education, *Annual Report, 1930-31* (Chicago: Bureau of Recreation, 1931), 10. The *Daily News* even had a city horseshoe tournament, and the *Tribune* had

1,400 matches in its 1930 golf tournament; from the *Tribune,* Sept. 14, 1930, part 2: 5.

Todd, *Chicago Recreation Survey,* 2 (1937): 76.

Thomas B. Littlewood, *Arch.*

15. Chicago Park District, *Fifth Annual Report, 1939* (Chicago, 1940), 169; Correspondence from Don Maxwell, of the *Tribune,* to E. C. Delaporte, Apr. 1, 1927.

Stagg and Stout, *Touchdown,* 240; *Chicago Tribune,* Nov. 23, 1930; Nov. 28, 1930; Nov. 29, 1930; Nov. 30, 1930. During this one-week span, five different Chicago-area high school football teams played in St. Louis, Little Rock, Benton Harbor, Michigan, Everett, Massachusetts, and in Chicago against a Detroit team. An unpublished study by Robert Pruter discovered over 250 interregional football games since 1900. A girls' field hockey team was also playing in a Philadelphia tournament.

Chicago Tribune, Apr. 6, 1930, part 2: 3; Apr. 30, 1930, 33; July 13, 1930, part 2: 2.

Lynn A. Barnett, "Developmental Benefits of Play for Children," *Journal of Leisure Research,* 22:2 (1990): 138-53; Riess, *City Games,* 152-6; Mormino, "The Playing Fields of St. Louis"; Rader, *American Sports,* 163-4, 198.

16. W. Packman Rankin, *The Practice of Newspaper Management* (New York: Praeger, 1986), 135, 138; Frank L. Mott, *American Journalism* (New York: Macmillan, 1942), 715; John Tebbel, *An American Dynasty* (Garden City, NY: Doubleday, 1947), 92, 108-10, 126, 146, 202; Linton, "A History of Chicago Radio Station Programming," 43-5, 122-7, 137, 199-200, 225.

Marquis, *Hopes and Ashes,* 26-7, states that 246 U.S. newspapers ceased publication due to lack of advertising revenue between 1928-1934.

John Schleppi, "Chicago's World Tournament of Professional Basketball, 1939-1948," paper presented at the North American Society for Sport History Convention, Clemson, SC, May 1989, on the continued competition among the daily papers for readers and the role of sport sponsorship.

Littlewood, *Arch,* 42.

17. PSAL suggested football schedule, 1928; Correspondence of Floyd A. Rowe, Director of Cleveland Bureau of Physical Welfare, with Delaporte, Feb. 1, 1929; Feb. 2, 1929; 1930-1931 PSAL Basketball Schedule; Pritzlaff memo of May 28, 1931 to Principals Committee on Athletics and Board of Control; Correspondence of Percy S. Moore to A. H. Pritzlaff, June 25, 1930; Pritzlaff letters to Board of

Control, Oct. 15, 1931; Oct. 24, 1931; Oct. 21, 1932, on continued abuses.

18. Ruzicka, 1933 Baseball Report, 3-4.

19. R. Crook game account, PSAL, Football File, 1931-1935. *Chicago Tribune,* Feb. 18, 1934, part 2:1, indicates that the state athletic association began an investigation of basketball rowdyism as well, since referees required police escorts in southern Illinois.

20. PSAL Soccer Files, 1926-40; Pritzlaff letter to Edward L. Burchard, April 27, 1936; Pritzlaff letters to Board of Control, Mar. 10, 1937; Sept. 13, 1938. Soccer Report of 1936. By 1938 soccer made a bit of a resurgence, as eight schools fielded teams.

21. H.R. Crook, Football Report of 1932; Ivan Lisagor, newspaper column clipping, 1940, in Football file, 1936-1940 of the Chicago Public Schools Athletic League archives on the Fenger issue.

22. 1937 football file; Pritzlaff letter of Dec. 12, 1938 to Dr. William H. Johnson, Superintendent of Schools, mentions Kelly's role in the Fenger issue; 1940 newspaper clipping, Ivan Lisagor, "Six Section Plan to Slash Prep Grid Cards," and Pritzlaff's rebuttal of the charges regarding football abuses to Lloyd Lewis, sports editor of the *Daily News,* dated Dec. 6, 1940.

23. *New World,* Feb. 2, 1934, 14; Dec. 13, 1935, 16; Nov. 27, 1936, 1; *Chicago Tribune,* Mar. 28, 1934, 25; Littlewood, *Arch,* 37-8, 49-58, 79-84; Linton, "History of Chicago Radio Station Programming," 271, 332; Todd, *Recreation Survey,* 2 (1938): 77 (quote).

24. *Chicago Tribune,* Jan. 30, 1898, 7; Littlewood, *Arch,* 49-52. Cohen, *Making a New Deal,* 83-94, correctly argues the reinforcement of ethnicity in secluded parishes but fails to consider the role of sporting relationships in diminishing such isolation. Alphonse Leone interview, Italians in Chicago, indicated intense conflict between Protestants and Catholics in Chicago Heights, but engagement in athletic competition between the hostile parties. The *New World,* the Catholic weekly, provided prominent coverage of both religious and secular teams.

Richard Sorrell, "Sport and Franco-Americans in Woonsocket, 1870-1930," *Rhode Island History,* 31 (Fall 1972): 117-26, provides an account of the process in that location.

25. Bishop Bernard J. Sheil, ed., *CYO Survey,* 2:6 (June 1953): 8; Roger L. Treat, *Bishop Sheil and the CYO* (New York: Julian Messner, 1951); *Chicago American,* Oct. 29, 1935, 17, 20.

The CYO was organized along the model of Visitation parish in Englewood, with Father Thomas Tormey, a parish priest, as the first

CYO athletic director. Racial confrontations in the changing neighborhood were thus channeled into athletic ones; from Lawrence J. McCaffrey, et al., *The Irish in Chicago* (Urbana: University of Illinois Press, 1987), 51-2.

See the *New World,* May 19, 1910, 8; Mar. 26, 1910, 1; Apr. 16, 1920, 6; Apr. 23, 1920, 6; May 7, 1920, 6; on Knights of Columbus tournaments, and the National Catholic Athletic Association, established in 1909, which served as the foundation for Catholic athletic activities that preceded the CYO.

See Gerald R. Gems, "Sport, Religion, and Americanization: Bishop Sheil and the Catholic Youth Organization," *International Journal of the History of Sport* (August 1993): 233-41, for analysis of the CYO.

26. Program, *1st Annual Boxing Tournament* (Chicago: CYO, 1931): 1, 2, 7; CYO (Chicago: CYO, n.d.), 5; *CYO Survey,* 2:6 (June 1953): 8; *New World,* Jan. 6, 1933, 10; Jan. 13, 1933, 10; Nov. 17, 1933, 15; Dec. 8, 1933, 13; Nov. 20, 1936, 12; Treat, *Bishop Sheil,* 1, 77-119.

27. Ken Blady, *The Jewish Boxers' Hall of Fame,* 111, 119, 227-30; Program, Silver Episcopal Jubilee of His Excellency, The Most Reverend Bernard J. Sheil, D. D. (Apr. 29, 1953); Program, BB40-CY0 All-Star Basketball Classic, 1957, states 23 years of friendly rivalry.

28. On Stagg's tournament, Axel Bundgaard, "The World's Greatest Interscholastic," unpublished manuscript. Steven Riess, *City Games,* 102.

Chicago Tribune, Sports Almanac, 206, 213, 226. *Chicago Daily Journal,* Jan. 10, 1925, 14; *Chicago American,* Jan. 10, 1925, 2; *Sandara,* Mar. 21, 1930 (FLPS); *New World,* Nov. 18, 1932, 12; Nov. 25, 1932, 10; Nov. 24, 1933, 14; Dec. 1, 1933, 1; Feb. 2, 1934, 14; Feb. 9, 1934, 15.

29. *Chicago CYO* (Chicago: CYO, n.d.), 5-7; *New World,* Jan. 6, 1939, 10; Riess, *City Games,* 102; Program, Silver Episcopal Jubilee. *New World,* Dec. 1, 1933, 11, claimed as many as 200,000 participants. Welfare Council Papers, Box 257, Folder 3, at CHS.

30. Archdiocese of Chicago, *Manual for Leaders: CYO Vacation Schools* (Chicago: Catholic Youth Organization, n.d.): 10-11; Program, *Testimonial Celebration in Honor of Bishop Bernard J. Sheil,* May 15, 1941; Program, Silver Episcopal Jubilee. See *New World,* Jan. 14, 1938, 10, for a warning to African-American parishioners against Communism.

31. *Chicago Tribune,* Nov. 30, 1930, 1; *New World,* Apr. 16, 1920, 6; Apr. 23, 1920, 6; May 7, 1920, 6; Feb. 16, 1923, 5; Jan. 31, 1930, 10; Feb. 14, 1930, 10; Mar. 21, 1930, 10; Mar. 28, 1930, 10.

32. Chicago Board of Education files, Third Meeting of the Executive Committee of the City Championship Football Game, Nov. 22, 1928, details the arrangements between Catholic and public league representatives and the commercialization of the game via broadcast and movie arrangements. *New World,* Nov. 27, 1931, 9, provides an early history. *Chicago Tribune,* Nov. 26, 1936, 33; Nov. 28, 1937, 1, pt. 2:1; Chicago Park District, *Third Annual Report, 1937* (Chicago: 1938), 168; *Chicago Herald and Examiner,* Nov. 27, 1937, pt. 2:1; 3,5. See Gerald R. Gems, "The Prep Bowl: Football and Religious Acculturation in Chicago," *Journal of Sport History* (Fall 1996), for a more comprehensive history and analysis of the annual spectacle.

33. Jelinek and Zmrhal, *Sokol, Educational and Physical Culture Association,* 44-9, 57.

34. *Denni Hlasatel,* Jan. 30, 1921; May 15, 1922; July 11, 1922; July 17, 1922. For other track and gymnastic activities, see ibid., Sept. 27, 1906; Apr. 16, 1911; May 23, 1912; Jan. 27, 1913; May 10, 1915; Oct. 12, 1918; May 21, 1920; Aug. 31, 1920; Mar. 30, 1922; May 7, 1922. The latter two issues state that the Pilsen Sokol was the American Amateur Federation gymnastic champion in 1921 and 1922. Pilsen was also the Cook County amateur track champion in 1914; from ibid.,Apr. 26, 1915.

Intra-Czech competition included soccer games between laborers' teams and middle class clubs; see ibid., May 3, 1917; and track and weight lifting contests between Catholic Sokols, known as the Blues, and their free-thought rivals, the Reds, see ibid., Aug. 23, 1915. *Chicago Tribune,* Jan. 9, 1933, 21; Feb. 18, 1934, part 2:2, on ethnic rivalries in soccer and the importation of players for key games.

Jelinek and Zmrhal, *Sokol, Educational and Physical Culture Association,* 52, 58, 61-3. The world *slets* were curtailed in 1938 due to World War II, at which time the Sokols became ardent supporters of the American cause. The 1941 Chicago *slet* included a pledge of allegiance to the American flag. On Czech programs, see CCC, NHC, Box LCCC, series IV: 6-8, and file 4/8.

35. *Dziennik Zjednoczenia,* Apr. 27, 1929.

36. *Denni Hlasatel,* Feb. 11, 1917; May 13, 1917; *Vita Nuova* (April 1925); *Dziennik Zjednoczenia,* July 9, 1927; *Bulletin of the Italian American National Union* (April 1925). All are in the FLPS. *Sokol*

Americky, May 15, 1932, 3. Helen Hrachovska, series of manuscripts on the sokols, Burgess Papers, Box 144, Folder 1. *Pamatnica,* 77-81, details the transition to English usage and American sports during the same period in the East, suggesting that such decisions emanated from national governing bodies.

37. Emil B. Meier, "Basketball," clipping from a Turner publication, c. 1924. *Denni Hlasatel,* Feb. 22, 1921; *Dziennik Zjednoczenia,* Mar. 8, 1930; Apr. 27, 1929; Jan. 16, 1929; Sept. 14, 1927; July 9, 1927; *Osadne Hlasy,* Jan. 3, 1930; Aug. 22, 1930; *Sandara,* Mar. 21, 1930 (FLPS); *Chicago Tribune,* Apr. 6, 1930, part 2:2. *Sports Almanac,* 1928, 193; Schiavo, *The Italians in Chicago,* 60-1. *Record Book of the Lithuanian Golfers Association* (n.p.,n.d.); *Jaunimas,* Dec. 25, 1936.

38. Hrachovska, "What Do the People Think about Sokol," May 10, 1931, 3-4, Burgess Papers, Box 144, Folder 1.

39. Ibid., "The Organization of Sokol Slavsky," n.p.; *Denni Hlasatel,* Sept. 21, 1921; and *Osadne Hlasy,* Apr. 13, 1934 (FLPS).

40. Roy E. Moore, "Gymnastics Over the Years," *AAU Golden Anniversary Book,* 12, 60; Charles A. Dean, "The AAU in the Midwest," *AAU Golden Anniversary Book,* 18.

Among the ethnic groups who held AAU membership were Germans, Poles, Italians, Irish, Swedes, Norwegians, Slovaks, Jews, and African-Americans.

Todd, *Chicago Recreation Survey,* 3 (1938): 117-18.

41. *Golden Anniversary Book, Amateur Athletic Union of the United States, 1888-1938* (AAU, 1938), 43; *Denni Hlasatel,* May 7, 1922 (FLPS).

42. Todd, *Chicago Recreation Survey,* 2 (1938): 74-5; 5 (1940): 74; *Chicago Tribune,* April 6, 1930, part 2:2; Jan. 9, 1933, 21; Feb. 18, 1934, part 2:2.

Italians in Chicago, an oral history project of the University of Illinois at Chicago, provides stories of Italian youths' increasing involvement in sports programs and forsaking chores at home for ballgames in the park. Umberto Magnaini, an Italian soccer player, was offered a job in Chicago and played for the Italian Maroons Soccer Club. Personal correspondence with Marino Mazzei, Italian Maroons Soccer Club, October (undated), 1987, verified the recruitment of new immigrants. The club constitution was written in English, but conversation at the club remains Italian to this day. Jebsen, "Assimilation in a Working Class Suburb," in Gallo, ed., *The*

Urban Experience of Italian Americans, 81, states that Italian youth had forsaken bocce ball for baseball and bowling by 1930. See Adria Bernardi, *Houses with Names: The Italian Immigrants of Highwood, Illinois* (Urbana: University of Illinois Press, 1990), 209-10, for the experiences of one player. Correspondence with Alfons Massel, president of the Hansa Soccer Football Club, and Hansa, *Golden Anniversary Program,* indicate that Germans were less affected by the immigration laws and were able to maintain local support and European recruitment until the 1960s. Older players came out of retirement to continue the team's activities in World War II. Steven A. Riess, "Sport, Race, and Ethnicity," unpublished manuscript, 44, n. 12, gives an indication of the recruitment problem.

John C. Pooley, "Ethnic Soccer Clubs in Milwaukee: A Study in Assimilation," in M. Marie Hart, ed., *Sport in the Socio-Cultural Process* (Dubuque, IA: Wm. C. Brown, 1972), 328-45, concludes that ethnicity is lost in heterogeneous groups. Andrei S. Markovits, "The Other 'American Exceptionalism': Why Is There No Soccer in the United States?" *International Journal of Sport History,* 7:2 (Sept. 1990): 230-64, argues that the working class enthusiasm for baseball and middle class interest in football left no room for the development and expansion of soccer.

43. File C-31, Chicago Recreation Commission, "City-Wide Plan," 62, in PSAL Archives; Glenn A. Bishop and Paul T. Gilbert, *Chicago's Accomplishments and Leaders* (Chicago: Bishop Pub. Co., 1932), 122.

44. Dawley, *Struggles for Justice,* 301.

45. Sam Darcy, *The Challenge of Youth* (Chicago: Young Workers Communist League, 1926); Weinberg, "Jewish Youth," 303-20; Dorothy Schaper, "Industrial Recreation for Women," *American Physical Education Review,* 27 (March 1922): 103-13. Mark Naison, "Righties and Lefties: The Communist Party and Sports During the Great Depression," *Radical America,* 13 (July-August 1979): 47-59; Bill Baker, "The Chicago Counter Olympics of 1932," presented at North American Society for Sport History Convention, Chicago, May 26, 1991. Cohen, *Making a New Deal,* 261, found only 2,000 Chicagoans as registered Communists, most of whom were foreigners.

Allswang, *A House for All Peoples,* 50; Kantowicz, *Polish-American Politics in Chicago,* 128, 180.

Dirk Hoerder and Christiane Harzig, eds., *The Immigrant Labor Press in North America* (Westport, CT: Greenwood Press, 1987), 3: 331, 390.

46. Amalgamated Clothing and Textile Workers Union, "Why Cultural Activity," 6.

47. Todd, *Chicago Recreation Survey,* 3 (1938): 153. Richard C. Wade, "The Enduring Chicago Machine," *Chicago History,* 16:1 (Spring 1986): 5-19; Amalgamated Clothing and Textile Workers Union, "Why Cultural Activity," 1940, 5-7, provided by Joe Costigan, union education department.

48. Todd, *Chicago Recreation Survey,* 3 (1938): 150-1. Less than twenty-five companies provided baseball teams, and only twenty-seven had basketball. Softball, with 264 teams, and bowling, with 1,702 teams in 225 firms, were the most popular provisions in the industrial programs. The number of bowling teams was actually higher, as twenty companies failed to report the number of teams sponsored.

49. Edward E. Ruzicka, "Chairman's Baseball Report, 1935," in baseball file, 1926-1935, PSAL Archives. On softball, see *Chicago Tribune,* Mar. 1, 1956, 2; *Chicago Sun Times,* Feb. 8, 1988, 18 on Yacilla; CHS, Italians in Chicago, Box 2, Zaranti interview: 13; Box 3; Herb Graffis, "Belles of the Ball," in Graffis, ed., *Esquire's First Sports Reader,* 161-87; Seymour, *The People's Game,* 365-70.

50. Bruno interview, Italians in Chicago, 51-2; the Di Liberto interview states that more than $1,000 was at stake in a local pool hall dice game. Dawley, *Struggles for Justice,* 365; Haller, "Organized Crime," 223; Burgess Papers, Box 135, Folder 4, and Box 139, Folder 3, detail gambling among North and West Side gangs. *Diamond Jubilee Book of St. Aloysius, 1884-1959* (Chicago, n.p., 1959), 101. Ruf Interview, Southeast Chicago Historical Project, states that semipro basketball players received $5 per game during the 1930s. Jim Fitzgibbons, "Tracing Baseball to Great Depression," *Daily Calumet,* Nov. 9, 1982, 10, 18, 20. Peterson, *Cages to Jump Shots,* 8, 125.

51. Women's International Bowling Congress, *WIBC,* 18-19, 22, 62-3, 65; Public Schools Athletic League, bowling file, 1939-1959; *National High School Bowlers' Bulletin,* 1:15 (May 15, 1939), 4.

52. Ross and Abramson, *No Man Stands Alone,* 74-6, 77 (quote), 82, 84-5. Blady, *Jewish Boxers' Hall of Fame,* 229-30, 245-6; Riess, "A Fighting Chance."

53. Littlewood, *Arch,* 79-84; *Chicago Tribune,* Dec. 3, 1931, 21; Jan. 7, 1933, 17; Feb. 16, 1934, 27, 29; Feb. 18, 1934, part 2:1; Feb. 26, 1934, 17, 21; Feb. 28, 1934, 19; Nov. 25, 1937, 37; *New World,* Jan. 13, 1933, 10; Dec. 1, 1933, 1; Dec. 8, 1933, 13; Mar. 23, 1934, 13; Nov. 20, 1936, 12.

54. The CYO program included football, baseball, basketball, boxing, softball, volleyball, skating, cycling, hockey, billiards, bowling, track and swimming competition in more than 60 percent of the parishes of the Chicago archdiocese. The Polish National Alliance included 320 locals, whose members included one-seventh of all Poles residing in the city. The PNA had twenty baseball teams in two leagues, and twenty softball teams were organized into three leagues; as were its twenty-three basketball teams. The Italo-American Union had four softball leagues with 120 teams.

55. Leonard J. Diehl and Floyd R. Eastwood, *Industrial Recreation* (Lafayette, IN: Purdue University Press, 1940), 5, stated that "79 percent of recreation leaders believed that the recreation programs established a friendly feeling between employer and employee which otherwise might not have been present."

The quote in the text is also from Diehl, cited in Earl L. Ferris and Floyd R. Eastwood, *Industrial Recreation Facilities* (Lafayette, IN: Purdue University Press, 1945), 9.

56. Todd, *Chicago Recreation Survey,* 3 (1938): 152, on the funding of industrial recreation programs.

Cohen, *Making a New Deal,* 169-83, 350-55, discusses workers' attraction and allegiance to industrial recreation programs among Chicago's largest employers. These programs proved the most beneficial to athletes in terms of release time and pecuniary possibilities. When the Commercial Baseball League tried to enforce strict amateur regulations, its membership quickly dissipated to insignificance.

57. Chicago Park District, *Fourth Annual Report, 1938* (Chicago: 1939), 142.

58. Ibid., *Third Annual Report, 1937* (Chicago: 1938), 143.

59. Ibid., 145.

60. Cohen, *Making a New Deal;* Dawley, *Struggles for Justice,* 334-95.

61. *59th Annual Report of the West Chicago Parks Commission, 1927-28* (Chicago: 1928), 14-15. *Report of the Citizens Committee, July 1938* (Chicago: Park District, 1938), 30.

62. Cranz, *The Politics of Park Design,* 193, 205, cites the *Chicago Park District Report, 1939,* 150.

63. Slayton, *Back of the Yards,* 193-6, 203. The Back of the Yards Neighborhood Council eventually managed to buy an old railroad yard at 47th and Damen for recreational purposes.

64. Ibid., 201, 210-11, 214, 216.

65. Ibid., 205; Saul Alinsky, "Prelate to the People," *The Progressive* (Madison, WI: June 1951) clipping at the Archives of the Archdiocese of Chicago, presents a portrait of Sheil. Alinsky organized such efforts on a national level thereafter. *Bishop Sheil and the CYO versus Anti-Semitism and Racial Discrimination* (n.p, n.d.) at the Archives of the Archdiocese of Chicago.

66. Slayton, *Back of the Yards,* 217-21.

NHC, CCC, Box ACC, file 3/12 gives details of the Centurions, another self-help organization formed in the Austin district in 1936. In addition to securing land from the Chicago Rapid Transit Authority to build a playground, the group fielded teams in bowling, baseball, basketball, softball, football, tennis, golf, swimming, shooting, archery, and track.

See Pacyga, *Polish Immigrants and Industrial Chicago,* 288, n. 1, on the Russell Square Community Committee.

67. Todd, *Chicago Recreation Survey,* 5 (1940): 86, states that of the city's 1,850 churches, with 1,650,000 members, two-thirds provided English classes. De Liberto interview, Italians in Chicago, attests to a perception of self as middle class, the retention of traditional food and language in the home, and the use of English outside of that sphere.

Christopher Tomlins, *The State and the Unions*; David Brody, *Workers in Industrial America.*

Chicago Park District, *Third Annual Report,* 1937, 145-53.

CHAPTER 7

Conclusions

Chicago was a cosmopolitan, if not quite a melting pot, city as the Depression hit. One-fourth of its residents were immigrants, while another 40 percent were second generation ethnics. Its cosmopolitan nature could be judged by the fact that it contained more Poles, Slovaks, Czechs, and blacks than any other city in the world. It ranked as the third largest city in the world for Italians, Irish, Swedes, and Jews. Its diverse population still exhibited social antagonisms, but most residents adhered to some common values and practices, one of which was an abiding interest in sport. Diverse groups might disagree on social issues, but they had found a measure of community in competitive, commercialized leisure practices.[1]

The culture-making process, however, had been a long and stormy one. The rapid growth of Chicago from a frontier settlement to a full-fledged city by the 1840s was marked by a distinct change in its cultural patterns. As easterners settled in the area, they quickly subsumed both the Indian and French-Canadian influences to produce a dominant mode of culture. Commercially oriented Yankees replaced the subsistence economy of the earlier settlers, and particular groups, such as the Jockey Club, began to promote sporting activities as profit-making ventures.

The Civil War enabled the commercial and industrial interests to extend their grasp on the city's economic life as they enhanced its stature in the national economic picture. The quest for greater efficiency, productivity, and profit led employers to impose regulations for greater work discipline on their employees. Following the war, workers began to question the equality of the wage labor system. When such regulations were imposed upon the leisure lives of laborers, they reacted forcibly. Often led by European immigrants who espoused socialistic or anarchistic beliefs antithetical to capitalism, workers challenged the established system in a series of confrontations and armed clashes over the next century.

Employers maintained their positions of power by force throughout the nineteenth century, but they also had begun to employ alternative means to control or coerce their work force. George Pullman began to organize his workers' leisure activities as early as 1881, but, like his successors, Pullman's efforts were reactive measures. In many cases, the workers and their children had already organized their own leisure pursuits. Among the ethnics, European fraternal associations bent on nationalism were simply transplanted in the New World. Organizations such as the Turners, Sokols, and Falcons served political and social, as well as fraternal, ends. These groups presented an obstacle to the American nativists who strove for greater cultural homogeneity.

It remained for the "progressive" reformers to try to forge these diverse elements into a more homogeneous society. They seized upon sport as a means to teach the desired values of teamwork, cooperation, and discipline. The reformers instituted a broad-based program of competitive sports and games in both public and private agencies to instill the prescribed values to the foreign population and its offspring. It was largely this second generation, the children of immigrants, who merged the competing ideologies and cultural values of their parents and the native Americans by adopting and adapting the progressive programs.

The process of producing an amalgamated culture had already begun in earnest with the massive immigration of Europeans in the nineteenth century. Because each group operated within different cultural and personal experiences, their perspectives could never be uniform. Immigrants' children, trying to make sense of their ethnicity and the expectations of natives, grew up in two worlds. The dominant culture's schools taught discipline, conformity, and "American" values, while home life adhered to ethnic customs. Children found their leisure in the public spaces, such as streets, parks, and playgrounds, where they adapted the progressive programs to the street culture they had created. The process proved to be one of accommodation where native, commercial, and middle class moral values interacted with preexisting ethnic, youth, and working-class cultures.

Before World War I, the various immigrant and native groups still largely expressed their own preferred values in sport. Employers conducted sporting enterprises in a fashion congruent with their business practices. They attempted to encourage wholesome leisure pursuits among their employees to improve productivity and reap commercial benefits. For the social reformers, sport became a means of addressing the moral and health concerns of an ailing society. Workers and ethnics, however, found in sport a respite from their toils, a way to preserve some communal traditions, and a source of additional revenue to augment meager wages. Sporting practices allowed the working class to retain a measure of self-esteem, recognition, identity, and occasionally even a profit.

Especially after World War I, however, a common, mass popular culture, combining native and ethnic practices, had begun to emerge. Americanization programs preached conformity, while immigration restrictions stemmed the lifeblood of ethnic cultures. The ongoing process of accommodating conflicting cultural values produced a new set of social relations fostered by the practice of common leisure activities and particular sport forms. The centralization of such activities in the public spaces incorporated the diverse groups within commercialized leisure structures, such as leagues or athletic promotional events, under the administration and regulation of the dominant group. Such regulation did not guarantee acquiescence, however, as the persistence of alternative group values challenged compliance and negated full domination. Native commercial interests, largely male and Protestant, fashioned an "American" sporting culture in which all shared some commonalities, but participation within that framework still remains colored by particular ethnic, racial, class, age, and gender perspectives that resist full incorporation.

Common Activities

Particular sport forms or practices often accentuated social barriers in the nineteenth century. Fox hunts, yachting, and polo matches distinguished the social elites from their inferiors. Middle class tennis, cycling, and golf clubs also provided evidence of leisure practices distinctly different from those of the working class. The privatization of particular sport practices and the social connotations of elite country clubs and urban athletic clubs reinforced distinct ranks all too obvious to subordinate groups.

Progressive reform efforts used sport to alleviate social gaps and portray a cooperative society to the children of the outcasts. Compulsory education laws required school attendance, where mandatory physical education and the public school athletic league indoctrinated students with the values of discipline, respect for authority, teamwork, and cooperation. Park and playground administrators tried to inculcate similar ideals among a less captive audience and with less success. By the twentieth century even the most nationalistic groups had adopted the practice of American sport forms, particularly baseball, football, and basketball. As children shared such cultural artifacts as bats and balls, they took the first steps in distinguishing their differences with their parents. As their leisure took on new forms in a new country, they took on a new life and a new identity. Common sporting interests fostered a cultural bond, as associations and alliances eventually incorporated ethnics, Catholics, Jews, women, and workers into the commercialized leisure structure by World War II.[2]

Within that structure both the schools and the media promoted the virtues of competition as they extolled the character-building qualities of sport. These promoters often tied athletic spectacles to American patriotism by scheduling events on national holidays. Symbolic displays of the American flag or the playing of the national anthem reinforced the association. The rhetoric of democracy, equality, and opportunity permeated the dominant ideology of sport and fed the expectations and aspirations of subordinate groups. Sports promoters, such as the media and schools, not only presented information, but interpreted it, shaping common practices into structures for commercial profit.[3]

Perhaps nowhere were the American dream and the perception of sport as a meritocracy—and ultimately the melding of native and ethnic ways—more evident than in the interscholastic athletic program. Middle class administrators operated school teams for profit, prestige, and publicity, much like Spalding and Brunswick had done in promoting their businesses. Ethnic and other working class members of such teams found self-respect and status based on physical abilities rather than academic success. The media extolled and promoted such physical prowess, and principals knew that winning teams meant media coverage and more patrons at their games. They condoned lost class time for interstate competitions, promoted intracity and religious rivalries, and often accepted whatever conduct it took to gain victories. The rough play, use of ineligible players, and other coping mechanisms of coaches and players, along with the boisterous and unsportsmanlike conduct of the patrons, were familiar to working class participants and supporters. Athletic events allowed them to display and cheer their prized physicality in a rowdy manner, consistent with their traditional lifestyles. Commercialized athletics thus met both the needs of middle class bureaucrats and the working class communities.

The interest in sport penetrated most corners of this urban society, and the process of consolidation was nearly complete by 1940. In addition to the YMCA, park, playground, school, and industrial leagues, churches provided athletic facilities and organizational structures for more than 1,000 teams. The Catholic Youth Organization alone provided athletic activities for more than 100,000 participants in 167 of its parishes, and the B'nai B'rith Youth Organization fielded 153 basketball teams by 1938; the Chicago Baseball Federation numbered another 233 teams. Catholic and public interscholastic athletic leagues provided leisure activities for many more thousands.[4]

As the Second World War approached, all of these sporting practices had become "American" in nature. Most Chicagoans' sporting practices coalesced around the "American" games of baseball, football, and basketball. Moreover, local teams simultaneously represented regional and civic pride and linked Chicagoans to a larger national sporting network. Such associations as the National and American Baseball Leagues and the National Football League contributed to the sense of cohesiveness in sport. Although the *Tribune* and the CYO managed to bring boxing into the mainstream with a veil of respectability, the nature of the sport continued to demonstrate alternative cultural values. For blacks, ethnics, and the working class, boxing symbolized the continued struggle for dominance and survival in an alien world.[5]

As with World War I, world events caused the next generation to examine their loyalties. The impending war also provided a common focus and crystallized feelings of Americanism. This emergent Americanism, accompanied by a waning sense of ethnicity, built upon the common activities of numerous groups. These shared experiences, often practiced on a common ground, bonded otherwise divergent elements into a larger whole.

Public Spaces

Philanthropic donations of land, equipment, and prizes also gave private individuals and particular interests, such as the Commercial Club, the opportunity to shape programs in the city parks and playgrounds. Although never fully implemented, the Commercial Club's Burnham Plan tried to restructure city spaces to increase efficiency, aesthetics, and profit. The centralization of leisure activities within the designated public areas allowed the dominant group to define expected behaviors within such spaces. Competitive programs transformed play by developing good work habits, discipline, and cooperation to achieve success. Architects and administrators pursued a particular moral agenda as they deliberately isolated the sexes and races in the planned public facilities and programs. Moral regulations such as public decency laws regarding swimsuits, antigambling restrictions in the parks and playgrounds, temperance and vice campaigns were all aimed at defining acceptable and unacceptable leisure practices. By repression and persuasion, the nativists tried to reduce the influences of the alternative cultures of the ethnics and the working class.[6]

Urban growth further limited alternative play sites as independent groups lost their fields, and the informal street culture became formalized within the supervised and regulated municipal spaces. The incorporation of alternative groups within such spaces fostered the practice of particular activities but it did not guarantee acceptance of the inherent ideology. The parks and playgrounds could not accommodate the masses, and working class petitions and demands for play space caught park and playground administrators within their own rhetoric of equality and opportunity. To answer such cries, aldermen and city officials constructed baseball backstops and football goal posts on the city's vacant lots. Such unsupervised play areas became the domain of local teams or athletic gangs, who carried on their gambling activities and the alternative street culture. Moreover, school and park records attest to ongoing conflicts with youth over gambling, eligibility, rowdy behavior, and unacceptable tactics. Without sufficient police to force compliance in the parks and playgrounds, gangs and other wayward youths simply transferred their private activities to the public spaces. Such areas remained a point of contention and demonstrated the lack of cultural consensus. By the mid-1930s the parks had been forced to change their programs to meet local expectations, and control reverted to neighborhood governing boards.[7]

Such hard-earned working class successes proved detrimental to the resurgent radical movement of the 1930s. Neighborhood coalitions used ethnic and patronage networks to win local concessions during that critical period of enforced leisure. Such minor victories reinforced rather than challenged belief in the established political system. Despite the trauma induced by the Depression, the offspring of those crushed at Haymarket and Pullman felt greater inclusion in New Deal welfare programs. The local Democratic machine, with its roots in the ethnic and working class wards, and the burgeoning Congress of Industrial Organizations, seemed adequate champions of the labor cause.[8]

Leisure Structures

In the late nineteenth century the progressive reformers had initiated legal and educational measures that brought ethnic youth closer to the mainstream culture. Mandatory education laws made schools the primary caretakers of children and limited parental authority. Commercial interests introduced a vocational education curriculum into the schools that was designed to fit their labor needs and market requirements. Rather than provide a liberating experience, such education taught conformity and obedience to authority.

Native white Protestants controlled the established American institutions and held the financial reins of the capitalist economy. During times of crisis, such as the Haymarket affair, the Pullman strike, or World War I, the natives relied on government interdiction to repress the alternative cultures and forestall labor unrest. In such a manner, Antonio Gramsci's dictum that "the state served as the instrument for conforming civil society to the economic structure" proved true for Chicago.[9]

After some ethnic Chicagoans resisted, the commercial groups found a more subtle means to influence employees. As the dominant group, reformers brought greater regulation and standardization to sporting practices that reinforced the middle class standards. In 1901 Ban Johnson organized the American League, with headquarters in Chicago, to serve as a moral alternative to the rough play and intemperate behavior of the National League ball players. In 1906 the National Collegiate Athletic Association formed to address the issue of brutality in college football, and the Playground Association of America started in 1907 to bring the proper guidance to urban youth. By 1912 the federal government banned the interstate transportation of boxing films, largely due to the flamboyant lifestyle of the black heavyweight champ, Chicagoan Jack Johnson, whose behavior challenged the standards of white decorum.[10]

Chicagoans enacted similar reforms on the local level, as reformers managed to ban horse racing by the mid-1890s, after gamblers had taken control of most of the racetracks in the Chicago area. A boxing ban followed in 1901. Beginning in the 1890s, adults increasingly took control of student-initiated extracurricular activities, particularly the sporting ventures that involved gambling and money prizes. By 1898 school administrators gained control over the high school athletic teams of the Cook County Athletic League through a faculty board of control. The league formally reorganized under the supervision of school authorities and commercial sponsors in 1913. Commercial interests, such as the City Club, newspapers, and private individuals, guided league policies over the next twenty years. Sponsors provided funding, prizes, and event organization, while particular groups dictated appropriate behavior.[11]

As the work environment and public recreation became increasingly structured, the nativist values tended to become institutionalized in administrative practices. Athletic leagues and public agencies, in general, required greater standardization, regulation, and conformity. But independent promoters, semipro teams, and neighborhood athletic clubs made their own rules, which often conflicted with the values of the dominant culture. When the class-based ideology of amateurism espoused by the regulating bodies met with the reality of professionalism in the park district leagues, administrators were forced into concessions.

Independent teams that had gained the rights to fields by victorious challenges or brute force had to request park permits as they lost their vacant lots to urban development. Within the public regulated spaces, they had to temper their activities to tacitly comply with middle class standards. Such impositions had limited success— they brought such groups into the mainstream but failed to curtail traditional practices. A citywide survey found extensive gambling and a persistent street culture in 1937.[12]

The administrative structure of sporting enterprises varied by sport form and affected the extent to which subordinate groups incorporated with the dominant culture. Sports such as baseball assumed modern administrative structures and regulations similar to commercial businesses. For players, professional baseball simulated the work experience by the late nineteenth century. Other sports, such as football, basketball, and bowling, modernized at a much slower pace. The transition from independent to semipro to fully professional activities in such sports occurred, for the most part, in the early twentieth century, concurrent with the greatest period of mass immigration to America. For immigrant children exposed to the evolution of new sport forms, the process engendered a proliferation of teams and a free market in which to peddle their athletic abilities, whereas the industrial process offered little opportunity or autonomy and seemed oppressive. Most sport structures paralleled the premodern stage of the independent craftsmen. Independent teams and neighborhood softball leagues forged their own destinies, while success in individual sports such as bowling or boxing depended solely upon one's own abilities and proved a quicker route to social mobility for many. For skilled athletes, the loosely organized semipro and barnstorming circuits of the early twentieth century provided a wealth of opportunities and more closely fulfilled immigrants' expectations of democracy.[13]

Social Relations

Common sporting interests undoubtedly brought divergent groups together. More than just social events, such practices transcended economic, political, and psychological spheres of existence. The clash of preexisting native, ethnic, and class cultures in the nineteenth century gradually gave way to greater compromise and accommodation thereafter.

The ethnic athletic clubs that espoused nationalism and maintained European lifestyles faced the erosion of their alternative styles in the twentieth century. With the decline of the radical labor movement, with which some of the early ethnic fraternal associations had been allied, the clubs continued to pursue their athletic interests. From the 1890s onward, such competitions became increasingly administered by national and native governing bodies. The membership of the ethnic groups in such middle class agencies allowed them to gradually be drawn into the sporting structures and practices of the dominant native culture, even as they continued to engage in international contests with their European parent organizations.

Unlike the elitist native clubs, the ethnic athletic clubs bridged social divisions to some degree. As fraternal associations, they organized along ethnic rather than class lines. The Turners, Falcons, and Sokols brought laborers, craftsmen, and middle class businessmen closer together. Originally initiated to retain ethnicity and traditional lifestyles, the clubs produced a perception of democracy and merged communal activities with commercial ones as they were increasingly drawn into the dominant sporting culture.[14]

Native clubs, on the other hand, recruited superior working class athletes for their own purposes, while blacks, Jews, Asians, and women often met with complete exclusion. Only a select few working class athletes were ever admitted to such hallowed environs, and then only to further the prestige and social status of the dominant group. As conditional members, their position reinforced the dominant hierarchy. Theirs was a plight similar to that of the athletes of industrial teams, who gained publicity and profit for the company. Both were exploited by their social superiors.

But the athletes also knew something about exploitation. If sport reinforced the status quo, it could also be a means to empowerment, however limited. Athletes used their physical abilities for personal gain within the established commercial sport structures. The financial opportunities available to members of industrial and semipro teams provided many with additional income. For others, gambling on such games was consistent with the fluctuating rhythms and fortunes of working class life. During the Depression, working class groups readily formed neighborhood softball leagues that provided income unavailable through employment.

Ethnic and religious factionalism unintentionally aided the industrialists' efforts to infuse the capitalist ideology. As World War I divided ethnic loyalties, competing groups often directed labor antagonisms internally, blaming and opposing other working class rivals and subjugating class consciousness. Employers pitted rivals in competition to increase productivity in the work place and organized industrial teams to divert athletes from ethnic interests in their leisure time. Social reformers and the middle class media channeled such internecine quarrels into more acceptable forms of competitive conflict in the athletic games conducted in the schools, parks, and playgrounds. The promotion of athletic events often emphasized ethnic, racial, or religious affiliations, thereby focusing attention on particular identities other than class. As the municipality entered into the growing national sports network, civic boosters and the media cultivated a localized geographic identity that transcended parochial factionalism. The formula reinforced internal divisions while producing external unity.[15]

The process of consolidation became even more complete with the Americanization of the Catholic church. Nationalistic parishes, particularly those of the Poles, steadfastly resisted the movement. But even they succumbed to the CYO program, whose leadership under Bishop Sheil more closely exemplified traditional paternalism. The inherent anti-intellectualism of the working class, its reliance on clerical leadership, and the church's ardent stance against Communism greatly limited any semblance of radicalism. Sheil's own labor activism, conducted within the established system, demonstrated the extent of radical Catholicism. Religious sentiments proved stronger than those of class or ethnicity, and each of these factors had become incorporated within the commercialized leisure system.

While numerous other issues continued to exacerbate differences between groups, leisure lives intermingled. Sport served not one, but several cultures, that shared some of the same sport forms and held some common values. Competition had become ingrained for both the middle and working classes. Middle class athletes sported in a manner congruent with their working lives. They sought victory through superior organization, efficiency, specialization, and a better strategy. They placed their emphasis on intellectual and analytical abilities. Within ethnic sport associations, they invariably assumed the roles of entrepreneurs, promoters, or managers. For others, such as Halas and the workers whose salaries were contingent upon their performance on company teams, labor and leisure coincided. They played for pay and relied upon their brawn to sustain their status, which proved temporary. Most returned to working class occupations when such skills diminished. But for a select few, athletic careers provided a quicker and more lucrative means to the American dream and fueled the perception of sport as a meritocracy.[16]

Each of these alternative groups, forced to operate within the middle class bureaucratic structures, learned to adapt traditional values and practices to the established system. They adopted American sport forms but practiced them within organizations such as the Catholic Youth Organization or the B'nai B'rith, which reinforced their religious values. Organized leagues in the parks, playgrounds, and schools lent themselves to regularly scheduled contests for gambling. They also reinforced the ethnic and neighborhood rivalries that the reformers sought to allay. Patrons of such teams united in a support network and communal fund raising endeavors that were familiar to the southern and eastern Europeans. As their work and religious lives became more Americanized, sporting practices allowed them to retain a sense of ethnic identity, and competitive contests provided a showcase for ethnic pride and the demonstration of physical prowess so esteemed by the working class. Widely perceived as positive, or at least as an innocuous activity devoid of political and economic overtones, sport served as a common ground for the practice of both shared and divergent values.[17]

The Meaning of Sport

For ethnics and other laborers, work often defined one's identity. For those who were often denied the realization of their expectations in the work place, sport offered an alternative identity, provided opportunity, and sustained the perception of a democratic meritocracy. From the 1880s onward, increasing numbers of immigrant offspring gained stature and occasionally substantial remuneration for their physical prowess, particularly on professional baseball fields or boxing rings. With the advent of basketball, indoor baseball (softball), and professional football in the 1890s, similar opportunities became available on a year-round basis.[18]

Until the emergence of a national sporting culture in the 1920s, local standards prevailed. Any youth with good skills might aspire to supplemental income and status on the numerous independent and semipro teams. Within such a context, many youths devoted an inordinate amount of time to the development of their physical skills. For many itinerant ball players, sport became a way of life and the primary occupation. For the less skilled, sporting activities provided the opportunity for gain through entrepreneurial ventures and gambling. While many ethnics, such as the Poles or Hungarians, often took in boarders to make up deficits, gambling offered a quicker, though riskier, means for advancement. It was also a behavior that conformed to the general instability and temporary gains and losses of working class lives. Despite the moral intentions of reformers, regularly scheduled contests within the commercialized athletic leagues actually offered more opportunities for gambling and perpetuated this element of the alternative lifestyle. Such practices met the working class need for immediate gratification, both psychologically and, if lucky, materially.[19]

Commercialized leisure activities, and sport in particular, provided workers with an acceptable means of economic mobility or social status. In the case of Barney Ross, a reluctant mother overcame religious misgivings to become a supportive fan when pugilism triumphed over poverty. For the few, such as Ross, Halas, or Weissmuller, sporting prowess translated into material gain and status. For others, however, wealth and any change in social status were often transitory. Age especially diminished physical skills in both workers' work and sporting lives, and, as did workers, athletes retired or sought lesser employment in the minor leagues.[20]

Competitive sporting practices and organizations also enabled sport promoters and other commercial interests to infuse capitalist ideology with democratic ideals in a more subtle guise than the legal and militant impositions of the nineteenth century. Industrial recreation programs appeased some working class athletes who found in them the means to better their social or economic status. The perception of sport as a meritocracy, an avenue of opportunity, a means to character building and the fostering of communal spirit, were values shared by middle class natives, aspiring ethnics, and workers who were denied other means of promise.

Sporting practices also helped to resolve the divergence of high and low cultures by creating a common element in the popular culture. Sport offered drama, where working class ethnics expressed themselves through the traditional physical means of strength, speed, or power inherent in sporting performances. They held in esteem those who succeeded through brawn rather than brains. The prodigious feats of a Babe Ruth, a Jim Thorpe, a Red Grange, or a Joe Louis attested to the triumph of the individual over adversity in a manner congruent with working class lifestyles. Moreover, such heroes' personal lives reflected those of the working class, who identified with the behaviors thought to be boorish by their social superiors. Identification with such athletic heroes, whose earnings allowed them to transcend their birth status, promoted the perception of sport as a meritocracy and muted the sense of class consciousness. For impressionable young males, sport seemed to serve vital roles as both an assertion and a measurement of their masculinity, as an entré into American society, and as a means to greater socioeconomic status.[21]

Boxing and other power sports held particular esteem and cultural significance among ethnics and others in Chicago's lowest stratum. Thrasher's study of Chicago gangs asserted that, next to the team sport of softball, football and boxing proved most popular, due to their personal, direct, and dangerous nature.[22] Working class youth established their honor, their prowess, and their territoriality with their fists. In describing an earlier era, Elliott Gorn has stated that "pugilism was an autonomous expressive form that symbolically opposed the drift of modern society...boxing captured the values, the ethos, the distinct culture of countless working men who felt dispossessed...."[23] This was no less true in Depression-era Chicago. The immediate success of the Golden Gloves and CYO programs during the 1930s rested entirely upon their blue collar participants, who were mostly members of ethnic groups residing in low-income areas. The composition of the Golden Gloves tournament was duly noted by the city's officials:

> Boxing has long been regarded as a means of self-defense; therefore, it is entirely consistent that the greatest number and also the highest ratio of competitors to the population

should be in those areas and among those groups where
survival of the fittest was long dependent upon one's ability
to defend his rights with fists rather than words.[24]

Strength and toughness were not only admired, but they
were also necessary in homes of the economically marginal.
For young men denied access to material success, sport
became essential to the retention of their masculinity, particularly during the Depression. The CYO boxing program enrolled thousands of participants in quest of both. Champions
won not only honors, but four-year college scholarships, and
even runners-up earned new suits and international trips as
alternate competitors.[25]

The physical and communal nature of working class life led
ethnic workers, especially, to place greater emphasis on particular sports. Team sports—football, softball, baseball, and
basketball—allowed participants and their neighborhood
supporters to band together in a social network familiar to
southern and eastern Europeans. Teams often emanated from
parish social or athletic clubs, which allowed ethnics to selectively participate in the American system while retaining
their religious and cultural values. Neighborhood, park, and
parish teams often reinforced ethnic or religious solidarity
rather than foster the homogeneity that nativist reformers
desired. In that sense, the ethnic sporting cultures of the early
immigrants who confronted the capitalist system were
brought closer to the mainstream, yet they retained some
sense of separate identity and cohesion.[26]

Sport thus served a ritual function. Hilmi Ibrahim states
that "it puts emerging cognitive patterns in the service of a
general vision shared by the community....It provides the
psychological foundation for the gradual shift from one status
to another."[27] That shift in cultural evolution is readily apparent in the study of leisure practices. The nineteenth century
practices of ethnic immigrants were not only separate, but
often antagonistic to the native culture. Americanized ethnic
youth transcended cultures in their commercialized leisure
pursuits during the initial decades of the twentieth century.
Radical volatility gave way to a fluid stability that accommodated pluralistic needs within the established structure.[28]

In promoting a national sporting culture, the media further homogenized the culture by establishing norms or standards of reference for all. The media incorporated the interests of the alternative groups to popularize a common culture with the same sport forms and some common values and beliefs. The media promoted a sporting language, images, and memories of past events and heroes, often ethnic ones, that bonded generations within the American sporting culture. Jack Johnson invoked comparisons with John L. Sullivan, just as Muhammed Ali did with Rocky Marciano.

Sport spectacles also fostered the sense of a shared experience. Despite their isolation in segregated communities, antagonistic groups met on a common field of play. The annual Chicago Prep Bowl filled Soldier Field, itself a monument to American patriotism, to participate in the celebration of a religious rivalry in the form of a football game. Participation implied at least a degree of cultural consensus, and winners were crowned "city" champs, no longer merely secular or parochial figures. Athletic victories thus preserved social honor and blurred perceptions of dominance; but like the movies, the dominant group could shape such spectacles to produce particular images, invent traditions, and construct a seemingly shared history without changing the real balance of power.[29]

By the onset of World War II, the interrelationships engendered by sport had transformed both natives' and ethnics' lifestyles to produce a relatively common culture. A pervasive interest in sport marked the society, consolidation of the American sport forms had been achieved, commercialized leisure practices won acceptance, alternative and occasionally antagonistic class and ethnic values had been muted, competition was recognized as the trademark of American culture. But sport continued to hold different meanings for the diverse residents of Chicago. Ethnics retained some communal traditions and a sense of identity. The working class still adhered to the rowdyism, gambling practices, and intemperate behavior so disdained by the social reformers, and physical prowess still held greater value than education or commercial success.

Culture could not be dictated. It was, and is, a continuously active phenomenon rather than a passive process. Early ethnics resisted the impositions of the dominant culture, while their offspring adapted and accommodated particular elements of the mainstream culture with their own values. The reorganization of the park district in the 1930s acknowledged such pluralism, allowing for local self-government by community groups as it sought to accommodate and incorporate all within the American system. As the Back of the Yards Neighborhood Council declared, "we the people will work out our own destiny." The sporting practices of the various peoples served a prominent role in that process.[30]

Notes

1. Hogan, *Class and Reform*, 3.

2. Sage, *Power and Ideology in American Sport*, 7, 38-42, 62.

3. Ibid., 119-20; Jones, *Sports, Politics, and the Working Class*, 61.

4. Todd, *Chicago Recreation Survey*, 2:39, 41-3, 67, 79; 3:61-2, 68, 70-1, 73, 97, 101-2, 115, 121-4, 130, 133-5; 5:61, 74-6, 85.

5. Michael Oriard, *Dreaming of Heroes: American Sports Fiction, 1868-1980* (Chicago: Nelson-Hall, 1932), 58-60.

6. Gramsci, *Selections from the Prison Notebooks*, 217; Roberta Park, "Review Essay," *Journal of Sport History*, 15:3 (Winter 1988): 364.

Special Parks Commission, *Annual Report, 1911*, 5, states a plan for racial segregation of public playgrounds, and "A Breath of Fresh Air: Chicago Parks in the Progressive Era," Chicago Cultural Center Exhibit, July 22 - Nov. 11, 1989, displayed the initial architectural drafts.

7. *Chicago American*, Jan. 12, 1925, 14, relates the story of a semipro team rescued by a politician after the loss of its ball park. Todd, *Chicago Recreation Survey*, 2 (1938): 66; map opposite p. 74 shows only 8 independent football fields by 1937. McDonough, *Annual Report of Municipal Recreation, 1924*, 5, 7, 19; David Whitson, "Sport and Hegemony: On the Construction of the Dominant Culture," *Sociology of Sport Journal*, 1 (1984): 64-78.

8. Allswang, *A House for All Peoples: Ethnic Politics in Chicago, 1890-1936;* Oral Histories of Chicago Polonia and Italians in Chicago, Chicago Historical Society; Chicago Park District, *Journal of Proceedings, 1934-1935*, 188-91, 206, 261-2, 265-6, 351, 357, 396, 399, 464, 491.

9. Gramsci, *Selections from the Prison Notebooks,* 208.

10. Randy Roberts, *Papa Jack: Jack Johnson and the Era of White Hopes* (New York: The Free Press, 1983).

11. Haller, "Organized Crime in Urban Society," 214; ibid., "Bootleggers and American Gambling," 106, in Commission and Review of National Policy toward Gambling, Appendix I; Wendt and Kogan, *Lords of the Levee,* 28-9, 50-8; Riess, *City Games,* 183-7.

12. Todd, *Chicago Recreation Survey,* 5 (1937); De Liberto interview, Italians in Chicago.

13. Guttmann, *From Ritual to Record,* characterizes modern sports as regulated, specialized, rationalized, and quantified within bureaucratic structures. Only professional baseball and bowling fulfilled such criteria in 1920.

14. R. Young, "The Sociology of Sport: Structural Marxist and Cultural Marxist Approaches," *Sociological Perspectives,* 29 (1986): 3-28.

See Riess, *City Games,* 96-9; "The Aurora Turnverein," in Keil and Jentz, *German Workers in Chicago;* Metzner, *History of the American Turners;* Jelinek and Zmrhal, *Sokol; Pamatnica;* Polish Falcon Papers; on aims and social composition of fraternal groups.

15. Lizabeth Cohen, "Learning to Live in the Welfare State: Industrial Workers in Chicago Between the Wars, 1919-1939," Ph.D. Dissertation, University of California, Berkeley, 1986, 219-47, 412, states that a 1939 Gallup Poll found more than half of those surveyed realizing their low-income status, but yet considering themselves to be middle class.

16. Zelenicki, ed., *The Poles of Chicago,* 145-8, 159, 167, 189-256; Droba, *Czech and Slovak Leaders in Metropolitan Chicago,* 37-70, 216-92; Schiavo, *The Italians in Chicago,* 58-61, 79, 165-89; Hemmer and Kenna, eds., *The Western Bowlers' Journal;* Slayton, *Back of the Yards,* 58-9.

17. Numerous researchers have addressed sport and the process of socialization. See John Loy, Gerald Kenyon, and Barry McPherson, *Sport, Culture, and Society* (Philadelphia: Lea & Feriger, 1981). Among those who have analyzed ethnic adaptations, see Maria T. Allison, "Sport, Ethnicity, and Assimilation," *Quest,* 34 (1982): 165-75.

18. Paul Willis, "Masculinity and Factory Labor," in Alexander and Seidman, eds., *Culture and Society,* 183-95.

230 Conclusions

19. Michael J. Ellis, *The Business of Physical Education* (Champaign, IL: Human Kinetics, 1988), 163; James H. Frey, "Social Risk and the Meaning of Sport," *Sociology of Sport Journal,* 8:2 (June 1991): 136-45.

Larry Hugick, "Odds Are 7-3 That You Gamble," *Chicago Sun-Times,* June 11, 1989, 8, states that a Gallup Poll found that 71 percent of Americans gambled each year, 31 percent on a weekly basis. On gambling during the period under study, see Riess, *City Games,* 183-94; Haller, "Organized Crime in Urban Society"; Rader, *American Sports,* 200-02; Landesco, *Organized Crime in Chicago,* 45-85.

20. In the stockyards, elderly workers lost the positions of status and higher pay, which required greater strength and stamina, when they could no longer keep up with the demanding pace of production. In sport, particularly within the fraternal, religious, and community organizations, a diminution of physical skill might still allow opportunities for management, coaching, or promotional roles.

Ross and Abramson, *No Man Stands Alone.* See *Baltimore Sun,* July 20, 1948, 19, on the decline of baseball star Hack Wilson.

21. Hoare and Smith, eds., *Selections from the Prison Notebooks of Antonio Gramsci,* 210; Michael S. Kimmel, "Baseball and The Reconstitution of American Masculinity, 1880-1920," 55-65; and Michael A. Messner, "Masculinities and Athletic Careers: Bonding and Status Differences," 97-108, in Messner and Donald F. Sabo, eds., *Sport, Men, and the Gender Order: Critical Feminist Perspectives* (Champaign, IL: Human Kinetics, 1990).

22. Thrasher, *The Gang,* 1963 ed., 45-8.

23. Elliot J. Gorn, *The Manly Art: Bare-Knuckle Prize Fighting in America,* 147.

24. Todd, *Chicago Recreation Survey,* 2:79. For descriptions of boxers see *New World,* Oct. 16, 1936, 12; Nov. 20, 1936, 12; *Chicago Tribune,* Feb. 16, 1934, 27, 29; Feb. 26, 1934, 21, 28; Mar. 29, 1934, 22.

See *Chicago Tribune,* November 1, 1920, 17, in which George B. Arnold, chairman of the Board of Education Finance Committee, advocated boxing to settle ethnic disputes in schools. The policy was already in effect at the Webster, Haven, and Parental Schools by that time.

25. Roger L. Treat, *Bishop Sheil and the CYO,* 59, 77-88; John V. Grombach, *The Saga of Sock* (New York: A. S. Barnes, 1949), 123. The CYO provided new clothing, complete with underwear, and

chartered travel throughout the U.S., Europe, Hawaii, and other exotic locales.

26. Parish histories at the Chicago Catholic Archdiocese Archives detail the ethnic nature of social and athletic activities. The matter is also treated by Zelenicki, ed., *The Poles of Chicago;* Slayton, *Back of the Yards;* Pacyga, *Polish Immigrants and Industrial Chicago;* and in Steven A. Riess, "Race and Ethnicity in American Baseball," *Journal of Ethnic Studies,* 4 (Winter 1977): 39-55.

27. Hilmi Ibrahim, "The Nature of Ritual," *Journal of Physical Education, Recreation, and Dance,* (Nov.-Dec. 1988): 26.

28. Victor Turner, *The Ritual Process: Structure and Anti-Structure* (Chicago: Aldine, 1969), 94-5, 125, 166-72.

29. Robert E. Park, "The Urban Community As a Spatial Pattern and a Moral Order," in Ernest W. Burgess, ed., *The Urban Community* (Chicago: University of Chicago Press, 1926); Elvin Hatch, "Theories of Social Honor," *American Anthropologist,* 91:2 (June 1989): 341-53.

Ove Korsgaard, "Sport as a Practice of Religion: The Record as Ritual," in John Marshall Carter and Arnd Krueger, eds., *Ritual and Record: Sport Records and Quantification in Pre-Modern Societies* (Westport, CT: Greenwood Press, 1990), 115-22, discusses the importance of ritual to Catholics. Kammen, *Mystic Chords of Memory,* 4-6.

30. Slayton, *Back of the Yards,* 1; Chicago Park District, *Fourth Annual Report, 1938,* 145-7; *Fifth Annual Report, 1938,* 150, 159-63; Elizabeth Halsey, *Development of Public Recreation in Metropolitan Chicago* (Chicago Recreation Commission, 1940), 116-18.

Index